More to Life

By

Maureen Moss

ISBN-13: 978-1542955096
ISBN-10: 1542955092

Cover by Kelly Leonie Walsh

Published by Acclaimed Books Limited

www.acclaimedbooks.com

.

Acknowledgements

My thanks to the Acclaimed Books Publishing team, especially to Kelly Walsh for the superb cover design, and to Peter Lihou for his ever- patient guidance. I also acknowledge the contribution made by the Torrevieja Writers' Circle for their encouragement and advice, and my long-suffering family, without whose spirit of adventure this book would never have been written

Itinerary

UK: Guernsey – London

India: Mumbai – Goa (Vagator/Chapora, Mapusa/Baga beach) – Mumbai – (via Ahmedabad) – Udaipur – Pushkar – Jodhpur – New Delhi – Ranthambore NP – Jaisalmer – Mount Abu – Ahmedabad - Mumbai

Singapore

Thailand: Bangkok – Koh Samui (Lamai/Namuang/Ang Thong NP, Chaweng, Big Buddha beach) - Surat Thani – Chiang Mai – Chiang Rai – Chiang Kong

Laos: Pak Beng – Luang Prabang – Vientiane – Hinboun - Vientiane

Vietnam: Hi Chi Minh/Saigon

Kampuchea (Cambodia): Phnom Penh – Tuol Sleng – Choeng Ek – Siem Reap – Angkor Wat (Banteang Srei, Bayon, Ta Phrom)

Vietnam: Ho Chi Minh/Saigon - Cu Chi – Mekong Delta – Dambri Falls - Langa Lake – Bao Loc – Dalat - Lam Ty Ni Pagoda – Chicken Village – Nha Trang – Po Klang Garai Cham – Danang - Mieu Island – Fairy Mountain -- Qui Nonh – Nguyen Van Troi - Marble Mountain - Buu Long Mountain – Dragon Lake - Hoi An – Cua Dai beach - Hue (Thien Mu Pagoda, Forbidden Purple City) - Hanoi – Halong Bay - Hanoi

China: Guangzhou – Wuzhou – Yangshuo – Moon Hill – Xing Ping - Guilin – San Jiang – Ping An – Longsheng – Guilin – Hong Kong (Lantau island)

Australia: Sydney

London

Guernsey

Mumbai

Bangkok
Ho Chi Mihn

Singapore

Sydney

Author's note:

I have tried to recreate events, locales and conversations from my memories of them. In order to maintain their anonymity in some instances I have changed the names of individuals and places, and I may have changed some identifying characteristics and details such as physical properties, occupations and places of residence.

More to Life

Prologue
1950

I am three and a half years old. My brother is in his pram, content, blowing bubbles. My mother has sewn *Andrew* on his pillow because I insist on introducing him to everyone as my new sister Linda Irene.

I edge over to look into the pram on my tiptoes. A dead bumblebee lies on the pillow, and my brother has gone. I promise I won't be a naughty girl again.

***

Guernsey
1996
To: Wendy McKintock
From: Rachael Green
Subject: Catching up
May 15

Hi. Long time no read. Hope you're faring better than me. Have got divorced since we last wrote. Our college teaching days seem like decades ago. I should have been in touch before, but have been so preoccupied. Anyway, now we can email so can catch up with each other more often. So, how are you?

***

My flippant reference to the single most ghastly experience of my life belied the agony it had brought me. Ours had been a fairly typical, British sort of marriage; a partnership in which we both knew the boundaries: some things better left unsaid.

9

David and I had been the two new kids in town. We had fallen in love when we recognised the outsider in each other, and this had propped us up for twenty-odd years. I couldn't say why I loved him; I just knew I did. He was somehow vulnerable—he seemed lonely and unloved, as if he was lost—despite his biting humour and scathing criticism of those he considered unworthy. I immediately wanted to protect him; to make sure he felt secure. I couldn't imagine betraying him—that would have been my failure, not his. And then something happened to him: discontentment, like an insidious odour, crept in, barely noticeable even when it had taken hold. He was no longer prepared to muddle along side by side. I felt that something was wrong, but didn't want to express it.

***

To: Rachael Green
From: Wendy McKintock
Subject: Catching up
May 15

Dear R

Oh dear, poor you. As you know I never met David, but I'm sure you're better off without him. It was so lovely to receive a message from you, despite your bad news. You're right: my oh my it's been a very long time since I put pen to paper. Oops, force of habit...emailing is the new fad over here in the good ol' U.S. of A. You're duly chastised.

W

***

He began by detaching himself from the invisible bonds of marriage. He started dismantling his particular chains after a three-week, long-distance hike alone, where he'd experienced freedom from others' expectations. He didn't have to be a marketing executive, a member of the Lions Club, a father, a brother, a husband. When he came back, he behaved like a tamed-but-angry feral, suppressed fury alternating with ever-deepening, powerless gloom. He stopped coming to the beach, for walks and other family outings, stopped shopping with us in town, stopped attending parents' evenings and dinner with relatives, until, finally, he stopped coming home, choosing to stay out all night partying with colleagues.

Searching for answers, I quizzed him incessantly, like a pneumatic drill probing into vulnerable flesh. *Why, why, why?* I alternated between treating him like a naughty schoolkid who wasn't behaving as expected, and interviewing him like a condescending counsellor. I did not understand him; he must have something wrong with him: how could he not be content with our situation if I was?

He was lonely, he said. Well, talk to me then. Explain. We can sort it out. Anyway, how can you be lonely? You're surrounded by people who love you!

When he announced the end of our marriage, it was as if a nuclear bomb had gone off in our family. That was five years ago, and we were all scarred by it—he with his guilt; me with my loss; our children with their confusion. I didn't find out for many years how much he had suffered. Our tacit silence in the early days kept our feelings of alienation from the world a secret from us both. He felt alone. That was that; there was no reason. Enough questions; he wouldn't play the game anymore.

***

To: Wendy McKintock
From: Rachael Green
Subject: Moi
May 19
Thanks for replying so quickly. You obviously have nothing better to do. You're right. Things are not good. Am not suicidal, just

seeking attention. Lots of it. I miss you: it seems like ages since you left for the USA but it was only at the end of last term! More later. TTFN, xx

***

I didn't know about the physical symptoms of grief and shock: waking after two or three hours' sleep, my body either numb or tingling, gasping for air, lying stiff, blank-eyed, gaping out into the darkness. I smoked, like a thing possessed, until the poison level numbed my brain. Later, I used food and wine in the same way. These strategies worked. Nicotine, alcohol and excessive food stopped the hurting, and successfully laid me out on the settee like a zombie, devoid of all emotion, glued to the television screen. I don't remember much of the first two years. I held down a job, saw friends, walked the dog, shopped, and fed the children, but I wasn't there. Whatever it was that had happened, I thought I would never feel secure again. I would be standing on the edge of an abyss and, unless I stood firm, I would fall.

***

To: Rachael Green
From: Wendy McKintock
Subject: Catching up
May 19

Why don't you come and see me? Austin is charming. All rolling hills and lakes, quite unlike any other city I know. Of course it's far from being another Florence, and doesn't come stocked with delicious Italian stallions to pinch my behind and croon 'O sole mio' into my ear...but then it does have its fair share of gorgeous sturdy Texans and of course, there's the musicians. Seventh heaven, whatever. I digress into fantasy.
Studying takes up the most part of my day; it reminds me of us both shivering in that awful garret room at Reading, huddled

around the two-ring gas burner warming our hands…oh, my, however many years ago now?

Are you still suffering? Are things truly awful for you?

***

I bumped into a colleague in the school stationery cupboard one morning. She asked how I was coping.

'I'm not coping. I'm overeating, drinking, smoking, taking anti-depressants and seeing a shrink,' I told her.

'Oh, but you are coping. Not coping would be sitting in the corner of the room, sucking your thumb, rocking backwards and forwards.'

Those few words brought back my power; the power to make decisions and choices. One by one, I began discarding my props. Once out of the darkness, I would never be afraid of going back in. I emerged like a butterfly, with new-found confidence, and proceeded to indulge in a sensuality I didn't know I was capable of. From now on, I was going to live!

Or so I thought. Because now, five years later, although I no longer stuck my finger into the butter to wipe it around the back of the bread bin to collect crumbs of cakes and biscuits which I didn't even like, nor swallow large glasses of wine in two drafts, pausing only to drag on a cigarette or to change television channels, my self-esteem was artificial. Deep down, I was still the abandoned wife, the failure, she-who-could-not-keep-her-husband.

When I went out, I was convinced I could see others' pitying stares, silently acknowledging my "lowered" status. Every time I passed a mirror, I would look at myself and demand to know why he had left: *who is this person who has driven him away?* Oh, the shame of it, mingled with bewilderment, anxiety and despair.

***

To: Wendy McKintock
From: Rachael Green
Subject: You?
June 5
Well, not that bad. Apart from school. The students get dimmer by the month. We now have to teach them how to read so they can resit their eleven plus. Last important news I heard from you, you were shagging some thirty-year-old. What happened to him?
X

To: Rachael Green
From: Wendy McKintock
Subject: Ooh young man
June 10

Goodness me the Guernsey grapevine is still functioning, then! Yes, I am seeing a rather delightful male companion. Simply couldn't resist him, don'tcha know... He treats me like a princess and calls me his 'li'l lady'. A dreamboat indeed. I'm very happy.

To: Wendy McKintock
From: Rachael Green
Subject: With envy
June 20
So, drop-knickers gorgeous, is he? And a Texan, to boot (get it?)! Did he call you ma'am when he removed his Stetson? How big is his cigar?

To: Rachael Green
From: Wendy McKintock
Subject: Texan Stetsons
June 22

A lady never divulges private conversations. Suffice to say I am slightly more out of breath than usual. Our strolls to the college shop were not adequate training. I'll have muscles like a boxer soon.

xx

To: Wendy McKintock
From: Rachael Green
Subject: Skint
June 24

Good for you. Does he have an older brother? Short-sighted, desperate? Actually, no. Am so sick of casting myself as the middle-aged, dumped ex-wife. Have lost a stone, given up fags and anti-depressants, only go to therapy once a month now...and down to a bottle of wine a night. Well...nearly. Surely, after all this effort, someone will notice me?

Have a summer job teaching EFL with a private school using college during the hols for classrooms. So can sit in my own room and mark whilst the students do written work. Should be a doddle. Am so skint, already have a lodger in every cupboard, and two jobs. This is not good.

***

Our stuff had been duly divided into his and mine; no longer ours. He came to collect his when I was out of the house. The remaining furniture taunted me. Once the symbols of a life, they had now become reduced to what they were: inanimate objects; mere dead matter. I even missed his junk, his mementoes and old clothes. What had previously irritated me had also offered me the womb-like comfort of familiarity, security. There were spaces in the house where he had been; holes in my world. They would mock me, those spaces, like empty fish eyes reflecting a lost life.

At night, I would dream that he was holding me in his arms, reassuring me that he still loved me, that everything was alright. Then I would wake and sob. I felt like a child again, helpless, fearful and isolated. Where was my optimism now? I was no longer an automaton, but five years had gone by since my so-called power returned, and I was no further on.

To: Rachael Green
From: Wendy McKintock
Subject: Beware of dodgy lodgers
June 30

Oh my word, pass me the Prosecco! I should imagine you'll need more alcoholic sustenance, not less, to cope with teaching in hols time. Who are your lodgers? Where did you find them? Surely Guernsey doesn't have an abundance of accommodation seekers, unless you are sheltering refugees working in hotel kitchens?

To: Wendy McKintock
From: Rachael Green
Subject: Oh la la
July 3

Guess what?! Haven't met Mister Right but have met Monsieur Possible. One of my EFL students. Has a Dalí moustache but, to compensate, twinkling eyes, and is extremely witty. Works as a translator in Paris. He calls me Rashelle, sounds a lot sexier than Rachael. So not a kitchen porter: non, non, non, mon dieu! We've been to dinner; also the beach, where he got quite amorous amongst the seaweed. The possibility of a long-distance romance is enticing: if it all goes wrong, no one here will know. Now plotting romantic weekends in La Belle France. Thought I'd better prepare the kids for Mum's first boyfriend in twenty-two years. They immediately insisted on taking me out to buy condoms. I had no idea what to ask for having been on The Pill till his midlife crisis did us part, so we duly traipsed off to the chemists where my children described—in hysterics—the various benefits of each brand, thickness, colour and flavour (flavour?), whilst my headmaster stood behind us pretending not to hear. Is this how post-divorce love life usually works?

To: Rachael Green
From: Wendy McKintock
Subject: Beasties
July 10

My word you do live an adventurous life. Which flavour did you go for in the end...oops, perhaps I'd better rephrase that...er, finally?
Do be careful of wee beasties...in the sea, I mean. A friend here got bitten by something and her foot expanded so much she thought it would explode.
Keep me posted with developments!
xx

To: Wendy McKintock
From: Rachael Green
Subject: Frogs and kids
Aug 1
The romance is on! I have done ze deed with ze Froggie! His name is Roland and the kids have nicknamed him Roll On Roll Off. We arranged an assignation in France as I didn't want to scare the family with a Frog in the bathroom. I took the ferry to Saint Mâlo. He met me with roses, and we walked hand in hand through the gates of the old town. His home is intra-muros, no less, and very charming in a dusty kind of way. We had champagne and lobster salad...and so to bed. It was sooo weird touching another man's body after sleeping with the same person for half my life. I lay awake for hours, terrified I might rumble, snore or fart in my sleep...or, even worse, that he might reach across for my tummy and notice how flabby it is. It's really hard to get to sleep with drawn-in muscles.

PS Thanks for the tip about the indeterminate crawlies in the seaweed. Haven't been bitten and blown up like a barrage balloon yet—at least not so you'd notice.

To: Rachael Green
From: Wendy McKintock
Subject: Kissing Frogs
Aug 21

How is the romance going? Have you now recovered from David separation syndrome? Hope your Frenchman is keeping you happy?
TTFN
x

To: Wendy McKintock
From: Rachael Green
Subject: Oh dear
Aug 29

Oh la, la... 'E is becoming a little trop 'eavy pour moi. 'E sinks eet weel be bon if 'e comes 'ere to leev. I am not so 'appy about zees. A leetle early for such propositions, hein?

So, he is getting to be embarrassing. He came over for a weekend and made a fuss because he wanted us to shower together and had to wait for both my girls to use it, by which time there was no hot water left. So he Went Out For A Walk. An hour later, having figured out that I was not coming after him to Beg Him To Return, he strolled into the kitchen and told me sheepishly he wanted to spend the rest of his life with me. Yuk. This is not such a good plan after all. Might even have to jettison him. Watch this space.

To: Rachael Green
From: Wendy McKintock
Subject: Crapaud in disguise?
Aug 31

How very ungracious of him to sulk. Not at all manly. Do forgive me if I sound negative but perhaps consider what he might be hoping for: your house is a fair size, yes? And he lives in a wee flat in the ramparts? Sounds like he's more like a toad than a frog!

To: Wendy McKintock
From: Rachael Green
Subject: Nascent plan
Sep 13

'E 'as been dumped. 'E 'as rolled off for ze last time. You were quite right: I am sure he had another motive for wanting to come here. Apart from my magnetic personality and irresistible body, that is. Thanks for the blow to my self-esteem, by the way. Call yourself a friend? I think my house was the most likely. Although I can't see why he would choose Guernsey over Brittany: they are almost identical. Anyway, I made a decision tonight, on the night of the new moon, 'cause that's when they (who 'they' are I have not the faintest clue) say that all Important Decisions should be made. More later!

***

September 13
So there we were, sitting in a semi-circle, tired and tetchy at the start-of-term staff meeting, dreading the new term; the "long" summer holidays instantly forgotten after a week of frantic preparation for the onslaught of adolescent monsters.

The Head rose to his feet, coughing nervously. 'Ladies and gentlemen, thanks to you all for your work last term. Not an easy one!' He smiled expectantly, but continued when no one laughed. 'There's just one announcement I have to make today. In view of the latest budget cuts, we're asking everyone to do a library duty. Just once a week. To save us the cost of an assistant librarian.'

'Does that mean we'll lose a free period?' someone ventured.

'Well, yes, technically, but I'm sure we can count on your goodwill. It's unavoidable. Every school is having to make cuts.'

Whenever the Head couldn't justify asking us to do something he always resorted to counting on our goodwill. As if we had any.

'What will it involve?' I asked.

'Stamping library books that the students bring in, taking cards out of the books they borrow. It's quite straightforward. The librarian can show you.'

'So will we be able to do our marking while we're in there?'

'Not really. It depends on how many students come up to the library. There's usually quite a few, so it's a bit hard to concentrate on anything else.'

'Last time I was in the library, there was a nest of first years in there. They really have to be discouraged from social behaviour.'

Nodded agreement all round.

'Yes, well. Can we get on? The library has been a problem area. We are, of course, asking all members of staff to help with any discipline problems.'

Someone muttered something about that being because the kids didn't know how to read, but I was outraged.

'Why does this *request* not surprise me?' I stood, chin up, and enunciated very clearly. 'I'm afraid to say that this is the straw that has broken this particular camel's back. I'm a teacher, not a librarian. I don't have a problem with librarians. It must be a fascinating job. But it's not what I chose as a career, and I choose not to do it. If that is a problem, please can I see you as soon as possible?'

Never one for thinking before acting, I wrote my letter of resignation that same evening. When it was done I went out for some air. Alone in the deepening dusk, numbed by the cold wind, I sat on the stone step outside my house, gazing into the shadows of the garden, sucking at the final centimetre of my cigarette. Charcoal-coloured clouds swept overhead, urging life on Earth below to flee from some impending terror.

***

Sep 14

To: Rachael Green
From: Wendy McKintock
Subject: Curiouser and curiouser

Hey R!
Hm, a decision. Made on the night of a new moon, no less. You've got my attention now. Can't wait to hear what you're up to!
xxx

***

I loved my Georgian house, finally bought from David by working at two extra jobs and filling the place with lodgers. Every morning when I walked down the stairs, I would whisper a thank you for its warmth, its fun, its elegance. I knew I would never again find a home of such fine proportions, such perfect dimensions, such solidity.

David had decorated in discreet colours which enhanced the quality antiques he had purchased. I had replaced these with plants; their life a substitute for the oak, walnut and mahogany that he had removed. What had happened? Why was I—were we—robbed of our future? I had dreamed that we would grow old together in this house. Our kids would look back on it with fond memories of trips to the beach, garden picnics, barbecues, family parties, and the privacy of their own big bedrooms, where they could hide out from the parents, listen to their own music, dream their own dreams.

Suddenly their home was an alien environment, full of strangers with their raucous laughter and drunken parties. But, for me, this new environment represented another chance at a life. The lodgers didn't see me as a failure. Instead of a baggy, washed-up cast-off, I could be a newly single, mature woman with a great body and bags of confidence. They made me laugh; they took me out for drinks. They were the sort of people I would never have normally met in the married couples' set I had previously socialised with. There was a downside, though, and a significant one. In the lodgers' company, I lost fifteen years, but I also lost my kids. I was so insecure that, instead of commanding their respect, I needed their approval. I dropped my mother role and tried to become their best mate, encouraging them to participate in my new lifestyle. Then I wondered why, one by one, all three moved out. Well, the two older ones at least. Sophie still spent half the week with me, but it felt like my frantic attempts to avoid loneliness had driven away my whole family.

Where was the responsible protector now? Who was I looking after now? I mentally shrugged. I was useless at the age of three and I always would be. No matter how hard I struggled to look after them, I would be sure to fail. Because I was a bad sister, a bad wife, and now a bad mother... and nothing could change that, could it?

***

To: Wendy McKintock
From: Rachael Green
Subject: Run away! Run away!
Sep 20

Good lord, you are turning into an American. What's with this 'hey!' greeting? And you a Jean Brodie soundalike... what is the world coming to?

Okay, here it is. Am fed up. Just thought I'd remind you again. But I have a kind of plan. It's a week since I made up my mind. Involves running away, kind of... I blew my top at the staff meeting. I can't face another whole year of dreadful kids and ticking boxes.

***

The night I made up my mind, I resolved not just to go on a journey but to make the going happen, come what may. Any other decision would have involved leaping over emotional or psychological hurdles. All I had to do was decide the order of procedure: resign first and risk having no income to pay the mortgage, or put the house on the market and risk having nowhere to live while I worked out my notice. I did both on the same day: gave up my job and put the house up for sale. And it was easy. So easy, in fact, that I wondered why it had taken me so long to come up with the idea.

I'd always subscribed to the theory that if things aren't working, do something different. Pity I hadn't put that into practice in my marriage. I guess it was because I didn't know it wasn't working until it was too late. My desperate pleadings fell on deaf ears: he was committed to his path, convinced there was nothing left to retrieve. I would never understand, he said. And he was right. I wouldn't, not till I'd learned to see the world in a different way, through different eyes.

***

To: Rachael Green
From: Wendy McKintock
Subject: Run away! Run away!
Sep 21

Oh sinner woman, where're you gonna run to? Are you planning to do something stupid? Good girl!

To: Wendy McKintock
From: Rachael Green
Subject: Happy Birthday to me
Oct 7

My birthday today. Forty-nine years old and have now officially given up on romance. Am going to try self-pity on to see if it suits me. Then join a nunnery. If my cunning plan doesn't work, that is. Will tell you more details when I have the confidence to share my risk-taking behaviour with anyone other than a counsellor. Sorry I haven't been in touch for a while. Big things going on for me. Big decisions. My two big kids have just moved out of home into flats of their own. Little Sophie spends half the week with her Dad. Time for me to move on. Couldn't quite bring myself to write it all down for fear of inviting criticism/reality check/derision…i.e. stuff I don't want to hear! Basically, I've done it again: acted before thinking, opened mouth before putting brain into gear. Only this time I haven't changed my mind. Yet.
How are you?

To: Rachael Green
From: Wendy McKintock
Subject: Happy Birthday!
Oct 7

I wish you a lovely day today, forgetting all the tough times you've had this year.
As for me, I'm as happy as a purring pussycat. Hope that doesn't sound faintly rude. When my guy dazzles me with one of his smiles I can hardly believe my good fortune. He has beautiful teeth, he's tall and slim, has a nice personality too, and he makes me laugh. What more could a girl want? My apologies in advance for making you feel queasy!
So, out with it! What news?

To: Wendy McKintock
From: Rachael Green
Subject: Choppers
Nov 4

Am so glad your Yankee 'guy' is cavity free. And yes, it does sound faintly rude. Ultra-white choppers, eh? Does he floss at night? Are you sure he doesn't take them out before he goes to sleep? These all-American smiles are highly suspect, you know. And what's this about a 'nice personality'? You know very well we only say that about seriously ugly people.

Well, here goes: I'm off. Travelling. For a year...in search of whatever pieces of my jigsaw are missing. India, Thailand, Vietnam, Oz, home via the US (in search of your Texan's older brother), or maybe Mexico...oo-er!

***

November 30

I'm nothing but a character in a story I have invented, I thought as I grabbed my coat to go outside. *I have very cunningly programmed myself to survive.* I have the same old thoughts, over and over again. I feel like a bloody robot.

I had to get outside, to the beach; my head was spinning with the implications of what I planned to do.

Although I was bored, I hadn't been able to find a way to escape. Every day for thirty years, I had watched the sea alternately caress and assault the granite coast of my island home, as if mocking my own see-saw of emotions. Sure, I was secure in the repetition; the routine. The odd storm would liven things up, but basically it was in, out, in, out, in, out. Reliable. Safe. Monotonous. This was not the life I wanted. I would give it all up, cast off my fears and be bold!

I strolled along the pale silk sands of the beach, two minutes' walk from my home. *Now the decision is made, the rest will fall into place*, I thought, looking up at the new moon just visible through the clouds. *Now I've said it, I'll make it real. It will happen.*

Within seconds, doubts set in. The deserted coastline stretched ahead of me, waves cresting into spume. Why was this not enough for me? I figured that most people would give their right arm to live where I did. And I had to go off globetrotting, looking for the meaning of life.

I breathed in the tang of the sea and pulled off my sandals to paddle.

Christ! It's freezing! Okay, Wander Woman, you win.

***

To: Rachael Green
From: Wendy McKintock
Subject: Your plan
Dec 2

My goodness! How very exciting! I am impressed. Brave girl! Don't disappear, will you? Let me know where you are and what you're doing. I'm speechless. Coming to the USA for a sabbatical is one thing; this is a whole new level of daredevilry! Good luck!

To: Wendy McKintock
From: Rachael Green
Subject: Eek!
Dec 18
End of term. End of previous life. Sold the family home, given away all the furniture, wept buckets—no change there, then. Bye-bye, friends; bye-bye, family. What have I done? What was that I said about not changing my mind?

To: Rachael Green
From: Wendy McKintock
Subject: The future
Dec 24

I wish you the very best this Christmas, dear Rachael. I will miss our email contact as I guess it won't be easy for you to find internet cafes till you come west. Of course you must visit if you possibly can; it would be so good to see you and hear all your stories. We have known each other a long time! When you married David I would never have guessed that your future held this whole new life. Don't let this marriage break-up have you forget who you are. I know you have been struggling with painful emotions. Please be kind to yourself.
W
xxx

To: Wendy McKintock
From: Rachael Green
Subject: Joyeux Noel
Dec 25
HAPPY XMAS! Are you gobbling (turkey, that is) with your Texan?
      So...here we go...am taking the kids with me! Made enough dosh from the sale of the house to support us all for the year, though the older two will have to get jobs at some point when we're in Oz 'cause I'm too ancient to get a work visa. Want to stay there a while and that will be quite pricey. Anyway, we're having a grand finale, last family Xmas in the house. Watch this space...

***

Maybe it was a mad idea, but I really wanted us to spend our last couple of weeks in Guernsey all together under one roof. And what better roof than the family home? David agreed to drop our youngest, Sophie, off on Christmas morning, even though it wasn't my 'turn' to have her. I invited him to stay for the day and, to my surprise, he accepted. Our older children, Sara and Conrad, had moved out of their flats the week before so they could pack up the stuff they'd left at the house when they'd moved out. I felt I was on the threshold of a whole new future; a whole new life.

Now the rooms in my house, once filled with the optimism of a future, looked like they had been hit by a hurricane. Dog hairs floated in the sunlight, grimy stains accused me from untouched corners of the kitchen, and torn edges from cardboard boxes betrayed weeks of disposal. For that's what I had been doing: disposing. Of pots and pans, books, trinkets, souvenirs, gadgets, CDs, albums, cassettes, clothes—heaps and heaps of matter "no longer required". To avoid acknowledging the void this frantic activity had created in my once comfortable, middle-class home, I hid my face behind my hands, like a child who thinks that if he can't see you, you can't see him. *Come what may*, I'd thought. Those words would haunt, and taunt, me.

***

January 1997

What was I looking for, then? What would I find on this journey around the world? What, actually, was the point of it all?

I had packed up my life as if it were the easiest thing in the world. I had a vague plan of travelling as far away as I could get from the routines I'd spent my life so far establishing. And for what? And, worst of all, what on earth was I doing taking my children with me?

Reactions from friends and family had ranged from outright admiration to 'What are you running away from? Problems always follow you, you know'. Smart arses. I preferred to believe I was an intrepid explorer, and talk of me dragging my kids around the world for no apparent reason did nothing to deter me. After all, what better way was there to learn about the world?

So I ploughed on—selling, buying, ticking off checklists, creating new ones—all the while refusing to let any negative thoughts push me off track. Until I came to the first hurdle: Sophie lived with her father for half the week and with me for the other half. And he refused to let her come with us.

'She can come out to you in the school holidays,' David had insisted. 'Educationally, it wouldn't be such a big deal, but socially, it would affect her big time. She'd be coming back into a class full of kids a year younger than her, and all her friends would be in the year above. No, it's not on, Rachael. I won't let you take her too.'

A blow beneath the belt. I felt winded; stunned. I hadn't reckoned on this. Truth was, he was right, and that's what hurt the most. It wasn't the right thing for her. She was still young, needing security, routines, familiarity. Family life as she knew it had already ended—it wouldn't be right to uproot her too.

I walked into the travel agency feeling dejected. 'I'm afraid we have to make a change to our plans. It won't be four round-the-world tickets, only three. And a return ticket Heathrow to Sydney in April, and another return Los Angeles–Heathrow, probably in August, but I don't know exactly when yet. The April dates are...'

How could I leave her behind? How would she feel when we all set off without her? Would she feel rejected? Would she be scarred for life? Would she hate me forever or, worse, spend her life thinking that she'd done something wrong; that I was punishing her? I tried to imagine how I would have felt at the age of thirteen in the same situation. I couldn't.

***

I thought I knew my older daughter. Sara had always been an easy child; personable, willing, eager to please. Now, at 20, she was lively, sociable and bubbly. At least she had been...until she fell for Michael. Since then she often seemed morose, at least to me.

The evening I had driven round to invite her on the trip, I had seen her standing at her apartment window, looking down at the street. She could see cars coming up the road from there. The street had been glowing. Lots of green tinsel, red baubles and golden pine cones were reflected in the shop windows. She'd been living in a quiet area of St Peter Port, at the top of a hill above the town, in a tall house divided into flats, close to bric-a-brac and antique dealers.

I'd parked and climbed up the stairs to the fourth floor. On reaching her flat, I knocked and opened the unlocked door. She had been deep in thought, swaying to rock music, as I turned the doorknob.

'Hi, darling. Only a few weeks till Christmas!'

'Mmm? Sorry, Mum, I was miles away. What did you say?'

'Are you okay, darling? You're not still fretting, are you? I mean, he...'

'Leave it out, Mum, please.'

'Look, he didn't actually promise, did he?'

'Actually, he did. He promised he'd be back on the island for Christmas. To see me. But he obviously lied. Anyway, I don't want to talk about it.'

"He" being Michael, one of my ex-tutees at the college where Wendy and I had worked together. I had been supposed to pick her up at the airport a couple of months earlier but had some mindless meeting or other and had sent him instead. I'd figured he was her sort: indoors type, hunky and funny, and tall. She'd told me off for saying hunky, said it was straight out of the seventies, made him sound like either a weightlifter or shirtlifter. But she did feel comfortable with him straightaway.

When I next saw her, she had prattled on excitedly about him. They'd had a laugh at the other passengers storming to Baggage Enquiries. Hers had gone missing too, as they do, but she was too obsessed by what she called his 'gorgeousness' to care.

As I said, I thought that, after nineteen years, I knew my daughter. Not well, obviously. For a start, I didn't know she could do a good impression. She mimicked his first words to her. 'Hi. Michael, at your service. And you're Sara, right? Cool you're on time. Do you have any luggage?

'I told him it was probably somewhere the other side of Turkey. We weren't told it was lost until after we'd been waiting half an hour at the carousel. I muttered something about going to get in the queue, and he offered to fetch me a drink.'

Not that she'd remembered his every word, of course.

'I told him he was a star and asked for vodka and Red Bull. About two hours later, we got home. Then we ran to the takeaway in the rain.'

Then back to her place and the canoodling, I suppose. I haven't asked her for more details about that. He apparently said he really liked her and wanted to see her next day. He was due to go to Thailand a few days later with some friends. Asked her if she'd be here for Christmas. She told him she'd make sure she was. And there'd been no communication from him since.

When I had knocked on her door, I knew she would be steeling herself to be pleasant. She'd be in no mood for mothers and would not be about to talk about the effect Michael's apparent rejection was having on her. I would have wanted all the details and she would have been feeling embarrassed enough already. So I didn't ask.

She'd been fiddling with her long, dark hair. It was a habit of hers, twisting it into tight curls. It wasn't as if she didn't have enough waves already. No matter how fed up, she was always immaculately made-up and stylishly dressed; what my mum would have called 'well groomed.' How come all my kids were tall and slender and I was a dumpy little upturned mushroom?

'Mum, when you came down the road I'd just closed my eyes, and I was willing his car to turn into the road. I recognized a car and...'

'Yes, I know how it is. I bet you gasped, thinking it was him...and then sighed with disappointment at the sight of my jalopy wobbling its way towards the building? Am I right?'

'No! Well, yes. Sort of. But I'm not going to let him ruin my Christmas.'

It was typical of her to act nonchalant. She used to stand by the playschool window, bravely waving goodbye to me with a smile, tears streaming down her cheeks. Nowadays, as a young adult, she hid her lack of confidence by insisting on luxury in everything: designer clothes, comfort. ('A half-hour walk to work? Are you mad? That's why God created taxis, Mother.')

'Can you turn the music down, love? I've got something to ask you.'

The Red Hot Chili Peppers silenced, we'd sat down, Sara sighing with irritation. Her light hazel eyes had been dull. My ever cheerful little girl had lost something. Her spontaneity, perhaps? She wasn't yet cynical, but certainly disillusioned.

'Well now, I have something to say which I think will cheer you up. You know I've been planning my big journey. You've been so fed up. Do you think a round-the-world trip would be 'just the ticket', as your grandma would say?'

'Oh God, Mum, even for you that's a bad one.'

'So, how do you feel about you and Conrad coming with me?'

It had taken several seconds to sink in.

'Oh, Mum. That's like a dream! Are you really sure you want to take us? No, don't answer that. Where are we going? When? Oh my God, it's fantastic!'

Brooding about Michael would have to wait.

'What did Conrad say?'

***

Conrad had been a chubby little boy. He would chuckle and smile to himself as he'd accepted extra biscuits from his older sister. She was going to be an actress, she'd told him, so she had to be thin. His sister was stupid, he'd said. Why give up biscuits just to be on the telly? He, on the other hand, was Spiderman, and needed plenty of fuel.

As he grew, his body fat quickly disappeared until, at nineteen, and six foot, he was what his grandma called a "beanpole". When I was self-medicating with wine and food, he used to wobble my belly with his hand and smile. 'Jelly belly, tub of lard.' Little shit.

He could never figure me out. Used to tell me off for moaning about being lonely, then staying in and stuffing myself. He decided that women were weird. He had to hand it to me now, though, he said. After years of droning on about changing my life, I had actually done something he approved of.

'D'you fancy taking a year off work and going round the world?' I asked.

'Certainly could manage that, I reckon. You paying?' His barely noticeable squint lingered for a second or two in his right eye.

'Well, you'd actually be coming with me. You know I've sold the house. I should be able to get a smaller place in a cheap country like Spain when we get back.'

'The travelling sounds good. Not so sure about going with you, though.'

'Sara's coming. She's thrilled. She immediately wanted to know what you'd said. She obviously wants you to come as well. I reckon it's an ideal way for her to get over that Michael. She was so disappointed.'

'She probably thinks she'll bump into him somewhere. Anyway, I'm busy right now. I'll think about it. Dunno if I fancy it, to be fair. I'd probably end up missing my mates, and work's not been so bad lately. Thanks for the offer, though. Cool.'

***

'For God's sake, just make a decision!' I yelled. 'Do you want to come or not?'

Patience eluded me. I was frustrated at Conrad's and Sara's seeming lack of urgency. They wanted to go, I knew that, but seemed so slow at getting themselves organized. I also knew they needed to adjust to their imminent departure from friends and familiar routines, but I had to keep reminding myself that, having casually cast off my own past, my children had no intention of casting theirs off so quickly.

At first, they had called it my "hare-brained scheme"; another of my idealistic, impossible dreams. Then I showed them the tickets: three round the world, and Sophie's returns for Sydney and Los Angeles. If I bought her tickets now, I believed, she would know that she was definitely coming out to see us, and this was supposed to comfort her.

'You do know why you can't come with us, don't you, darling?' I tried to guess what Sophie might be feeling.

She looked back blankly. 'Of course, Mum, you've told me a million times.'

'What has your dad said?'

'Nothing.' Why are children so infuriatingly uncommunicative? Couldn't be that we've somehow taught them to keep their mouths shut, since no one really listens to what they say, could it? Right now I wished I could turn back the clock and encourage my child to prattle on instead of repeating my time-old parental cop-out: 'In a minute, darling, Mummy's busy right now.'

Truth was, I had no idea at all about what she was thinking or feeling, and had no point of reference in my own childhood as a starting point. My mother wouldn't even leave me with a babysitter, for Christ's sake. She really should have been more thoughtful and abandoned me at some stage so I would be able to empathize with my child.

I felt helpless, and shabby. All I could do was reassure her that I loved her, but it sounded so hollow. *'I love you, but oh, by the way, I'm off for a year and I'm leaving you behind.'*

***

'Andrew, brother dear, can you do me a favour?'

'Sure, sis. Hold on while I take you off loudspeaker. Louise keeps pressing the wrong buttons on our phone, and before you know it you're broadcasting private conversations to the whole street. Okay, done. What do you need?'

'I want to find out how the kids really feel about coming away on this big trip with me. I don't want to force them.'

'Force them? Are you mad? They should be bloody grateful!'

'Yeah, I know, but I don't want them thinking they have to come, to please me. Will you just see if you can find out for me?'

'Sure, sis. No problem.'

'Oh, and by the way, we're all having Christmas lunch together at the house. Will you and Louise come and have a Christmas drink with us before you go and do your own thing?'

'I'll have to ask the boss!'

'Is she okay now? You said she was being a bit off with you lately.'

'Seems okay to me. I think she was just going through a bad patch. You know how excitable she can get.'

Excitable? My sister-in-law? I don't think so. But I replaced the receiver without saying any more.

Andrew sometimes didn't notice what was going on around him. Ever since the bee sting incident, I'd felt the need to protect him, but the truth was I didn't really know him that well. I knew I loved him. We were not only brother and sister; we'd been best buddies since early childhood. Never needed anyone else, and always stuck together in defiance of our parents. If one or the other did something naughty, we'd both own up to confuse them, and both end up being punished, but we didn't care. As we grew up, we drifted apart a bit, but the sibling bond remained.

***

After a morning walk on the beach, I relaxed. I did a quick check on the food. Andrew's yappy Yorkie was in the kitchen, trying to talk the turkey out of the oven. You'd think that, after ten years, he'd give up on this annual ritual. One of these days, I'll put him inside and roast him instead.

We filled the spacious sitting room—Andrew and Louise with their son Solomon, on leave for Christmas in Guernsey from his army post, David and me with our three. Our first family meal together since he left. If we were going to be separated for a year, we could manage a few hours together, surely?

I looked around. In the next few days, I would finish clearing out. For us all, this was the last time our house would resemble a home. Conrad and Sara had spent the last few days making piles of the remaining possessions in their rooms to leave with trusted friends, and would soon only have the contents of their backpacks to their name. Sophie had moved everything of hers into David's cosy but elegant cottage.

I poured a glass of Sauvignon Blanc for David and Chardonnay for Andrew.

'So you said you took Conrad and Sara out for a drink the other day. Where did you go?' David asked Andrew.

'Can't remember the name of it; that minimalist bar place on the seafront, opposite the marina.'

'The one with the spotlights and flashy blue stools? Full of skinny people sitting at those tall steel tables?' I interrupted.

Not my scene at all, that bar; way too pretentious. Andrew, on the other hand, thrived on being a trendy businessman, and enjoyed taking his niece and nephew out every now and then for an after-work cocktail.

'What did they say?' I whispered to my brother. I couldn't wait to find out.

'I think the exact words were *'It's going to be difficult, spending a whole year with Mum. We'll have to take care of one another.''*

'Well, thanks a lot for dobbing on us, Uncle Andrew!' Sara materialised out of nowhere. She's sharp, that girl of mine. Misses nothing.

'Look, Sara, your mum just wanted to be sure you really want to go, and weren't agreeing just to please her.'

'Okay, but I'm not trusting you again!'

Andrew looked crestfallen, until he noticed her grinning.

'It's alright. We knew what you were doing.'

'Phew. Is that why you said all that mickey-taking stuff about my big sister?'

'What mickey-taking stuff?' I proffered a bowl of peanuts.

'Stuff like: *"We'll have to make sure we do what we want or we'll be dragged round a load of boring museums"*, I seem to recall. Sara had to shout over the pounding dance music, sis. Said something like, *"She's sure to want to look at some of her weird ancient sites and jabber on about Indians and piles of stones and old gods. You know what she's like."'*

'Sara! You cheeky madam!' I couldn't help laughing.

'Well, you've got to admit you were a bit scary, saying you were going to buy us all special towels that look like dishcloths,' Conrad joined in.

Oops. I bit my lip: a couple of those towels were lying wrapped in Christmas paper at the base of our tree.

'And a weird pump for purifying water.' She was remorseless. 'Do you reckon we're going to be drinking mud?' she chuckled.

'And trudging around for hours? She'll love that, playing at explorers!' Conrad winked as he nudged his sister.

'In her clumpy boots and baggy old trousers.'

'Oi, you two! *She* is right here, you know!'

'Yeah, and that naff trekking jacket.'

'Stumbling along, weighed down by a huge backpack!'

Andrew giggled. Actually giggled. My brother. Oh God, somebody please put me out of my misery.

'They took a solidarity vow: them against you in all arguments. Then we all ordered more Sex on the Beach.' Andrew recovered his composure.

They think they're so smart, kids. They have a good laugh about you; then tell you all about it so they can laugh all over again. Even Andrew thought they were quite funny. Ha, ha.

David, meanwhile, shook his head slowly, his eyes fixed on Sophie.

'We'd best be off, Andrew. Our turkey will be cremated.' Louise had his coat over her arm and extended it to him.

'Hold on, Louise.' I indicated her front teeth where particles of peanut skins were wedged.

'Thanks. I always seem to get into a mess with peanuts. Remarkable, really.'

'We need to have a farewell hug. Lord knows when we'll see each other again.' I felt a sudden surge of melancholy: we'd had a lot of fun in the early days, Louise and I. Dinner parties, dog walks. Although never close, we had formed an easy friendship. And my little brother was about to lose his big sister. Like a lot of men his age, he didn't have close friends. Somewhere inside me I felt a tiny flutter of fear for him. I walked them to the gate and stood there alone for a moment waving goodbye, before turning back to the house.

'Okay, folks, let feasting commence!'

We gathered at the table laden with festive food and proceeded to devour the starter of smoked salmon on brown bread, Sara, Conrad and I quaffing copious amounts of Chardonnay, while Sophie sipped quietly at her Coca Cola and David at his Sauvignon Blanc.

'You okay, Sophie?'

'Yes, Mum. Why wouldn't I be?'

Why indeed. Maybe it was the wine, but I was unable to respond.

David coughed. 'It's time for a toast,' he announced. 'This year is going to be hard for Sophie and me. We're going to miss you. Here's to a successful trip. Let's hope it's worth it for you all.'

Trust him to put a damper on the meal before the main course was served.

'Well, I think we should focus on today. Who wants to pull a cracker?'

'Mum, are these home-made?' Conrad eyed me with suspicion.

'Yes, sunspot, why?'

'Erm, just wondering. What the hell is this?' Conrad laughed. I had put a small gift in each cracker.

'It's called a pack towel. It's really good. You can wring it out and it dries in minutes. Saves carting heavy wet towels in your pack. I got you one each...'

The laughter drowned my last few words.

'I was joking when I said you were going to take dishcloths!' spluttered Conrad. 'I should have known better!'

'Sophie, let's pull yours, darling.'

We tugged her cracker apart.

'A tiny notebook...great.' She was clearly underwhelmed.

'A diary, sweetheart. So you can write down what you do each day, like I'll be writing to you. Only you can bring yours with you when you come to Australia, and we can read it together there. Do you think that's a good idea?'

'Okay,' was all she said. 'I'm hungry. Can we have our turkey now?'

'Your wish is my command.' *Thank God, she's smiling. I so want this to be a happy day*, I thought.

'Mum, Sophie's got massive handwriting. How much do you think she'll be able to write in a fairy-sized book like that?' My son was guffawing. Time to change the subject. I'd had enough criticism for one day. Especially Christmas Day. I got up, fetched the turkey from the kitchen and handed the platter to David to do the carving. He could play head of the table one last time.

'I know, let's have a "what about when?" session!'

'Good idea, Sara. You go first.'

'Okaaay...what about when we went skiing? And you and Dad fell over watching us ski past you after we'd only had one lesson?'

'We were so proud of you,' David said.

'Your turn now.' Conrad turned to his father.

'Why me?'

'Because that's the rule.'

'You just made that up, son.'

'So?'

'Alright, hold on while I think.'

'This could take all day,' I quipped.

'What do you mean by that?' David's face was stony.

'Nothing, just trying to be funny.'

Why didn't I leave it at that? What's with the self-destruct button we humans sometimes push?

'But come to think of it, it must be hard for you to remember something good about our past.' *Oh, no. I really didn't mean for that to come out of my mouth.*

'Mum!' all three yelled in unison.

Emboldened by alcohol, I wasn't about to back down. 'Well, we wouldn't be giving you and Sophie such a "hard year" as you've just called our adventure, if you hadn't... If...things had turned out differently.'

'You bitch,' he mouthed. Then, louder: 'I'll never forgive you for doing this to us.'

'Dad!' shouted Sara.

'Well, she started it,' Conrad rejoined.

'Calm down, everyone, please. I apologise for saying those things. I don't know what's the matter with me. David, I'm obviously still more upset than I thought I was, but that's no excuse for being nasty. I didn't mean it. I'm really glad you came today. Let's wipe the last few minutes out of our memories and start again. Agreed?'

David smiled, a false smile. 'You always were good at that, dear heart.'

I wanted to ask him what he meant by that, but deep down I knew. Whenever I felt bad about something, I'd pretend it hadn't happened, until I eventually convinced myself it hadn't. Could that be why he'd had enough of me?

'Okay, whose turn is it?' Sara took on the role of peacemaker.

'What about when we used to go camping in France?' I suggested.

'Yay, you two used to go off to the bar and leave us in the tent, and we thought up all sorts of tricks to play on you.' Sophie smiled at her brother and sister. I felt like my heart would break as she spoke.

I looked over to David. The wine had mellowed him and he looked relaxed, enjoying himself even. He'd forgotten his anger and was more like his old self; the fun-loving dad he used to be. I gulped away the pain of unfulfilled hopes, blinked away the hurt, breathed away the loneliness. *Focus on happy times*, I told myself. *Focus on happy times.* You are lucky to have these memories. Some people have never even known love. *Be grateful, not sad.*

***

A week after Christmas, my neighbour Sally peered in through the stained glass window of my front door, rang the door chimes and walked straight through the hall into my kitchen. We island folk didn't do locked doors.

'My God, Rachael, look at all those boxes! Are they all full of kitchen stuff?'

'Yep. Chaos. But I know I've made the right decision. Teaching's been getting harder and harder, the students are an unruly mob, and for what? A pension? I don't want to sell my soul for a bloody pension. Mine will be crap anyway because I haven't been teaching long enough to get a decent one.'

I don't for one minute believe I sounded convincing. My fear was that everyone would find out before long that I was an imposter, and that my rise to fame as a cutting-edge Head of Languages would turn into a spectacular downfall. My reputation was based on nothing except a certain charisma in the classroom, with no back-up skills such as record keeping and actually knowing which kids were which in my groups, let alone how much progress they were making. This fear of discovery had been rising and was now too close to the surface for comfort. The excuse that my husband had abandoned me could only mitigate the situation for so long.

The phone rang. 'Home for the Permanently Bewildered, Rachael speaking... Oh! Hello, darling...'

It was Conrad. He was on the top floor, but insisted on using the phone to communicate.

'Thanks for calling back. Can you pop downstairs a minute?'

I had to concede that, as he was watching Man U, this was out of the question and I'd have to wait until tomorrow when he was next due to come downstairs for some food.

'What's all this stuff?' Lodger *numero uno*, Steve the butcher, eased his ample buttocks into one of my flimsy plastic chairs which, despite buckling ominously, just bore his weight.

'Unwanted, unloved kitchen stuff,' I told him. 'It's all got to go. Can't take it with me; can't sell it; charity shops don't want it.'

'I'll have it. I'll take all of them boxes out your way.'

I thanked him, and was taken aback to see that he began moving them out straightaway. I had never seen him do anything quickly before, so this was quite a surprise. I wondered about his true motivation - was he planning to sell my stuff? -but decided to let it drop for now.

'What's going to happen to your lodgers?' Sally asked.

'Oh, they've already found somewhere else. I gave them good references. They both pay on the dot every Friday. They come in, put their rent money on the kitchen table, then it's straight out to the pub! They're only moving up the road, next door to the Co-op.'

Sally and I stared vacantly as Steve hefted box after box out of the house and into his old banger of a butcher's van, which occupied a generous portion of the drive.

'Kitchen looks nice and bare now. Truly minimalist,' Sally commented.

'I was definitely unencumbered by logic when I made that decision. He's taken everything, apart from a couple of mugs and the kettle. Hmm, smart move, Rache. What do we eat off till we go? Not that it's a long time. Only a couple more weeks...'

'You could live off fish and chips and Chinese takeaways, I suppose.' Steve grinned.

'*Plus ça change,*' Sally said.

***

I was daydreaming again, sitting in my kitchen, thinking back to my childhood days, and the hawthorn tree. It was the best place of all in the garden, where I could climb, stretching all my muscles, to reach higher and higher among the heavily scented blossom, sit astride a branch and look over the house, the garden and the potato field behind—on top of my own world. Then I saw the men carrying my dining table out of the front door, and returned to present reality.

I stirred my tea and snivelled a weak greeting to lodger *numero dos,* aptly named Roger (at least that's what he told us to call him), as he barged into the hall in a grubby Stoke football shirt and kneeless jeans, whiffing of stale sweat.

'What's up wi' you?'

'I'm indulging in a few moments of intense nostalgia,' I told him. 'I have so many happy memories of us all sitting around that table. And now it's being carted off to an ignominious auction.'

'What's one o' them, then?'

'Let's just say my antique mahogany table deserves a better fate.'

'Listen, love, the table is a bit o' wood. The memories are in your 'ead.' He strode off to make himself a coffee in what was left of the kitchen, and where my sister-in-law Louise was attempting to find a kettle.

'Remarkable, the state of your kitchen. Looks like a bomb site.' She peered over my shoulder to read my checklist: visas, medication, inoculations, clothing, water-purifying pump, mosquito nets. 'My God, that lot must be costing you a fortune!'

'Yep. Money has been haemorrhaging out of my account. I had to go to London to get visas for us all. That cost an arm and a leg. The staff at school gave me a backpack. I've filled it with so-called essentials.' I swigged my tea. 'You know: insect repellent, sun cream and stuff.'

'Torch? Swiss army knife? Medical kit?'

'Yep, and guide books, first aid bits.'

'Tampons?'

'Thousands of them, plus a year's supply of HRT.'

'What's left on your list? Good Lord. Money belt, padlocks, and special quick-drying towels. There's no room for clothes!' Louise grinned. 'Hey, I've got a pair of size twenty-two knickers left over from when I was pregnant. You could take them as an emergency tent.'

'Hmm, camping... You know, I've been a fresh air fiend ever since I was a kid. I used to run from mysterious enemies through the grass, and play Pooh sticks at the beck, and clamber up onto tin roofs, and jump from great heights.' I gazed into my cold coffee. 'I can't remember ever playing with dolls. I had a couple. I propped them up against the back wall of my wardrobe, with their terrifying bead eyes staring. Cold and hard things, horrible to cuddle. I hated them.'

'Oh, I loved my dolls. Used to tell them all my woes. Them or the dog. Whenever I was at home in the school hols, that is.' Louise had been sent off to boarding school at a very young age.

'Not me. There was an abandoned works site at the end of the avenue. It was the ideal obstacle course for Andrew and me. Even in bed, I would dream about being outside. I used to make hills with my knees and make my three-legged rubber horse—called Beauty despite his sex and obvious disability—wander up and down the hills and valleys on top of the bedclothes as I sang "I love to go a-wandering" at the top of my voice.'

'Good Lord, you were sad even then. Ah, found the kettle. In the larder cupboard, where else?'

I caught sight of my reflection in the kitchen window. 'No wonder I'm fat. We had cakes for tea every night. I had to lay the table. I had a checklist—bread, butter, milk, cheese, sugar, jam, cakes. We were really into healthy food in our family.'

'At least you can remember family meals. At boarding school, we had dinners at long tables with nuns rapping your knuckles if you forgot your manners.'

'I had a great childhood, I suppose. On Sundays, we used to listen to "Two Way Family Favourites". When we heard the tune "With a Song in my Heart" it was the signal for us all to sit down. The dog used to sit at my dad's feet, ever hopeful. All he ever got was a smattering of ketchup when Dad shook the bottle really hard and Mum hadn't screwed it closed properly. Poor dog looked like road kill.'

'Remarkable. I can just picture your father getting worked up into a frenzy. He rather liked to look good, didn't he?'

'Mmm. You know, it was a cosy world for me. Routines and security. I used to daydream a lot.'

'No change there, then.'

'I suppose I could because I felt so secure. Every day was an adventure. I'd look through that window and fly off to play with fairies or gypsies.'

'Yes, I know what you mean. I used to love watching "Champion the Wonder Horse". It was a special treat for finishing prep early.'

'Me too. And "77 Sunset Strip", with that cool guy called Kookie or something; just seemed to hang around looking broody all day. The only cookies I look at now are of the biscuit kind.'

'We weren't allowed television at school. I only saw it in the holidays. I read a bit. "Wind in the Willows." Ratty and his riverbank. I had a bit of a thing about rivers.'

'I used to read loads. Still do. My favourite books were "*The Water Babies*" and "*Heidi*". You know, my whole morality is based on Mrs Do-As-You-Would-Be-Done-By and Mrs Be-Done-By-As-You-Did. And I blame that bloody Heidi for me loving every fattening dairy product on the planet. All that butter and cheese…'

When I drifted to sleep later that night, my internal monologue began again. I had always felt a vague longing for what I thought were times past, something so elusive that I couldn't give it a name. Was it melancholy, or anticipation? Was it fear, or excitement? It was a compelling, intoxicating and enlivening sensation, making me feel filled with optimistic energy, but it also made me feel sad because, whatever it was I yearned for, it was not happening now. No matter how excited I felt, there was something missing.

I lay still, breathing deeply to relax. Memories rushed at me, of exiting the school gates on winter afternoons, my hands sore with chilblains when I waited at the bus stop outside brick-built Bracebridge Juniors, my nose running, my woolly gloves full of holes where the cold pierced my flesh, hoping my mum would make me a hot cup of tea when I got home, and toast some bread on the fire. I used to hum "What D'you Wanna Make Those Eyes at Me For?" and felt truly sophisticated, or mimed Queen Elizabeth waving at the crowds.

As a teenager, I was embarrassed by my parents' continual praise. I didn't realise until much later that what they were giving me was support. I didn't know, then, that there are children whose parents not only never praise them, but ignore or criticise them, or worse. My twin older brothers had died at birth. My parents considered me a miracle and I basked in that adoration until I contracted the ever-critical ingratitude of adolescence.

I saw school as something I had to tolerate, as a means to an end. I was about to be expelled for recidivist insolence, until 'The School French Exchange' came round. The School French Exchange promised escape; no rules, no uniform. I couldn't wait, and was horrified when the headmistress banned me from going to France. ('You are an unfit representative of the country, let alone the school.')

France was out, but there was still the carrot of Germany later that year. All I had to do was conform. Not being one to make a pointless stand, I selflessly devoted the next few months to creeping, and even began thinking about doing some work. The longed-for trip came around. Yes! I was allowed to go.

I returned completely changed. I fell in love with a German boy called Pit who didn't even notice my existence, but this motivated me into wanting to speak better German. I visited the tiny village of Bielefeld in the hills near Limburg-an-der-Lahn, host to a beer festival, and, at fifteen, had my first dance with an adult male who wasn't my relative.

I slept in a bed covered by crisp white lace over a dark wine red sheet visible beneath. The bedroom overlooked high-roofed Einzelhäuser which formed a barrier between the village and the tall pines covering the hills behind. The yeasty smell of warm, fresh bread wafted up each morning from the bakery next door. After that school exchange, my future was determined: I swore to experience as many foreign places as I could, and that meant learning as many languages as I could.

When I eventually became a languages teacher, it was natural to organise similar school exchanges for my students, as much for my benefit as theirs. At last I had my opportunity to travel; to fulfil my childhood dream.

***

My brother and I were torn away from familiarity in the early nineteen-sixties, when I was in my early teens, and taken to Guernsey where our parents had dreamed of returning ever since our father left to go to war as a young pilot in the RAF. We knew the island. We had visited our grandparents frequently for summer holidays. Long, salty, wet days on the pebbly shores of Fermain Bay.

Andrew and I stared out of the rear window of our father's royal blue Vauxhall Cresta and made a drama of leaving Lincoln, our friends, our home, our avenue—our whole life. We were victims of circumstance. I could not say that I was taken out of my comfort zone, as I had not been comfortable there.

I had already made myself into an outsider after an incident at primary school when my third year teacher uttered the words, 'Of course you can do it. Everyone else can,' which I interpreted as meaning that I was different from the others in my class, and in some way odd, stupid, slow.

A few—no doubt well-intentioned—words changed my world forever. I was no longer safe. I spent the next forty-odd years living my life according to those two beliefs about myself: I was different from the others, and stupid. A lifetime based on less than ten words.

To: Wendy McKintock
From: Rachael Green
Subject: Your fault
Jan 12

Oh God, we're going in a couple of days. So excited I can't breathe. Surviving on nicotine, actually. Haven't had oxygen for weeks. Actually, you kind of inspired me to do this, going off for your year in the US. So, if it all goes horribly wrong, I'll blame you. Just thought I'd let you know. Will email when I can. You have to keep me posted about the Texan—what's his name, anyway?

***

January 16 1997

The scene at Guernsey Airport was not unusual: a group of adults and one teenager were seeing off two young people accompanied by a middle-aged lady. There were a few tears, but no great drama was discernible to passers-by. I held on to Sophie, willing her to feel the warmth of my body for a hundred days while I would be on the other side of the world and she was going about her daily school routine. In the small airport we could see through to the security gate; very soon we would be disappearing through it and out of her life.

I looked over at David, his eyes belying a fixed smile. What had happened to us? Our early years together had been fun. We never got bored and, as a couple, we eased into the local social scene. We never discussed serious stuff like money, buying a house, children, nor even what we both wanted for our futures. We just played, went out to parties and dinners, and sailed other people's boats around the islands. Then we did what everyone in our circle did: bought a home, started a family, and gradually the fun stopped and responsibilities took over. We were smart and fairly successful, with three beautiful children.

Now, he looked crestfallen. 'I'll look after them, you know that, don't you?' He didn't respond for a moment, then whispered. 'Yes, I know you mean to. I just wish I could believe you're capable of protecting them, though.'

When Sophie was born, we were ecstatic. It was as if Life had given us a bonus for being good people. She was an easy child: compliant, contented and thoughtful. As she grew, she tagged along with whatever her siblings were doing, never questioning or making demands.

I watched her nodding to her Walkman, listening to heavy metal, no doubt. By the age of thirteen, she had begun to develop her own style: chain bracelets and necklaces, rings on most fingers, skimpy tops, jeans, boots. She wore her long, dark hair with a fringe that covered her brown eyes, believing it would detract from the freckles sprinkled across her nose. She was tall, with big feet and long legs, and hated to be interrupted, shouting to be heard. Despite her aggressive surface, she was a softie, and loved romantic films and novels.

None of the rest of the family liked her favourite food, sashimi, so I would buy her a Japanese takeaway from time to time. As she grew into a teenager, she relished her individuality. After years of following her older siblings' lead, she was beginning to choose her own direction. Now, I would not be part of that. I would miss her new tastes in food, music and clothes. I would not be there when she felt insecure; when she and her best friend Katy fell out; when she had period pains.

When the time came to let go, I tried to picture the moment she would be walking through the arrivals door at Sydney Airport, to embark on what would surely be one of the most exciting adventures of her life. I handed her the return ticket, London–Sydney, and urged her to keep it safe. Somehow it felt that, by this act, I was promising her that I would not forget her—a pretty meagre token of consolation for my absence. True, not many thirteen-year-olds travelled so far for Easter. At the dismal, foggy airport though, the thrill of Australia and its sunshine seemed a very long way off.

As we walked through to the departure gate, Conrad and Sara turned back for a last look at their dad and little sister. For a second I thought they might run back, but they both waved, then smiled at each other. The ground crew man at the gate wished us a pleasant flight to London, and I couldn't resist saying, 'Oh, we're going a lot further than London, we're going round the world!' Before he could reply I moved towards the gate door. Then I turned back for a last goodbye wave, and my heart felt like lead. I couldn't even summon up a smile. This was somehow wrong, this whole crazy idea.

It was an effort to put one foot in front of the other to board the plane. Once seated on board, I closed my eyes and tried to blot out images of Sophie aged nine months, toddling towards me, arms outstretched. The sadness began to subside a little as the aircraft rose, and a surge of excitement and anticipation dizzied me. I looked across at Conrad and Sara and beamed. Next day, we would be flying from Heathrow to Mumbai. The pain of separation was still there, but it was less acute, displaced by butterflies.

***

India

We spent our last night in the UK in a guest house near Hatton Cross, not far from Heathrow, celebrating our imminent departure drinking a bottle of champagne out of plastic cups. Well, I did. The kids took a sip and moved on to beers. We stayed in our spacious triple room before walking—in my case, staggering—to a nearby Chinese restaurant for an early dinner. We had a 04.30 am check-in. Just before embarking on my journey of cultural enlightenment and spiritual awakening, I had joined the "drunk in a Chinese restaurant" brigade.

As a taxi ferried us to Terminal Three next morning, I began to feel anxious. What if I'd forgotten something vital?

'What's up, Mum? Having regrets already?'

'Just having a quiet panic, Sara.'

'Oh, great, now she tells us,' Conrad mumbled.

'How will you cope with no red wine, eh, Mum?'

'Can we smoke on the plane?'

'I have no idea, son. I just hope we get through check-in and security quickly. Maybe we've cut it a bit fine. It's already three-thirty.'

'And that's not early enough?' Sara asked with a touch of sarcasm.

But before long we were shuffling slowly along the queue, me pulling my pack along the floor by the straps, to the amusement of one or two other passengers. Once on board, we all fell asleep, exhausted from the boozy evening, our excitement, and the shock of the pre-dawn wake up.

***

Mumbai

'Bloody hell; it must be thirty degrees down there!' I groaned.

The captain announced our descent into Mumbai. The first thing we had to do before joining the immigration queue was find an ATM to get local currency: rupees. I had some from the currency exchange in Guernsey but we'd need more.

'Just hang on while I get some more cash.' I fumbled in my day pack. 'Oh shit, where is it?'

'Where's what?' my children cried in unison.

'My card!' I'd brought my credit card. It hadn't occurred to me that we'd be in big trouble if it got lost or stolen. 'Oh God, no. Please don't let this be happening...' For a few horrible seconds, I thought our grand journey was going to be over before we got out of Mumbai airport. However, in my panic, I'd shoved the card further down in my pack and had to withdraw every single item before retrieving it from the very bottom.

It was past midnight when we emerged into a blast of heat. I took a few seconds to adjust my breathing. A sea of open-necked shirts over white dhoti swayed and shouted in front of us.

'No, we don't need a porter. No, we don't need any freelance taxi-finders! No, thank you. We have already booked a hotel.'

Voices were buzzing around us like humming flies.

'This way, madam.' A uniformed man led us to one of a dozen black and yellow Humber cars.

He shook someone lying on the back seat.

'I am not waking up! Leave me alone!' was the slurred response.

'But they can pay. They have rupees. Look!'

With a reluctant grunt, the taxi driver fell out of the rear door and tottered into the front, breathing alcohol over us. My thoughts spilled out in panic. Who was the uniformed man? What was in it for him? We should have used a freelance taxi-finder after all. My first mistake. Not bad for five minutes after leaving the airport.

Oh jeez, he's swerving all over the place! We're going to be killed amidst the rubbish on the streets.

There were rotting vegetables and damp cardboard boxes piled up everywhere, and, despite the lack of windows, the car was filled with the acrid smell of cigarette smoke.

We hurtled through the gloom. The driver pulled up outside a mediocre-looking hotel and made no move to budge from his seat. The road was patched with fresh tarmac.

'He's still seething drunk. Can't be bothered to help us. After all, we're only the customers,' Sara muttered.

'Okaaay. Let's open the boot and get our backpacks out. I bet he'll move if we just start to walk off.'

'No tip! No tip!' Now fully awake, the driver staggered out of his seat.

'Oh my God, he's following us into reception!' I whispered.

'No bloody tip! Bloody foreigners! All the same, the bloody lot of you!'

'Ow!' He had pinched my bum, really hard. This was no flirty gesture.

After collecting our keys from reception, we trudged up to the third floor and into a large room partitioned into two sleeping areas.

Conrad threw his pack onto the floor and stretched out on the bare mattress. 'What's on the menu? I'm starvin', Marvin!'

'You've got to be joking. I've been sucking in hot air, and my clothes are sticking to my body,' Sara groaned.

'It's really humid, that's why. Plus we're all knackered. Come on you two, let's forget about eating and get some sleep.'

Heads spinning, we collapsed onto our grimy beds with not a thought of washing.

Seconds—well, okay—seven hours later, I awoke from a comatose stupor. Then I remembered where we were, and why, and winced.

What was I thinking of? Based on a couple of school trips abroad, a few long-haul flights and family holidays in Europe, I was about to drag half my family around the world for a whole year. I had no experience, no clue about where to stay, no preparation for emergencies, nothing. I didn't even have basic first-aid knowledge. Was I planning to wave a magic wand if anything went wrong? I was never known for my practical skills. This could be a complete disaster. Too late now. Here we were, and I was hungry.

'I suppose it's far too early for you to digest anything, Conrad?' Sara said. 'I'm having bread and eggs. They're the only things on the menu I recognize. Oh, should've known. No table in here. Ha ha, they said they'd bring us breakfast in the room. Nothing about where to eat it!'

She sat on the bed, her plate balanced on her lap, trying to spear fried eggs as they slithered around in a pool of grease. I felt so proud of bringing my children to this luxurious place. Not.

'Sorry, guys. We'll have to risk another taxi to the national airport to get to Goa.'

Two hours later, we were leaning against our backpacks on the terminal floor. Conrad and Sara were having a smoke ring blowing contest.

'Okay to get some food, Ma?'

'Sure, sunspot, here's some money. See if you can get a departure time while you're over there.'

'Goa flight indefinitely delayed,' Conrad muttered when he returned, in between mouthfuls of dahl, veggie curry and rice.

Sara sighed. 'That meal looks manky, Conrad. Those chapattis smell foul. And that weirdo chef was grinning inanely. I reckon he's either off his head or trying to poison you.'

When the flight finally left, three hours later, Conrad's face was pasty white, his eyes narrowed with sleep after the early start.

'Why are you moving seat, Conrad?' Sara asked, ten minutes after take-off.

'The woman next to me keeps putting her feet up onto my knees. And she's mingin.'

***

Goa

After landing, we took a taxi to Chapora, about an hour from Goa Airport. We arrived at dusk, and parked in a narrow street outside a dingy looking café squeezed in between dilapidated shacks with rusty, corrugated iron doorways hanging off their hinges, and Subscriber Trunk Dialling booths.

'Hey, look, Mum! The café's advertising rooms for rent,' Sara said. 'Looks a bit naff, though.'

Stunned into indecision, I suggested we have a drink. The heat was oppressive; my neck was clammy.

'Look, there are loads of dodgy men watching us,' whispered Sara. 'And they've got shifty eyes. Why are they all hiding under the trees?'

'They're not hiding, love. They're just sitting. Probably been there all day, keeping out of the sun. What about that taxi ride, then?'

'Yeah, well weird!' Conrad said.

'I saw a woman balancing a huge basket of bananas on her head,' I said. 'And those wriggling little pigs squealing like mad, strapped across the back of a scooter!

'Check out the cows in the middle of the traffic! And did you see that family? There were five of them on one motorbike, calmly weaving along through the cars.'

'Look, there's a money change place opposite. We'd better get some now in case we have to pay in advance.'

I stooped to enter a gloomy hut where a grinning man sat at a card table with an enormous open cash box in front of him. Inside were neatly stacked wodges of notes, held together by long metal staples the width of my little finger. There was obviously no hope of using my card here.

'You will have to go into Mapusa, madam. Here cash only.' I felt queasy as I stood before him, unable to avoid seeing his tobacco-stained, tombstone-shaped teeth.

'Oh, okay, thank you.'

'How'd you get on, Mum?' asked Sara.

'Let's just say it's a good thing I couldn't use my card. They sell notes in massive thick blocks with metal spike things and, to get one off, you'd end up tearing the notes to shreds!'

Sara clearly hadn't been listening. She looked around anxiously. 'My pack is heavy. It's getting dark. I'm hot and dirty, and this café is full of mosquitoes. Can we not go and find some rooms now?'

I approached the moustachioed owner. 'Please show us your rooms.'

'There is only one room available for sleeping. Look, come looking here, madam.'

'There are three of us. It is six metres square, with a dirt floor, one double mattress on the floor, no furniture, no electricity and no windows. No, thank you. This won't do,' I replied.

I stifled the urge to panic. My hair was plastered to my forehead; my flimsy top was sticking to my skin.

My stomach clenched. I held my breath for too long and began to feel dizzy. For a second or two I was back in the garden, aged three and a half, and I relived those moments. *There is a searing screech from the pram. Something goes wrong in my tummy. It goes hard, it's tight, and I'm frightened. I sit up. My chest hurts, and my throat is so dry that my in-breath feels like hot sand in my mouth. I get up and run into the corner of the garden to hide as Mummy rushes outside, her pinny covered in flour, to scoop Andrew up. She is crying. She ignores me. It's my fault. I have caused this dreadful scene because I don't want him. I am a bad sister.*

We trudged on towards Vagator, about a kilometre away according to the cafe owner, Conrad and Sara following me wearily along a shadowy path. I saw a glow from candles on rooftop tables. I crossed my fingers as we approached a man sitting on the red-painted stone verandah steps of the building.

Yes! Rooms to be had; price to be negotiated.

'Wow! A whole house! With a terrace! Let's take it, Mum!'

'And an outside shower! Look, you two, a tap high up on the wall with a bucket underneath!'

'And an *American Toilet!*' Conrad's false enthusiasm was evident.

'What's an American toilet?' Sara enquired innocently.

'Whatever it is, it's filthy, it stinks, and there's no loo roll.'

The house owner beamed proudly, his fingertips joined as if in prayer. 'Ah yes, madam, very luxurious. We have every comfort here.'

'Hmm.' I glanced at the dusty cobwebs in every corner, the horsehair mattresses and thin cotton covers on the beds. 'No pillows, I see. Every comfort, as you say.' I decided to go for it; we were too tired to walk any further. 'Yes, we'll take it. Thank you.'

'Thank you, madam. I am happy you are liking my home. Yes, yes, very comfortable.'

'Your home? Where will you be sleeping?' I asked.

'My family and I have a room at the back, madam. We will be most comfortable there.' He shuffled out of the house and headed towards a makeshift iron shed.

Sara was staring at a holy shrine on the wall. 'Great. Keep me safe from evil. Just my thing.'

I didn't register that it was unusual to find Catholic icons in a Hindu country until I spotted "Our Lady of Knock, preserve us" engraved on a small image of the Virgin.

Preserve us, indeed. We chose a bedroom each. My head banged down onto the lumpy pillow improvised from my day sack. I was asleep in seconds

***

That night I slept fitfully, waking every hour or so after dreams in which my children and I shouted at each other angrily, each of us nervous, tired and unreasonable. I was relieved when the light of dawn called me into consciousness. Fool. It wouldn't be long before those dreams became reality.

I lay still for a few minutes, taking in the scene. I was lying on a narrow bed, staring at desiccated insects stuck to the bare light bulb. The whole room smelled of mothballs. I dozed off again, and awoke to a tinkling of bells. I scrambled out of bed and looked across at the path leading to the village.

'Quick, wake up you two! Come and look at this!'

An elephant was shuffling towards me like a giant fatty, a large red Om sign painted on its trunk.

'Donation, madam?'

'Stuff that,' replied Conrad, emerging from the darkness of his room. 'I haven't got enough for beers let alone bloody elephant donations.'

'I can't give you money for beers. It's costing me enough to feed us.'

'I didn't ask you for any money, did I?'

Here we go: an argument. And so soon. I quickly changed the subject.

'I'm going to do some washing. My clothes are thick with red dust. Want anything doing, Conrad?'

'Nah, you're okay. I'm gonna live in these shorts for at least a week.'

'Ha ha, I notice you didn't ask me, Mum. Favouring your little "sun spot" again, by any chance?'

'Sorry, darling. Of course I'll do some for you if you want. It's just that...'

'No need to explain!'

The owner's well-padded wife led me to the laundry: a row of plastic buckets arranged around a well in the backyard; a flat, smooth rock with a natural channel running lengthways down its incline; and a bar of green soap.

I stared at the washing lines sagging between the trees like broken telegraph wires, laden with dripping, tie-dyed T-shirts and dirt-grey socks, which looked like gnarled twigs suspended from oversized wooden pegs.

After ten minutes of bending, filling and carrying heavy buckets of water, and hand-wringing each item against the rock, I stood up to stretch. 'Bloody hell, I can't cope with this.'

'You have a washing machine at home, madam, yes?' Smart arse.

'Er, yes. Is there a laundry service in the village?'

'Oh yes, madam. I will take care of it. Very best service. Clean clothes always. Leave your garments with me.' Her grin irritated the hell out of me.

'Come on, Mum. How long are you going to be?' Sara had her hair tied back in a loose ponytail, her pale cream shirt open to reveal the curve of her breasts. She looks beautiful, I thought. I hope she doesn't attract any dodgy characters.

'You go ahead, Sara. Have breakfast on the main track and go down to the beach. I'll find you. I want to find a post office so I can post my letter to Sophie. I promised I'd write every day.'

'Bit rash, wasn't it? Are you planning to spend the next year in post offices?'

'I said I'd write every day. Doesn't mean I have to post a letter every day. While I'm out I'll get us some beers to keep at home so we can have a drink on the terrace at night. I saw a fridge in the owners' kitchen.'

Dear Sophie

This is just a quick note to let you know we are in a place called Vagator, near Chapora, in Goa. If you look on a map of India it's down the coast from Mumbai (used to be called Bombay if your map is old) and the nearest big town is Panjim. You wouldn't believe the taxi ride we had to get here from Goa airport! There were yapping dogs running around in circles in the middle of the road, and dead ones lying at the side, left to rot. It was horrible to see them, but the taxi went so fast it was like watching one of Grandpa's old home movies, all jumpy and jerky and going too quickly to see anything properly, or to dwell on what we were seeing. Kids chased each other around old oil drums with no sense of danger. I was shocked by the sight of barefoot urchins running alongside the taxi with their hands outstretched. They looked almost the same as the monkeys that were scattering lopsidedly into the bushes when we got near!

I'll write again later darling, and post it in a couple of days. I want to spread the letters out a bit and post them regularly, rather than send big long ones every now and then.

I'm already missing you, and I know this is going to be much harder than I thought. Please always remember how much we all love you,

Mum, Sara & Conrad (they'll add their own letters to mine in future—want to get this one posted off quickly to let you know we're safe)

xxxxxxxxxxxxxxxxxxxxxxxxxxxxx

***

The track to the beach led through thick jungle. Sara and Conrad sat at a small table at a café where the track met the sand. They'd decided to wait for me before ordering breakfast, bless them.

'Sorry, loves. They don't have cans for sale here, only bottles. And I didn't bring a bottle opener! I guess we won't need the corkscrew—I haven't seen any wine since we got to India. Anyway at least I posted the letter. She should get it in a week or so, apparently.'

'Right. Let's order. This guy has been hanging around us for half an hour, waiting for us to choose something; he must be the owner.' Sara said. Sure enough, a slightly built man in a multi-coloured t-shirt was hovering beside our table.

'Welcome, welcome, madams. Welcome, sir,' a dumpy, round-faced young man greeted us eagerly. 'You will be having what at my café, madams, sir?'

'I'll have a papaya juice, and a banana and pineapple pancake, please.' I was determined to have a healthy breakfast every day, to compensate for the rubbish I'd been eating for years. In any case, I had planned a hard day ahead of lying on the beach.

'And a muesli with yoghurt, and white coffee,' added Sara.

'Bacon, eggs, beans and chips...and a coke. Ta. Hey, check out the cows on the beach!' Conrad smiled.

'I saw one just now on the way down here, eating a cardboard box. It stopped for a snack on its way down to the shore. Cool. It was just gonna lie down, chill out and catch some rays!' Sara beamed.

We spent nearly the whole day on the sand. It was fabulous: relaxed, warm and fun. The waves were a bit too rough for swimming, but it didn't bother us. Towards dusk, we hired scooters from a local rental shop for twenty-four hours, to make it easier to explore, and drove halfway up to the Portuguese coastal hill fort overlooking the village. We laid our bikes at one side of the track and walked to the top.

'Let's sit on the parapet, my loves.' Conrad and Sara exchanged one of their "here she goes again" glances. The wind silenced us for a moment as we looked out at the ocean. Straight ahead, as the crow flies, lay our island home and previous lives; friends and family. We watched as the sky turned from pink, to blue, to lilac, and the sea from green, to dark metallic blue, to grey, and finally to a pink-tinged silver.

'It really is like being on a different planet, isn't it, Mum? It's not that we're in a new country. It's more because we're leading a completely different life. It's like, by being here, we're already getting used to how other people in other countries live. I really get how we don't have to do things the way we're used to; how there are other ways to live your life apart from the ways we know.'

'I'm so proud of you, darling. You're quite right—there is nothing to say our way of doing things is the only way. We may think they're barmy here, but they probably think the same about us. And, looking at how happy they all are, I'd say they're the ones who've got it right.'

'Finished philosophising, Ma? Let's get back, eh?' Conrad rolled his eyes.

Stretched along the coast on both sides were endless swaying palms, patches of straw-coloured grass, deep-yellow sandy beaches, and coves where a blanket of trees swept right down to the shoreline. Everything glowed golden in the sinking sun.

So far, so good, I thought. We've survived the first few days without any serious arguments. The kids seem quite relaxed. Sara is already learning more about life outside of Guernsey. Maybe this will work, after all.

I hadn't yet identified my motivation for the journey. I just felt driven to keep going.

***

'What are you doing, Mum? Practising your dance moves? Will you be long?' Sara said next morning, leaning against the door frame.

I hopped around the sitting room with one sandal on, trying to insert an earring while looking into a poorly lit hand mirror. 'Just a sec, love. Won't be long.'

I gave up on the mirror and tried without it, but my fingers were too thick for the job and the butterfly dropped into my sleeve. 'Oh, can you do this for me?'

'Sure.' Sara bit her bottom lip in thought. Before moving, she looked around the room for a mirror.

'Why are there no wall mirrors in here? I can't check my hair! It's okay for you, Mum, 'cause you don't care what you look like, but I do!'

The butterfly fell out of my sleeve and rolled into a gap in the floorboards, like a perfectly executed putt. I squatted down to see if I could extract it, then conceded defeat. *Life's too short*, I thought.

'You weren't much help!'

'Sorry, Mum. I was thinking about...'

'Yes, I think I can guess. Michael, right? I bet you won't be giving him a thought after we've been here a month!'

After leaving the house we wandered down a dirt track where shacks leaned higgledy-piggledy against each other like a row of drunks. We headed towards a café, hungry. Goats and cows shared the street with chickens, pigs, emaciated dogs and dozens of scooters. Inside the café, in a smoky fug, sat thin, miserable-looking backpackers, dressed in sixties' hippie clothes.

'Look at that lot! See what drugs can do to you?' I fiddled with my empty crisp packet, winding it around my middle finger, a habit I found strangely comforting.

'Yeah, ruin your taste. Shit trance music. They think they're really cool, swaying around like zombies. Tripped-out techno time travellers.' Conrad looked worried. He didn't seem to know how to react to this strange new breed within his peer group. As the only male in our party, I guessed he was uncertain of his role.

Although he had left home and been sharing a flat, at seventeen he was too young to feel secure in the role of pack leader, and too mature to act like Mummy's little soldier. He had to assert himself, and had found a way of being different from us females by being derisive, but with humour, not malice. He was angry with David and me for getting divorced: it was just so embarrassing! Maybe this trip would make him more mature—it would be a real challenge, unlike anything Guernsey could throw at him—and give him the chance to prove his manliness to the world. Women would chase him; mates admire him. At least, that's what I hoped.

***

'Bloody hell, the ceiling in my room is grubby!' Conrad moaned. Although it was early afternoon, he had claimed he was owed breakfast, so ordered eggs on toast, which he gobbled down, and immediately followed them with lunch. Our hosts, we had discovered by chance when we saw strangers eating on our terrace, also offered meals, which delighted Conrad.

As he devoured shredded chicken and rice, Sara called out, 'Conrad, look! Hi, Steve! Oh my God! It's Steve! What are you doing in Goa?'

An acquaintance of theirs from Guernsey was meandering aimlessly along the track towards the house.

'Oh, hey. Good to see you guys,' he said with a lopsided smile. 'What you up to?'

He sat down at our terrace table, propped his chin up with one hand, and waved a joint in the other.

'Not much, just going round the world for a bit. You?'

'Hey…you know…like…it's so weird, like…you know how you get, like…a thought…you know…and you try to…like, hang on to it, like…you know…you want to hang on to that thought…Well, I was by this rock, you know, and…like…I walked over to the rock. Like, you know…and it's so weird, like…just to get to that rock, man...it took me...fourteen years, man... Fourteen years...know what I mean?'

He waited for a reaction. Conrad stared ahead, open-mouthed and dumbstruck. I couldn't look into his eyes for fear of exploding into laughter. Only Sara, ever the diplomat, managed a reply. 'Yeah, see what you mean, aha. Strange things happen, eh?'

'Do you remember anything about the fourteen years?' I enquired as gently as I could.

'No, man...I just know it took fourteen years, and I wonder if I can ever get them back...you know?'

This was the most coherent conversation we'd had so far with any of the other travellers, and I reckoned that prospects for acquaintances, though poor, were definitely looking up.

After this enlightening encounter, I retreated to my room to check our finances. A fat fly sat motionless on the windowsill. *What does the world look like to him?* I wondered. *Must feel a bit like those druggies on a trip, with his multi-vision eyes.*

'We've only spent two hundred and forty pounds so far.' I joined Conrad and Sara again after checking that Steve had gone. 'That's not bad for nearly a week for three of us. We'll have to get some more dosh in a couple of days, though, and book our travel up north. I'm going to hire us some bikes again and we'll drive into Mapusa. Let's go somewhere nice to eat tonight.'

'Mum, there aren't any "nice" restaurants here. Shabby little villages don't do red wine and fillet steak. The reason it's cheap is that it's crap. The sooner we get to a place with a McDonald's, the better,' Conrad complained.

I pondered varying definitions of crap, but said nothing.

***

Dear Sophie

Here goes, your first proper letter! We've been here a week so thought I'd post it off to you today. Hope you got my first quick one. I posted it on our first full day here. I'm already losing track

65

of time; the days just kind of blend into each other. It's brilliant, really relaxing! We didn't exactly get the palm-fringed beaches we hoped for. The sea is warm but you can't swim as the waves are so rough.

We've got to know a few local characters. There's Ambrose, who sits on the steps leading off the veranda, rolling cigarettes. He never speaks. He's got yellow teeth, stained from nicotine, with wide gaps between them. His skin is grey, pulled tightly above his thin lips, and his bony arms end in long, pointed fingers. His wiry, black hair looks like tiny springs flat against his skull. He wears the same outfit every day—a pale yellow T-shirt and faded multi-coloured knee-length shorts, with no shoes. His legs have got no hair and they're covered in shiny pink scars, especially around his knees. He smells of tobacco and sweat, and his breath…oh, yuk!

But the real character is Luis, who Conrad's renamed "Lost it Louie". He's the even skinnier alcoholic brother and keeps falling flat on his face when he brings our breakfast. He looks like the village idiot. He's got staring eyes, glazed over and unfocused, though they're hardly ever open! He sleeps on the floor in the washroom—he's banished from the rest of the house. He's the black sheep of the family. Conrad asked him to go on an errand, and gave him cash to buy cigarettes, a bar of chocolate and some beers. He didn't come back that night—they found him found thirty-six hours later, lying drunk in the hedge, clutching a tin of chocolate powder and a box of matches!

The food is okay, and better than I expected. Last night we ate outside an old temple, under a canvas shaped like an old-fashioned parachute!

Hope you are looking after your dad. Can't wait for you to come and join us!

Love you a zillion times round the world on a pogo stick backwards,
xxxxxxxxxxxxxxxxxxxxxxxxxxxxxxxxxxxxxxxxxxxxxxxxxxxxxxxxxx
xxxx

I put the letter down on the counter of the post office and closed my eyes, but the tears still escaped. Trembling, I turned to leave, then turned back, picked up the letter and held it to my lips before setting it down again and scurrying away.

***

'Slow down, Conrad, it's really bumpy back here. My bum's getting pummelled.'

'Might bash down a bit of the fat, Mother.'

Full of the previous night's crab masala dinner, we were biking off to an outdoor club, me holding onto my son's waist.

'Look! Over there! We'd better stop,' I yelled.

We pulled up at the side of the road to investigate a group wailing and wringing their hands.

'Can we help? What's the problem?' called Sara.

'It is unbearable. We have just lost our beautiful daughter.' A thin middle-aged man shook his head slowly as he spoke, while the rest of the group continued to howl.

'Oh, no, I'm so sorry. When did it happen?'

'Just now, madam, just a few moments ago.'

'How awful. How did it happen? Was it a road accident? '

'No, no, madam. There was no accident. Our daughter is not dead, nor injured. We had to sell her as we cannot afford to feed her anymore.'

Sara's mouth fell open. The wailing continued as we chugged away, all of us speechless. This time I was on Sara's bike, hoping she'd drive a bit more carefully than her brother.

For the next hour I was unable to get the image of that mother out of my head. The desperation of her situation overwhelmed me. Here was I, gaily trundling along on my great adventure, escaping my own emotional pain and trawling my children with me. I couldn't imagine the agony that mother was feeling now. *Imagine being in that situation*, I thought. How would you choose? Struggle to feed your child, or wonder forever what had happened to her after she was sold? It was too much to process; I had to move on. Self-preservation prevailed. We would certainly encounter further horrible situations. *Come what may.*

. When we arrived at the well-known bar to which we were headed—to experience the "Goa beach party" thing—I stared for a while, wondering what world I'd lived in up to now. It seemed to me that my persona was like a sketch, where the basic frame is there, but the details are still fuzzy. The right lines hadn't been gone over again to secure them in place. There were still a lot of alternative shapes, positions and locations, and I couldn't make up my mind which to use to complete the drawing of myself. Images of the Indian mother came flooding back. I compared her life to mine. I had believed I had been suffering, wavering between mother or friend. Ha!

Seeing so many people in and around the beach bar—there must have been hundreds—coming into focus and fading, swaying and jostling, unnerved and fascinated me simultaneously.

Travellers of all nationalities danced around a huge coconut tree with a fluorescent pink and yellow totem pole painted on its trunk. Red and yellow planets, stars and meteors adorned the walls and, above the menu board, the words "Primrose Experience" were daubed onto a large yellow-painted clover. A hundred and fifty people of all ages danced, oblivious to anyone outside their own groups. We sat on a low wall drinking weak local beer, watching them, envious of their carefree, tanned bodies, as they swayed and talked. Dayglo fractal shirts suspended along one of the walls added to the psychedelic ambience. I got up to dance.

'Oh no, she's going to make a fool of herself again,' Sara groaned.

My dear, sweet children watched me gyrating slowly. My response to music has always been physical rather than cerebral. If it has a beat or catchy tune, I like it.

Several beers later, we lay in the sand. I watched them pass each other a joint, which Conrad seemed to be able to roll with undue skill. That was unnerving; was that how he'd been spending the evenings in his flat? Should I say something disapproving? Mothers aren't supposed to encourage their children to take drugs, I suppose. But, since I'd spent most of my student years lying between two speakers stoned out of my head, I could hardly preach at them. And, anyway, I fancied a drag. I'd been musing on my life again and had come to the conclusion that the only purpose worth having was to be happy and loving. Back to the sixties from whence I came. Perhaps it was a good thing that Sophie wasn't with us; not only had she been spared images and circumstances that could have deeply disturbed her, but there were some situations which just wouldn't have been possible with a child in our group. Was I so bad, after all, to leave her behind? With her father, protected from the harshness of life?

'I spy, with my little eye, something beginning with B.' Sara giggled.

I squinted in the darkness. 'But there's nothing but black sky and stars.'

Sara's bindi gleamed like a diamond on her forehead against her tanned skin.

'I know: bindi!' I called out, as Conrad turned his back on us.

'Wrong,' laughed Sara, by now shaking with mirth. 'It's blackness!'

'What exactly are we smoking?' I struggled to get to my feet. It was a good job I wasn't driving, as God knows how I would have driven my motorbike home, although I was rapidly coming to the conclusion that the best way to survive India was to be as stoned as possible for as long as possible.

I was about to heave myself onto the back of Sara's bike when Conrad groaned. 'Oh shit! I can't find my bike keys.'

'You're kidding, right? We'll never find them in the sand.'

'Thanks for the vote of confidence, sis.'

We headed back to the beach where we each set about squatting again, this time gently smoothing our palms over the surface where we'd been sitting. My befuddled brain had no idea why we were doing this; I'd already forgotten about the keys.

After what seemed like twenty minutes, but could have been seconds or hours, Conrad raised his fists up into the air. 'Geronimo! Let's get moving.'

'I really, really, really wanna jig a jig, aah...'

'Calm down, Mother. Act your age.'

Far from being offended, I chortled. Until I noticed his death stare.

After we parked the bikes back in Chapora, an emaciated boy wobbled towards us on his cycle. As he passed, he stretched out his hand and grabbed Sara's left breast, squeezing it hard. He cycled on in silence, leaving my daughter dumbstruck—a rare occurrence. Twice in one day? India sure was bringing us some new experiences!

**

The day of our motorbike expedition into Mapusa dawned cloudless and hot. Our mission was to find a bank, and to book and pay for our return to Mumbai. It took forty-five minutes on busy roads to get to the noisy, crowded town, weaving our way among other bikes, buses, cows, goats, and people carrying large baskets on their heads, to find that the bank system was hostile at best.

A handwritten sign read *"open till 2 pm"*. Relieved, we entered at one thirty and were told that, although the bank was open for locals until two, foreigners had to get there by one. We gave up and drove back. Although we had failed to achieve our goal, we had by now lowered our expectations and were neither surprised nor disappointed.

It was a marked contrast from the glamorous world of private banking back home, where sparkling new glass and steel buildings were being erected all over town to accommodate the tide of new finance houses taking advantage of the island's low tax status. School leavers could walk into a well-paid job with few qualifications, fuel for the growing finance industry machine.

To my dismay, neither Sara nor Conrad had expressed any interest in further education. The offspring of a disillusioned teacher and a father damaged by boarding school, they had had enough of book learning by the time they were sixteen, and were ready to make their mark on a world beyond educational institutions. So, whilst my children enjoyed the life their bank career pay cheques supplied, I accepted their lack of academic ambition and watched them grow from teenagers into young adults, somewhat in awe of their courage, yet afraid they would one day regret the lack of a higher-earning, professional career.

Goa had been a good place to start our odyssey. Although different enough to be an adventure, it was not so different as to unnerve us. There were plenty of other travellers. We could hear Western music, and fast food like pancakes and chips was easily available.

***

We got on well those first weeks. All on best behaviour; very few arguments. The strain of travelling together hadn't begun to show, and I was still buoyed up at the prospect of spending a whole year with my two older kids.

Only towards the end of the month did I start to feel the pain of missing Sophie. I dreamed of her smile, I could hear her voice, and began wondering what she would say if she could see what we were seeing, eat what we were eating, hear the lilting Indian intonation.

Conrad, who until this trip had been easily bored and insecure, had refined his natural wit, and we'd done a good deal of laughing in the evenings, sitting around the wooden table on our veranda, smoking, and recalling the incidents of the day. Sara was a delight. She had a permanent expression of surprise—eyes wide, mouth open—and entertained us with stories of linguistic misunderstandings.

***

Dear Sophie

Today we went to Baga beach. I lay with my feet in the sea to keep myself cool. Conrad got roped in to haul one of the fishing boats up onto the sand. It took a total of twenty men over half an hour! Afterwards, he played football with the locals, who kept cheating! Every time his team scored a goal, their opponents said the ball was too high, claiming that the cross bar was only one metre off the ground. When they sent the ball soaring above our heads, they said the crossbar was five metres high!! Anyway, everyone had a laugh. After climbing up to the hill fort to watch the sunset, we sat singing silly songs, then came over to a rooftop café to eat. What chaos—the waiters kept bringing the wrong things. It's fine at breakfast, but obviously their brains go dead at night. They are so nutty you don't mind, though.

Next day

Oh dear, I made the mistake of ordering spaghetti bolognese last night, forgetting that it has meat in it, and you don't eat the meat in India. I left most of it as soon as I realised, but this morning I still had cramps so had to dose myself. Tonight I am sticking to naan bread and egg fried rice! It was so hot today we didn't go the beach till 3pm. The rocks are volcanic so, if you sit on them, you get a pock-marked, holey bum. Most of the travellers here are totally out of their heads on drugs and don't really speak to anyone, but we have met some friendly Argentinian girls, one of whom told us she'd been on the catamaran from Bombay. Apparently, you get a meal thrown in and a Hollywood movie. She told us only to use the buses if there is no other form of transport available. She also told us how to get rid of the hawkers: "I don't need anything" in Hindi is "Nahee chai yeh"…and it nearly works!

I've read three novels so far. My bed is hard and wooden and has an old, inch-thick horsehair mattress, but I'm sleeping like a log. We are hoping to go to a beach party soon but they don't start till midnight and we usually can't be bothered to move from our veranda. Oh, by the way, an elephant came for breakfast the other day, accompanied by people wearing saffron-coloured robes, ringing bells. Sophie, you should have seen our faces when it just turned up at our gate!

Hope you are seeing lots of Grandma and Grandpa. Don't forget to keep that diary for me (see, I can nag you all the way from India!) I re-read the words of that song you like today—"To a different beat". It feels like our world is moving to a different beat already. Love you lots and lots, Mum xxxx

***

Mumbai
We settled into our seats next day on the boat to Mumbai from Panjim.

'Please could you turn the sound up?' Sara enquired in her best well-brought-up voice. She had been fiddling with her hair and had twisted it into a knot which stuck up vertically from her scalp.

The movie on the ferry would be our first reminder of Western culture for weeks. We had spent two weeks in Goa, doing little but watching, thinking, and swapping our observations.

Sara, who had been so image-conscious at home, had cast off her teenage personality quickly and was now on a quest for enlightenment. She said she was impressed with the calmness of the local people, with their ability to tolerate so little comfort, whilst she had been a seeker after luxury, always asking for designer labels and celebrity-endorsed products.

'Oh no, madam. Very sorry, sound will not go higher. It is broken.'

We strained to listen, but the movie was competing with very loud Hindu music coming from another speaker. An hour or so later, it was time for the Bollywood movie, starring two famous Indian movie stars.

'The sound is so deafening we can't talk!' Sara spoke to the same man as before.

'Very sorry, madam, sound cannot go lower. It is broken.'

Sara let out a sigh of frustration, then shrugged and settled down in her seat to read—a futile exercise due to the movie noise. Instead, she nodded off.

'What's with the new hairstyle, sis?'

'What are you on about?'

'Go and look in a mirror. You've been asleep for an hour and you've got a massive bird's nest on your head.'

'Slight exaggeration there, son. But yeah, Sara, you have been tying your hair in a knot again.'

We were heading north, on the recommendation of friends, via Ahmedabad to Rajasthan, to see Pushkar and Udaipur.

I pointed at a fat, squashed Arc de Triomphe at the entrance to the port of Bombay.

'That must be The Gateway to India. Look, over there!'

After the eight-hour journey, we battled with more seething hordes of taxi drivers anxious to earn, and were settling down to sightsee as we drove to the railway station. What we saw was not what we expected. In fact, we didn't actually notice the buildings at all; we were so stunned by the sights in the street. People lay in the road, sleeping in drains. Mutilated beggars dragged whatever limbs remained to them on trolleys, or on home-fashioned crutches, through the squalor on the streets. The traffic noise deafened all thought. The air was thick with the acridity of pollution, and the smell of rotting rubbish attacked and overwhelmed us, like an insidious poison gas.

Against a backdrop of huge advertising hoardings, offering "high quality" Western consumer goods, makeshift stalls lined the road, some serving both as workplace and home.

'It's like the entire population's out on this street. Do you think it's a demonstration?' Sara's face betrayed fear.

My thoughts were elsewhere. I had expected to have some kind of spiritual experience in India; to find enlightenment. Big disappointment. I closed my eyes to avoid facing the reality. My experience of the first weeks in Goa was clearly not representative of the whole of India, and I felt diminished by my own stupidity in believing it might be.

The taxi slowed at a light. I scratched at an itchy patch on the top of my foot. A bead of perspiration ran down between my shoulder blades.

'What are you doing?' screeched Sara as a woman peered in, surveying our bags. She quickly wound the window up, but a hand was already halfway in. 'Mum! Help!'

Panicked, I shuffled across to the other side of the back seat. My stomach churned. Pus was dribbling from one of the many sores on the woman's face. A deep, threatening voice screamed unintelligibly. 'She' was a transvestite, now spitting aggressively through the window.

'Let's get out of this shit hole!' called Conrad from the front as our driver sped up, leaving the would-be thief standing in the road.

At the station, we pushed our way through crowds of screaming people.

'All full, no seats, come again tomorrow!' the ticket seller cried as he lowered his hatch.

I knew I had to compose myself or I was sure to be eaten alive by the throng at my back. So I resorted to elbowing the bony old ladies around me in order to reach the front of another queue, guilt now compounding the negativity flowing through me.

When I reached the counter, a surly face glowered at me. 'All trains to Ahmedabad are full for the rest of the weekend, madam.'

I returned to Conrad and Sara, waiting by the bags. 'We'll have to find a bus instead.'

We plodded through the throngs out onto the pavement where bus tickets were on sale at ramshackle booths. The fare we were quoted was three times as much as the train. As I dithered about what to do, a smiling, plump woman approached. Wrapped in a shiny golden sari, she looked like half of a walking *Twix* bar.

'Can I help?' she enquired. 'I am employed by the Mumbai Tourist Board. My name is Sandie. I heard you talking and I want to help. I can get you better priced tickets for your journey, but you will have to wait until tomorrow. There are no cheap buses tonight. I can find accommodation for you near here also.'

'She's obviously a con woman,' warned Conrad. 'Just tell her to fuck off.'

But I was tired and frightened, and afraid of coping with finding a hotel without getting knifed. So, against Conrad's wishes, I allowed Sandie to take us to a cheap hotel.

'This area is full of drug addicts, thieves and muggers. Do not go out into the street. I will come back in the morning and take you to the bus station.'

The one room available was bare but quite clean, with a functioning ceiling fan. Conrad went out to buy cigarettes, to my consternation. After twenty minutes of worrying, I ventured outside to find him smoking just outside the door. The atmosphere was stale and airless. We stood watching shadowy movements against the orange glow of the street lamps which veiled the endless traffic as it rushed by just a few feet away. Headlamps surged towards us like the roving gleam of predators' eyes casting around for prey in a gloomy mist.

'Let's eat. How do we get food round here?' Despite the circumstances, Conrad's appetite was normal.

'I'll go and ask at reception,' Sara volunteered.

'Thanks, darling. If he doesn't understand you, just use hand signals. Everyone can understand someone imitating eating.'

A few minutes later, Sara reappeared. 'Here's the menu!'

'Ah. Okay. No English version, I take it?'

'I couldn't mime *English*. And there's no dining room. We'll have to eat here in the reception.'

'But there's no tables!' Conrad seethed.

'Like it or lump it, kiddo.' I pressed down on the brass bell on the reception desk. Like magic, a chubby, grinning man immediately appeared from behind a beaded curtain.

'Yes, madam?'

We each circled our index finger over the menu, like playing the "tail on the donkey" game. Wherever your finger landed, you chose that meal.

The man on desk duty didn't even look surprised; maybe not many of his hotel guests could read.

'Best to keep your eyes open, Mum. You've just picked a paper napkin. Choose again.'

When the food arrived, I wished I had stuck with the napkin. It didn't take long to eat. It was all lukewarm.

'Okay, I'm off to bed. See you down here first thing. Don't wake me up when you come up. Remember we're all in one room together here!'

'Nah, you're okay. We'll go up now too, shall we?' Conrad turned to look at his sister. 'There's not exactly a lot to keep you up when you're confined to a crappy hotel.'

**

'Bloody hell, she's here!'

To Conrad's surprise, Sandie turned up next morning as we tucked into omelettes in the tiny foyer, once again balancing our meals on our laps. Tables were clearly a luxury item in Mumbai.

'Don't give her any money till she takes us to the ticket desk,' he said. 'Give the money straight to the ticket man or she'll probably run off with it.'

I nodded wearily, slightly saddened at my son's lack of trust in human nature.

**

To: Wendy McKintock
From: Rachael Green
Subject: skinny men
Feb? (have lost track of time, let alone dates…)
Hi, remember me? Have managed to find internet here in India—amazing! Thought I'd better let you know I'm still alive. Eventually

got going in January, flew from Heathrow to Mumbai and so far have been to Goa. Now back in Bombay/Mumbai or whatever it is now, on the way to Rajasthan where we take various trains and buses to Udaipur, Pushkar, Jaisalmer and Mount Abu. Also hope to go on a tiger tour if I can afford it. Then back here to fly to Singapore for a few days before heading off to Thailand. Still can't believe it's actually happening. Then again, have spent most of my life not knowing what's going on, so nothing new. Needless to say haven't met any men—well, only tiddly skinny ones or doped up backpackers who've lost the plot even more than I have. In any case, hauling the kids around is a bit of a passion killer. You never told me what happened between you and the Texan... Well, gotta go. The site is likely to time out before I send this 'cause the system's so slow here!

***

'Fuck! I'm having a *bad* day!!' Conrad shouted, after slipping on the slimy steps at the bus door. He'd alighted to get some air for five minutes. We'd been on the bus for four hours.

'Mum, this is the bus ride from hell,' Sara sobbed. 'It's a nightmare!'

At each stop, every twenty minutes or so, more and more passengers got on, carrying plants, chickens and snotty children. We were cramped in our seats, feet on top of our bags, the only foreigners. This had to be the cheapest form of local transport. Eventually, towards dusk, people were lying in the aisle, piled on top of one another. Loud Hindustani music blared from rattling speakers. *Come what may*, I'd said. *Remember that, Rachael.*

'Why are the other passengers staring at us so angrily?' Sara asked.

'Ten locals could sit in the seats we're occupying. They must resent us for that,' I said.

'It's not our fault, though. We paid for our tickets like they did.'

'That's not the point, though, is it?' Conrad quipped.

'Why do you have to be such a smart arse?' his sister replied.

I closed my eyes, but I could hear the arguing. *They're under such stress,* I thought. *They're not equipped for this, not after their cosy lives, cocooned on a small island. I wonder how long we'll all last before a real row starts.*

'What time do we get to Wotsitabad, Ma? I can't take any more of this! Fetid armpits, dog breath and farts. Someone must have a dead rat up their arse! It's gross!'

From time to time, one of the water bottles stored in the luggage rack above our heads crashed down onto our heads like a bomb, exploding loudly and soaking everyone in the two adjacent rows. But we were beyond caring. Moans of pain escaped from sleepy lips as the hours of darkness dragged by.

I tried to sleep. *Mothers aren't supposed to do this,* I thought*, put their children through hell and call it an adventure. What's the matter with me? Why am I such a rubbish parent?*

When we fell out of the bus twenty-two hours later, it seemed we'd spent most of our lives on it. I could not remember where we were going, nor why. I only knew that it was over, at last. When I looked at my children, ashen and drawn, I wanted to hug them. But I knew better than to try.

I spotted a "rooms" sign: Shanti pissful sleeping shop 500 rupees very nice and cheep.

'Ah, here we are…'

'What? We're sleeping at the bloody bus station?'

'Keep your wig on, she's only joking. We're staying near the lake. We are, aren't we, Mum?'

***

Udaipur

The lake at Udaipur sparkled; the fairytale palace in its centre glittered like a jewel. *At last,* I thought, *the India to inspire my soul.* The discomfort of the journey was instantly forgotten, like you forget the pain of childbirth the moment you see life in your baby's face. After checking in to our hotel, we negotiated a path through piles of shit along a narrow alley to order breakfast on a roof terrace, from where the view over the lake was stunning. We could have anything, the owner told us—eggs, bacon, sausage, bread. Delighted, we ordered bacon and egg, and settled down to watch tiny, squirrel-like creatures scurrying between the tables.

An hour later—we were in no hurry—we enquired about our order.

The waiter folded a tissue, wrapped it round his pinky tip and set about cleaning his ear. 'Oh yes, madam, the cook is coming back soon. Egg and bacon shop quite a long way.'

Later, after the longest breakfast I'd ever had, I went out to explore.

'Can I be of service?' A slender young man with dark, oval eyes and pock-marked skin looked up from my armpit level. He was neatly put together, though, I noticed. I continued ambling along the narrow dusty street, hoping to shake him off.

'I don't want to buy anything, thank you.'

'I am not selling, madam. I can accompany you to the Monsoon Palace if you wish. I am a guide. It is my expertise. I ask only a meal and you must pay for rickshaw.'

'I'm not sure I want to go to the palace, actually.'

'I am known here for my honesty. I will be greatly honoured if you will consider a visit to the palace with me. It is a most wondrous sight to behold.'

I was annoyed. Pressure like this—polite, honest man trying to feed his family—I didn't need. Besides, I had to buy train tickets to Pushkar, and had spent two and a half hours trying to book in the travel agency, where faded posters beckoned the poor of Udaipur to the glamorous hotels of Hong Kong, Sydney and New York.

'You understand, madam,' the agent had said, 'travel by train here in India is complicated. We must rule out such a journey to be organized in one day. Tomorrow will be more promising.'

'Tell you what,' I turned to Mr Honest Man. 'If you can magic me some tickets, I'll pay you a commission.'

'Tomorrow we can obtain the necessary items,' he assured me, his eyes narrowing conspiratorially. 'If you decide to go to the palace later, I will be waiting by the rickshaws at the bottom of the hill.'

I decided to spend the time wisely, and went shopping. Thirty minutes later, I was eight hundred pounds poorer, and a silk carpet was rolled and ready to wing its way to Guernsey to gather dust at David's house until my return a year later. To comfort myself after my recklessness, I entered another shop.

Later still, feeling hungover after a further hour of binge spending, I caught sight of Conrad and Sara sitting by the lake, silhouetted against the surrounding hills. The Lake Palace Hotel gleamed in the sunset and, behind it, the white Monsoon Palace perched on top of a nearby mountain. I decided to take up the guide's offer.

'Let's take a rickshaw up to that palace, kids. A wee man I met will guide us.' They glared at me.

'What?' I asked.

'Kids?' was all Sara said.

From the summit, we looked out to the desert beyond. The road was bordered by nothing but scrubland, dust and small rocks, with the occasional tiny shrine punctuating the otherwise monotonous route. In the light of the setting sun, even this barren area shone like gold. We fell silent. On the edge of the desert, some of the magic of the enigmatic country enveloped us as we gazed out over the darkening mountains, catching our breath with the sudden chill. *I wonder what Sophie would make of this,* I thought. *She probably wouldn't be impressed; maybe even still traumatised by the bus ride.*

Scrambling back into the black and yellow rickshaw where the driver perched, beaming inanely, a trickle of marijuana smoke wafting from his nostrils, I turned to our own personal Mister Fixit.

'Yes, yes, I know what is your concern,' he assured me. 'I will bring tickets to your hotel at eleven o'clock in the morning. Three for Pushkar on tomorrow night's train.'

'God, I hope the driver's not too stoned to drive us back down the hill safely,' Sara whispered.

'Oh, do not worry, madam. I only sold him enough for one joint.' Mister Fixit was obviously even more enterprising than I thought.

***

Dear Sophie

I'm sitting having breakfast on a roof terrace overlooking a really pretty lake and mountains in the distance. It's hot and sunny and very lovely.

Sara and I took a boat ride on the lake here yesterday. It was so peaceful. There's a lovely palace in the middle of the lake. As we approached it, we could make out a row of elephants lining the base of its walls. The view from the boat was stunning: the white stone steps of the City Palace, and the walls of other buildings led straight down into the water. At the "washing ghat" people were waist-high in water, either fully dressed in multi-coloured silk outfits, or naked apart from a linen cloth wound around their bony abdomens.

On the overnight bus from Bombay, I awarded Conrad the Olympic Gold Medal for Moaning. It was very uncomfortable, in fairness, but you just have to put up with it like the locals do. This country will drive me mad by the time we leave—everything takes forever. You order a meal, then they go out and buy the ingredients and come back to start cooking—and I'm not joking!! A two-hour wait for your meal is not unusual. And nothing works properly. Trains are either full or cancelled completely; things don't go, start or finish when they say. If you are in any kind of hurry, India is NOT the place to be. It's taken three days so far to get our tickets for the next leg of our journey—and we still haven't got them! We're going out for a meal now. Will write more later (if we get our meal before midnight, that is!).

Later. When we got back from dinner, the hotel arranged to put a telly on the roof terrace so we could watch a James Bond film called "Octopussy". It was filmed here (we're in a place called Udaipur, by the way). One scene was filmed in the street right below the hotel. The owner brought us blankets as it's quite chilly at night.

I can picture you reading this in your dad's kitchen. Do you remember when you used to dress up like Madonna and dance around your room? Sara and I were talking about it the other day, because we saw an Indian girl wearing elbow-length, black lace gloves—really weird!

Off to Pushkar tomorrow; it took us ages to get tickets. Onward and upward, Carruthers! (In case you're wondering, he was a famous explorer.)

xxxxxxxxxxxxxxx

***

That night a commotion woke me. Up till now, Udaipur had been tranquil.

'Police! Let me in!'

I turned over to look at my watch. Eleven thirty.

'Go and have a look, son, please.' I had to shout. Conrad was asleep in the adjoining room.

Slightly bemused, he opened the door to a man grinning in the dim light of the corridor.

'Only joking! Not police!' He smiled. 'I need a bed for the night. You have a very big room.'

'Only have one bed, though, mate. Sorry.'

'We can share your bed.' The stranger grinned lasciviously.

'On your bike! If you come near me, I'll knock your block off!' Shaken, Conrad shoved him away.

'Check he hasn't dumped anything on you,' Sara called out. 'It's an old trick. They plant something on you then get a pay-off from the police for a drugs bust. I'll go and get the manager.'

Seconds later, the manager appeared, sweating with exertion. Irritated, he dismissed our concerns. 'This man is only a drunk. It was all a joke,' he insisted.

'He climbed three flights of stairs to find my room!'

'He is always in the hotels. He is not right in the head. Probably he was merely looking for money.'

'If he comes back, I'll wring his skinny little neck, the smelly git.'

Despite his bravura, my son was unnerved, and didn't sleep again that night.

***

'Mum! Come and look at this!' Sara grinned. We were in the street, after collecting our railway tickets from our "wee man".

The sign read: **Fair Price Shop. Washing. Urgent service. Reasonable rate.**

Parked in front of it was a rusty bus, laundry hanging from every window. Pale blue underpants, long, off-white vests, cloths of indeterminate purpose, and various other items of clothing were draped over sagging curtain wires.

'Wonder what happens when the bus moves,' Sara said.

'They could have a delivery system,' I replied. 'When it's all dry, the bus takes off and, as it gathers momentum, the laundry falls into the street for people to collect. Bad luck if it lands in some cow shit, but more business for the Fair Price Shop. Who knows? This is India.'

***

Dear Sophie

Someone tried to break into Conrad's room last night, but he ran away when Conrad threatened him. It's all part of the

Indian experience. To them, the fact that we have been able to come to their country means that we must be very rich. Even though we have no valuables in our backpacks, the contents represent a year's salary for them. It is like nowhere I've ever heard of. It certainly hasn't been the spiritually uplifting experience I'd heard about when I was younger. I don't think I could cope with living here, but so far it has been a most fascinating experience.

I do hope you get all my letters. Sometimes it takes ages to find a post office; other times it's on the main street. And the queues! You wouldn't believe it. I can't figure out what stuff people here post, in great big brown paper parcels. Sometimes the parcels are bigger than they are!

Haven't got much time, darling, so will sign off now. Got a train to catch, doncha know!

Love you, as always, and miss you like mad!

XXXXXXXXXXXXXXXXXXXXXXXXXXXXXXXXXXXXXXXXXXXXXXXXXXXXXXX

***

At the rail station, duly armed with tickets stating "dep. Udaipur 18.00, arr. Pushkar 07.00", Conrad checked the itinerary posted on the station platform.

'The "overnight train" gets in at two-thirty in the morning. Shit. We'll end up trailing around in the middle of the bloody night in some ghost town.' *Not exactly a safe experience. Is this how I am fulfilling my childhood promise to myself to keep my family safe?*

'Don't start whining yet, we haven't even got on the train.' Sara glowered at her brother. 'Mum's doing her best,' I heard her whisper. 'It's not her fault the train system here is such crap.'

I spent the next eight hours wondering how we would find accommodation at that hour of the night. Conrad was convinced that all we'd have to do was push someone's door in. He really should have been a diplomat.

***

Pushkar

The station was deserted apart from one other traveller. He looked bemused to see a family of three lugging huge backpacks alight from the train in the middle of the night. He stood on the platform with a resigned expression, a small bag draped over one shoulder.

'You haven't by any chance lost any laundry, have you, mate?'

'Sorry, my son has an inappropriate sense of humour. Do you know any hotels round here that might be open at this time of night?'

He raised a limp arm and pointed, waving his hand up and down.

After a short walk in the direction he indicated, we banged on a blue-painted door, which was flung open seconds later. We staggered into the shabby hotel foyer to be greeted by a young man, grinning broadly.

'Morgan Freeman at your service, madam! I am thinking I look like my father, no?' *Doolally*, I thought, borrowing my sister-in-law Louise's favourite descriptive adjective.

Morgan ran the Relax Hotel. He showed us to a room in silence. His nonchalant manner made me think he'd been expecting us. Immediately after we reached the room, the building was plunged from gloom into total darkness for a few seconds. Morgan merely shrugged when the lights came back on. Power cuts were clearly nothing exceptional.

He carried a knitted, multi-coloured open shoulder bag whose contents were clearly visible: wide-toothed metal comb with black gunge and strands of hair between its tines; dried, hard knobs of chewing gum; crumpled tissues; a book of three unused matches; and a rusty ring holding about a dozen heavy steel keys and three large wooden ones. *His worldly goods?* I wondered.

As he turned to move away—still grinning—I noticed floppy shorts hanging loosely from his hips, where his bottom should have been. *Morgan Nobum would be a better name than Freeman*, I thought.

I tried to rest on my bed for a while to make up for the lack of sleep overnight. Relax? It's a bit hard to relax while swatting kamikaze flies and mosquitoes.

I wasn't the only one suffering from lack of sleep: I heard my kids bickering.

'For Christ's sake, Sara, stop trying to preen yourself in that mirror. You can't see a bloody thing, and it's not as if there's a queue of photographers waiting outside.'

'Cut it out, Conrad. It's not my fault we're stuck here. Just remember that.'

'Why are you two carping at each other? We're all in this together, so we'll have to make the best of it.'

Conrad turned to our host. 'So you reckon your dad's Morgan Freeman, mate?'

'Do you know who he is?' Sara smiled one of her patronizing smiles.

'Of course. I am not a fool. He worked with Robin Hood. And he is my father.'

Although worn out none of us felt like sleep, so we lay around on our beds, reading and listening to Walkman music. When there was enough light outside, we walked down to the lake to join groups of tourists receiving a Hindu blessing and a "Pushkar Passport"—a kind of friendship bracelet.

'We have to go and do the Pushkar Passport thing. I've been looking forward to it for ages. Becky did it when she was here.'

Although sceptical, I smiled. 'If it's good enough for your friend Becky, sweetheart, it's good enough for me.'

'Okay, don't go over the top.'

'Coming, Conrad?'

'Guess so, nothing else to do.' He turned to me. 'Best to humour her, I suppose.'

We were told to imitate the priest, so obediently threw flower petals into the lake, washed our hands in the water, and splashed some onto our foreheads and lips.

'A bit dodgy, isn't it?' quipped Conrad in a whisper.

'Tell me about it. The water doesn't look exactly clean,' I replied.

Kneeling with a half coconut in my cupped hands, wearing a bracelet tied on by a priest, I experienced an urge to rebel. Apparently we now had some god or other's permission to go down to the water at any time. After congratulating us, the priest went on to mark our foreheads with red paste, sticking bits of rice into it and sealing it all by sprinkling yellow saffron powder somewhat haphazardly over his work.

Throughout the ceremony, we had to repeat his chant. Finally, he mumbled, '…and I promise to give five hundred rupees to the priest as my freely given donation to cover the cost of all the expenses of this ceremony.'

I wasn't having this. 'I promise to give fifty rupees to the priest as my freely given donation to…'

'I promise to give four hundred rupees to the priest…' he repeated.

Conrad grinned at me.

'I promise to give fifty rupees…' I insisted.

'Oh, Mum, wasn't that lovely?' Sara beamed afterwards. I shot a warning glance at her brother.

Later, my face still smeared with red and yellow like a clown who'd been out in the rain, I sat, in the inner courtyard of the Relax, admiring the bright blue painted walls and wondering why the doors all bore padlock chains or bars. A smell of onions, cabbage water and diarrhoea wafted up from the drains.

As I stared at the locks a voice behind me said,

'If you lose your key, dear, the chances are that this will completely puzzle the hotel owners, who are surprisingly unprepared for such eventualities. This happened to me, would you believe? They had to send out for a locksmith.' She was four feet tiny, with huge glasses, a face like a river delta seen from the sky, and a voice so gravelly from tobacco damage that it was only possible to hear her at ten-centimetre range. We had met over breakfast, both eyeing up the remaining serving of banana porridge. Due to my well-practised teacher's death stare, I won, but, as I prodded my over-sweetened wallpaper paste, it was clear she'd got the better deal of muesli with creamy yoghurt. She coughed after every mouthful, her nicotine-stained fingers wrapped around a tiny fag end on which she sucked desperately on one side of her mouth after spooning her food in on the other.

'What is it about India that has you coming back every year?' I enquired a short time later over coffee.

'The place is perfectly ghastly, and the people... Well, we are talking pond life much of the time, dear. But, every now and then, one comes across someone who's not perfectly vile, and that makes it worthwhile. You know—the odd diamond. For the most part, though, they are awfully vulgar, I'm afraid.'

Her snobbery amused me. I persisted. 'So why do you keep coming back?'

'Do you know, dear, I really have no idea.' The liver spots on her cheeks creased as she gave me a crooked smile.

Maria had spent every winter for the last twenty years backpacking through India, apparently accompanied by a series of young boyfriends. So I was a little surprised when she volunteered the information, 'I am still a virgin, you know. Unusual at seventy, isn't it?'

'I thought you told me you had a daughter?'

Her eyes shrivelled earnestly. 'It was an immaculate conception, my dear. No one believes me, but it is the truth.'

'I prefer this place to Goa,' Conrad announced as he sat down to join us. 'The locals are not so mad.'

***

From a temple carved in orange-red stone, Sara and I looked out over desert and mountains. Everything was ornate; even the steps had tiny carvings on their top surface. Floors with marble inlays shone from within inner sanctums containing silver tubs of blossom, and shrines glistening with gold and silver were set on carved pedestals. Chubby little stone men with lingams twice their height grinned from a nest of enormous boobs and buttocks.

'Indian tradition, you see, was to worship fertility, so there was never any intention to shock nor disgust. On the contrary, arousal would be considered a fine emotion.' The smooth voice came from a slightly built young man behind us. Sara turned to smile at him and saw that he was experiencing his own fine emotion—no doubt from worshipping fertility—under his robes.

'Erm, Mum, I think it's time to move on.'

We thought better of making his acquaintance, and set off to walk back to our hotel.

'Hey, look, Mum! Guess who? I wondered where he'd got to.'

Conrad was caught up in a huge crowd. A procession weaved through the streets, illuminated table lamps held aloft, high above the participants' heads. To power them, they were towing an electricity generator at the end of the line. The group started dancing.

'Shall we go over and see what he's doing?' Sara went on.

'I'll leave you to it. I'm going for a lie down. See you back at the hotel.'

Sara walked over to join in without hesitation. Later, she told me about the procession.

'And the next thing we knew, Mum, we were invited to the prince's wedding! After the banquet, the king sat on his white horse wearing his bright red and gold robes and his turban, smiling and making conversation with people in the crowd. The press and television were in "obsequious attendance", as you are fond of saying. There was a sudden shove forward, and Conrad and I got photographed standing next to the king! All the Indians kept bowing to us. They thought we were special guests because we were white.'

'Yeah, it was quite cool. He was alright, to be fair. Seemed quite pleased to see us. Sends you his regards. I did try to bring you a bit of chapatti but one of the monkeys ate it.' Conrad placed his hands behind his head as he spoke, and lay back with a self-satisfied smile.

***

A week later we were sitting by the side of the road, propped up against our packs. We had woken at five to be transported by the ever-helpful Morgan in his Jeep to a nearby bus stop. He'd assured us that there was an early bus..

We were headed for Jodphur. I had no idea why; something about it being blue. It was time to move on from Pushkar. I was beginning to tire of Maria's fantasies, and Sara was feeling lonely among the many honeymooners the town attracts.

'We should have come for the camel festival, Mum. You might have found yourself a rich man with plenty of camels to spend on you. There were loads of them at the wedding.'

'What, camels or men?'

'Ha, ha. Anyway, Maria's probably worked her way through them by now. The men, that is. Then again, some of the camels in the postcards look quite sexy with their long eyelashes.' Sara smiled.

'She swears she has a young man in every town in India,' I said.

'Didn't know they went in for grab-a-granny nights round here. You could try your luck, Mum. You're a lot better looking than her.'

'Like I'd want a man with skinnier hips than me? God, the embarrassment! No thanks, I'll pass. Anyway, here's someone coming. Let's ask him.'

'Watcha, mate. Where's the bus, then?' Conrad called out to the approaching cyclist.

'Bus is cancelled. Come back tomorrow.'

'But we've been waiting for hours! By the roadside! Isn't this the right place to wait for the bus to Jodphur?' I pleaded.

'Main bus station. Look.' He pointed behind him. 'Go and ask there.' He wobbled off on his pushbike, his white robes hitched up to his thighs, revealing stick-thin legs.

'Hope you fall off your pushbike, mate!'

'No, Conrad, don't antagonize him. It's not his fault.'

But I was overwhelmed with despair. Why had Morgan brought us here? When would anything turn out to be straightforward in this country? Nothing worked, everyone seemed to lie about everything, and we were despondent. This was not what I'd expected. I came here to find inner peace, and all I was getting was frustration in huge measures. We staggered to the bus station, bought tickets, and crossed the road to a distinctly dodgy-looking restaurant nearby.

We had spent the morning sweltering. I was nervous about getting lost, so we hadn't budged from the so-called bus stop. We didn't dare move in case the bus arrived, and we were unaware that the main bus station was just along the road. It was, after all, pitch-dark when we got there. Now, however, it was eleven o'clock, the sun was high, and we were hot, dusty and thirsty.

'This has to be the most disgusting meal I have ever seen!' shouted Sara, uncharacteristically loudly. Her outburst was followed by a general hush, and all eyes turned towards her. She coughed to cover her embarrassment. 'I ordered toast,' she complained in a whisper. 'This is fried bread, soggy with grease. God knows what it was fried in. It tastes like a mixture of stale fish and motor oil. There's a coating of red sauce on the bottom. Oh, yuk! It's probably blood! I'm going to throw up!' She pushed her plate away, stormed to the toilet, and came back moments later, visibly paler, with a piece of toilet paper stuck to the bottom of her shoe. 'Don't go in there. And don't ask why.'

Conrad and I had ordered soup, but it was lukewarm with a layer of grease floating on top, so we left it, drank a Pepsi instead, and returned to the bus station to clamber onto a bus marked "13.30 Jodhpur".

A round-faced man, whom I took to be the driver, stopped us.

92

'This not bus for you. Come back at four o'clock.'

Something snapped. I screeched, grabbed him by the collar and hauled him across the terminal back to the ticket counter, shouting hysterically, 'We are getting on the one-thirty bus! We have tickets!'

Somewhat taken aback by his abduction, my hostage muttered unintelligibly to the ticket man who nodded and waved us back to the bus. Once we had boarded, I saw that the man I had manhandled so furiously was not the driver at all, but just another hapless passenger who now boarded after us, keeping a nervous eye on me. In fact, he didn't take his eyes off me throughout the whole journey—quite an achievement over a period of five hours. Once at our destination, I noticed that he appeared to have developed a twitch.

'Why did he tell us it wasn't our bus, Mum?'

'The ticket man said he thought we were going to Mumbai, 'cause our backpacks look like we're going on a long journey. So I guess he was trying to be helpful.'

'Trying to get money out of us, more like. He'd pretend to find us the right bus, then charge us a commission for getting tickets.'

Still as cynical as ever, then, my son.

***

Jodhpur

When we got to the Jodhpur hotel, I foolishly believed we would avoid price negotiations, as I had cunningly called ahead from Pushkar to book.

After a couple of minutes' heated discussion, Conrad took me to one side and whispered, 'Mother, do you know you're getting stressed over twenty pence? You are being really embarrassing. Again. Who gives a fuck? Just give him the money and stop trying to score a victory all the time. Why do you always have to prove you're right?'

'All I want now is a hot shower.' I turned back to the proprietor. 'You promise there is hot water in the room?'

'Yes, yes, madam, shower in room.'

We climbed three flights of steps and looked in: the usual bare room with corner washstand and a tap halfway up the wall. I couldn't see the promised shower anywhere.

'Don't get stressed again, Mum, please.' Sara sighed, then gave me her patronizing smile.

'I'm not stressed,' I growled, 'but I have paid for us to have a shower, and I'm not going to let them get away with not giving us one.'

'What do you expect? They come up and scrub your back? They haven't got the strength to even lift the scrubbing brush.'

'Thanks for your helpful contribution, Conrad. I'll bear it in mind.'

I clambered back down the stairs to the reception area, features set hard into forbearance.

'Please come and show me where the shower is.' I spoke with as much dignity as I could muster. 'I can't see it.'

'Hot shower in bucket, madam.'

'But I can't shower in a bucket,' I pleaded, by now reduced to whining.

'Yes, yes, madam,' he replied patiently. 'Cold water in tap. Hot shower in bucket.'

I was too bewildered to respond, and past caring about cleanliness.

When I told Sara, she let out a low growl of fury. Her calm, conciliatory mood disappeared. She stormed downstairs.

'I am sick to death of being dirty and smelly! My muscles ache from hauling my heavy pack on and off. Get us hot water NOW!' At that, the proprietor scurried off into the kitchen, presumably to fetch the bucket.

The cracks were beginning to show. I expected an almighty confrontation with my kids at any moment. I was no further on towards finding the meaning of life than I had been a month ago. And here we were, with only two destinations left in India.

I decided it was time for a treat and made a reservation at the Ajit Bhawan Palace Restaurant. We had a cold strip wash and put on fresh clothes.

Later that night, slightly intoxicated, I settled down to write to Sophie.

***

Hello darling

This evening we rattled along the streets of Jodphur in rickshaws, waving at each other as our drivers raced to arrive first at a palace where we were having dinner. The grandeur of the palace was almost overwhelming, after half a day spent in the roadside dust like beggars. Sara swept along the wide corridors to the dining hall pretending to be a maharini (that's an Indian princess, I think!). For the first time since leaving England, we saw tables set with cloths, place settings and napkins. I ordered a bottle of red wine. It was expensive and, apart from the very weak beer in Goa, the first alcohol we've had for nearly a month.

We felt as if we had been transported back to the days of the British Raj. (Ask your dad!) The palace was built for the Maharaja Ajit Singh and is still being run by the royal family. There was a huge table in the centre of the hall, laden with buffet foods ranging from fresh watermelon to various rice dishes. We were attended by silent, turbaned servants in traditional white Nehru jacket and trousers. There were delicately carved marble pillars and statues all around us, and scenes from royal life on silk tapestries—rulers being borne aloft in their howdahs; elephants, tigers and other large cats striding alongside the processions.

It took our minds off the muck and smells for a while and reminded us of what civilization felt like! I guess I've been trying so hard not to overspend I've probably gone to the other extreme… Anyway, we are on the move again soon—first to New Delhi to try to see a tiger; then to Jaisalmer, a fort in the middle of the Thar desert. I'll write from there, of course.

Love you and miss you so much xxxxxxxxx

***

'So much has happened today: we've gone from roadside to palace! After that lovely meal and the race through the streets, it seems like weeks ago that we were standing in the dark waiting for the bus. I never thought I'd cope with journeys like the ones we've had so far. Now I can see why the local people are so accepting of their lot.' Sara sat down on the end of my bed in her cobalt blue silk pyjamas, looking prettier than I'd seen her for a long time. She had a serenity about her that evening; a complete contrast to the twisted, angry face of the night before.

With a surge of pride, I acknowledged that not everything we had experienced had been negative. My daughter was appreciating the cultural differences between those who have and those who make do without, and to understand that comfort is not a necessity for survival.

'Poor buggers don't know any different really, though, do they? Thank God we don't have to survive here,' she added.

***

New Delhi
I lay back on my lumpy bed to rest and escape the heat. I could hear a cockerel, the humming of a generator, the chirping of birds and croaking frogs. Someone was playing the sitar, and children were singing and shouting in the distance. Close by, engines were revving and horns were honking. I raised my head to look out of the window, but my view was blocked by a huge mango tree and I had to get up.

A bottlebrush shrub tickled my face as I leaned out. Dozens of scooters were parked in front of the garage pumps opposite. It had to be the day for buying petrol. A young girl dressed in pink organza sat alone on a nearby doorstep as men passed by, spitting into the road. No one smiled.

We had made it to New Delhi. I watched a bus clatter past, its roof laden with belongings wrapped in rope bundles. Hopeless faces gazed out of each tiny window, looking as if patience had long ago replaced emotion, as if all hope for the future had gone, and each day offered only survival, not life. The bus belched black smoke, the gears wrenched and crunched, the wheels spun up thick soil dust. Men and boys lay on top of cardboard boxes tied with string on the roof. From my viewpoint, I'd had a glimpse into the driver's cab. A "no smoging" sign was sellotaped onto his door, where no one but he could see it. Maybe he was trying to give up.

Sara wandered into my room, screwing her hair around her index finger. 'Phew! I'm boiling to death here!'

I hadn't realised how humid it would be. The temperature felt higher than in the desert. One of the reasons for coming to New Delhi was that I wanted to do a tiger tour. It was not the ideal time of year, but I hoped we would be lucky. Feeling hot and languid, I shambled to the bathroom where a diagram next to the toilet warned against squatting on top of the pedestal. In the humidity, condensation shimmered on the window and dripped onto the rotting, swollen wooden frame below. Spider webs trembled with droplets. In the daytime sunlight, a daddy-long-legs had been caught and crisped in the mesh fibres of the curtains. I struggled to open these faded scraps of cotton, tugging them along their bare wires.

***

The train journey from Delhi to Ranthambore National Park took longer than I anticipated. The train was comfortable, but slow. We watched families with impeccably behaved small children, young couples gazing into each other's loving eyes, and one or two careworn businessmen. It was all very civilised, despite the acrid body odours. As we pulled out of the city, the countryside was barren. We passed villages where sari-clad women carried baskets of local produce on their heads, accompanied by their barefoot offspring and scrapping dogs.

We arrived late and had time to kill before dinner. We spent an hour or so lazing in the garden of our lodge before a supper of lentils, chicken curry and flat naan bread.

I wondered why so many people seemed to be covered in bright paint, and was told that we had arrived during the festival of Holi, during which giggling people throw coloured water and powder at each other.

'This is a completely different India from what we've seen so far, don't you think? There's something magical about it. Just look at those trees!' I said.

Lantana trees, heavy with white rhododendron-like blossom, were host to gnarled, trailing orchid roots. Women carrying baskets of rocks wove between stands of bamboo.

We rose for breakfast at five and were soon seated in a Jeep—the three of us plus our driver and guide. We drove around for two and a half hours, went back to our lodge for lunch and a rest, then set off again until dusk. Plenty of optimism, but no sign of a tiger. I began to doubt that we would see one; we had been warned that sightings were rare here. We pretended to be cheerful. I was glad of the opportunity to see some gorgeous kingfishers, peacocks and egrets, and tried to remain positive, despite our disappointment.

The pattern was the same for the next two days, although we did enjoy a rare sighting of a jungle wild cat.

At one stage, the guide said 'Look.' Our attention was diverted from tigers as we gazed open-mouthed at herons, giant storks, owls and woodpeckers galore.

After a full day's drive in larger Jeeps, we arrived at Bandhavgarh National Park, where a band greeted us and we were welcomed with heavily scented frangipani flower garlands and fruit juice.

'That's the most gorgeous scent ever!' Sara exclaimed.

'Makes a change from camel spit, true. That's the worst smell ever.'

'You're right there, Mum!'

On our first game drive here, the guide signalled for silence. We held our breath for several seconds then waited, every sense tingling, for thirty minutes. No one dared move a muscle. In the stillness, I heard the growl of distant thunder. The air was heavy. The only sounds were the chirping of large green berber birds, flies buzzing, and the Jeep driver's erupting burps. It was perfectly calm.

Our guide pointed into the bushes. 'Sleeping tigress,' he whispered.

We drew in our breath. It was only a glimpse, and she was too well camouflaged to photograph, but we knew our luck had changed.

The next two days were packed with anticipation and excitement as we observed another tiger, then another—a total of ten sightings. I was stunned by the size of one young male. His body spanned the width of the Jeep track so that, when he stood still, his front legs were on one side of the track and his back legs on the other. He moved with supreme confidence: there was no other animal to challenge him. He knew he was king.

We watched another young male attempt to catch a porcupine, his staring face curious and innocent, like a playful kitten.

'I feel privileged to be here, on his territory. Don't you?'

'Yeah, I guess so. How could anybody want to kill them, Mum?'

'Money, darling. It's always about money, sadly. Oh, look!'

A jackal was creeping across an open stretch of land amid silk cotton and orange and red flame of the forest trees. I breathed in the scent of thyme mingled with citrus, musk, mango and our guide's sweat. We mounted elephants and swayed into the jungle for closer tiger sightings, and we gaped at multi-coloured rollers and racket-tailed drongo birds among lilac gravellia trees.

That night my head was filled with close-up images of tiger faces and mesmerising bright eyes.

Here at last was the India I had anticipated. What spirituality had failed to deliver, Nature had, in plenty.

***

Dear Sophie
We are all entranced. I will bring you here one day. You have to see this place. We've seen TEN tigers!! Unbelievable! We had to wait a few days before we had a sighting, but it's been more than worth it. You know how you love cats. Well, the tigers are just like them, only massive. Young ones play like kittens while the older ones look on, wisely. Probably keeping an eye out for danger. Though they haven't got any predators 'cause they are the kings of the jungle. The jungle VIPs...da da da. Sorry, got carried away. I've even been dreaming about tigers, but it's worth coming here for other wildlife too. I never thought I'd be so into trees and birds. I used to think that was for old people with nothing to do. Ha ha, how wrong was I? Conrad and Sara have hardly said a word since we've been here. It's like we're all under a spell. It's really peaceful; the only sounds are birds singing. Everywhere you look there's something to see. There is in the towns, too, but here in the jungle it's a completely new experience. Sorry to rabbit on so much. You must be feeling jealous by now so I'll shut up. But I promise I will bring you here one day. No, make that next year. I promise I'll bring you here next year. How's that?
Love you so much I could burst, as always,
Mum
xxxxxxxxxx

***

Jaisalmer
Night train to Jaisalmer. The very words filled me with romantic notions of dusky desert heroes.

Jaisalmer rose on the horizon as the train rattled slowly to a halt. Straight out of the "Tales of the Arabian Nights", with golden ramparts rising from the sand. I felt as if I was moving backwards through time to the Middle Ages as we passed the haveli mansions carved from wood and yellow sandstone. The fort was built in 1156 and, from outside the walls, it appeared unchanged since then.

'C'mon then, let's get off and find our place to stay. I won't call it a hotel. We know better than that by now, eh? Here we go again, happy as can be; all good friends and jolly good company...' I chirped. I was in a really happy mood after our tiger experience.

I ignored the pitying looks. We staggered through the dusty streets, weighed down by our packs, keeping one eye on the dark-eyed boys and girls who leaned against solid stone walls, watching us with suspicion.

When we reached our guest house, we had to wait for rooms to become available. Jaisalmer was filling up fast for the Desert Festival due to start within the next few days. I began negotiating the room rate. Although we had agreed a price at check-in, the proprietor immediately put it up by fifty per cent once we had placed our bags in the rooms. I guessed he was hoping we would be too tired to argue.

I was furious. 'I have budgeted carefully. I am down to eighty thousand rupees for the remainder of our time in India and I do not like being conned yet again!'

Proudly, if somewhat nervously—I had no idea if there were any rooms left elsewhere—I called his bluff and walked out.

'Oh, for God's sake, Mum!'

Sara and Conrad were not happy. But we were in luck, found another hotel quite quickly, and began to settle in.

'You've cheated me out of a nice room,' Sara suddenly yelled. 'My room in the last place was lovely. This one is disgusting!' Her outburst seemed to come from nowhere, but I soon realised that this was the culmination of weeks of discomfort, stress and uncomfortable beds. The pride I'd felt earlier disappeared.

She had been screaming for a few minutes when the landlord interrupted to tell me that the room rate was based on taking a camel safari with him, which meant I would not be able to negotiate my own deal.

'Look, you two, according to Lonely Planet, the hoteliers in Jaisalmer are infamous for kicking out guests who do not take a camel safari, so I've agreed, but we'll move on again in the morning.'

By this time, Sara and Conrad had had enough. Moving from one place to another in the dusty, dry heat had been bad enough, but now I was proposing to flit in the early hours, just to save a few rupees.

'I know you're paying for everything, but you can't expect to keep pushing us around! We've slept in flea pits; we've travelled on disgusting buses and trains. It's supposed to be a holiday for us as well. Why did you ask us to come if you were going to put us through this?' shrieked Sara, tears welling.

'It's not a holiday, it's travel. That's not the same thing at all. We can't afford luxury accommodation—we either rough it or we go home early.' I was bluffing, and feeling rotten. I hated to see her so upset. I knew I was putting my kids through a complete culture shock, and, despite my flip answer, I did want them to have happy memories.

'We've only got a couple of nights here so, if we have a cheap lunch, we can still afford the camel safari. How's that?'

'Dunno what we can get cheaper than the shit we've been eating up to now,' grumbled Conrad.

***

Later that day, through the flimsy bedroom wall, I could hear them whispering. Trembling, I tiptoed to their open door and watched Conrad and Sara looking at a photo of Sophie. Would she ever be able to forgive me? Would she stop loving me? What kind of monster was I to leave her behind, splitting up my children?

Sara adored her little sister. Said she was timid, vulnerable. After the divorce, David and I had agreed that she would spend half the week with each of us. Sara often wondered how a teenager dealt with that: half your clothes and school things at one house, half at the other. Homework was, for me, an exercise in resource planning: which school books were at whose house?

As a child, Sophie spent hours in the garden making mud pies or playing with worms. She worshipped her father, and would sit watching him through her wavy, light brown fringe while he read the paper or gazed silently at a rugby international or favourite antiques television show.

Their grandpa had had a lot of influence on the three of them. He was, like so many old men of his era, a creature of habit. He always knew what he would be having to eat for each meal three days ahead. He went to certain shops on certain days, watered the garden at the same time every day, and put the grandchildren to bed with a story at the same time. The fact that he then let them get up again and play was quietly ignored by all. As Conrad grew, Grandpa taught him it was okay for men to get upset; that talking is better than fighting; that real men aren't impressed by "pomp and bullshit". He saw no need to discipline his grandchildren, and was able to give them unconditional love and instant forgiveness.

'That's what grandparents are for,' he would say. I continually admired his ability to be the father that children need and the grandfather that children want. With Andrew and me, he'd been a stern disciplinarian—a figure of fear sometimes—but, with his grandchildren, he was a complete softie.

I pictured Sophie asleep on his knee, thumb stuck in her mouth, the sight that greeted me whenever I was late picking my children up, which was often. Sara would be in the bedroom watching MTV; Conrad would be practising knee-ups in the study. And my mum would be in the kitchen, making cakes.

I started to weep—aching for my child, for my parents—overwhelmed by a feeling of loss. When I looked up, I saw that Sara was weeping too, and Conrad was fighting back tears.

'We need beers, Mother. Several.' He pressed his fingertips into his eyes.

'Forty days isn't that long,' I tried to console myself. 'Lots of families are separated longer than that if the children are away at boarding school.' Then I thought of the things I hadn't told her: about make-up, sex, boys, falling out with best friends, becoming someone's girlfriend…the things mothers and daughters talk about. Even away at school, they can phone each other. I was half the world away with no two-way contact at all.

As we strolled back to the hotel after a lunch of what Conrad called 'camel shit', Sara's sandal sank into a soft, deep pile. She instinctively shook her foot to get rid of it.

'Nice one, sis. Thanks.' Conrad laughed as the fresh, sloppy mess spattered his designer joggers.

A group of children approached, giggling. Conrad ran towards them, hands outstretched, shouting, 'Rupees! Give me rupees!' Startled, they fled in several directions, disappearing into the maze of cobbled streets.

'For God's sake, don't be so unkind!' Grinning whilst simultaneously trying to express disapproval is quite tricky.

Our hotel was situated inside the city fortress. On our way back there we wandered around inside the ancient walls, along narrow streets lined with intricately carved, honey-coloured havelis. A poster advertised the forthcoming festival.

'Listen. There are camel races tomorrow, with over five hundred camels. There's a Mr Desert competition which I think Conrad should enter, and a turban tying contest, camel dances, camel polo, decorated camels. It all finishes with a firework display. We must go and have a look.'

'Right. Look at this, Mother, here's the highlight. One for you to enter: the moustache competition!'

'Ha ha, very funny, son.'

Hours later on that same day, we were lying in the desert, watching the hotel chef cooking our dinner over an open fire. He was doubling as our tour leader and was dressed for the occasion in leather jacket, jeans and silver neck chain. We had reached the Sam dunes by Jeep, passing through a remote village of five or six dwellings and a few scraggy animals.

The silence of the desert enveloped us as we looked out over rolling sand hills, their shadows elongating as the sun went down. I felt as if I was on the edge of the universe. Conrad and Sara sat on the top of the highest dune, watching the sunset. As the desert turned pink, a huge, silver moon was revealed, hanging low in the sky.

As the chill of the night set in, only the fire's crackling broke the silence. The chef put on a Fugees' tape and our desert party suddenly began, complete with fireworks. It was watched by a few goats and sheep tethered with the camels ten metres away, ready for our safari next morning.

We swayed, or rather, lurched around in the sand, trying to show off our Western dancing to the camel drivers who looked on in stunned silence, sipping from small cups. The chef had brought along what he called "desert whiskey", which smelled and tasted like pure alcohol. An hour later, he was so drunk that he took off in the Jeep, sand clouds rising as he drove round and round, coming to a sudden halt with a loud thud.

'I was looking for a private place to vomit,' he explained on his return, failing to mention that he had managed to flatten a tyre in the process.

We continued to sing and dance with the camel drivers around the campfire.

'Help!' Sara groaned to the men. 'That'—pointing to me—'is our mother.'

I had consumed "just a few sips" of the fiery beverage, and having learned all the words to "Pardassi"—the hit song of the moment—had been valiantly singing it with the locals until I was now hoarse.

Sara then spent half an hour trying to show me the man in the moon—to no avail: I couldn't see him. I couldn't see much at all, in fact. My daughter wrapped me in a thick blanket, covered me with my sleeping bag, and spent the night trying to ignore the loud snores coming from my direction.

We woke at dawn and dozed until a breakfast of boiled eggs, toast, jam and coffee appeared. As we mounted the camels, the sun rising over the dunes cast an eerie, pale silver glow which crept over our empty sleeping bags, the embers of the fire, and our small packs propped up in a heap in the sand.

'Need some extra fuel, Mum?' called Sara, fortifying herself with double-decker Bourbon biscuit sandwiches. 'You never know, you might get asked on another date!!'

I had been propositioned the evening before by a young man—obviously visually challenged or inebriated, or both—who invited me to his village, twenty kilometres away, to go to the cinema.

'We do not have to use the camels. We can go on my scooter,' he boasted, grinning widely. He was tiny and bony, with rotten, red-stained teeth. I politely declined, to his astonishment.

My camel farted and spat a lot. Collecting a ball of slime in one corner of its mouth, it vibrated the gunk in a large pink sac, which hung from one side of its jaw, and shook it from side to side before evacuating it into the sand. All this as I was being raised aloft, swaying laterally as I rose, sheer terror setting in. I felt nauseous, due not only to the lurching ascent: the foul smell of the camel gunk, sucked up from his stomach, had reached my nostrils.

'Okay, let me down now, I've had enough. I've been perched up here for three minutes and that's more than enough. I'm riding in the Jeep.'

My children took off for a race to the horizon whilst I stomped off in a sulk.

'I don't care much for camels,' I stammered as our leader approached.

'Why, madam, did you then book a camel safari, I am wondering?'

'Nobody likes a smart arse,' I mumbled, already sweltering inside the Jeep.

***

We were strolling around the fortress when Sara surprised me with a proposition.

'Right, Mum. You've got to try this. We've had some already. It's a travel experience you shouldn't miss.'

Oh dear, this sounds ominous.

'What is it?'

'Bhang lassi. It's a drink.'

I never thought I'd find myself looking for a sign advertising "bhang" but my children were determined to find one, for me to try. *And laugh at me, no doubt.*

'Look, Mum, this is what it says in the guide book:

"If you're tempted to try, it's very easy to find a bhang lassi shop. Just look for a group of foreigners in a very relaxed state. In Rajasthan, they are government run and usually have signs outside."'

Just about everywhere we looked we could see groups of foreigners 'in a very relaxed state', so that wasn't especially helpful.

I resorted to accosting a young local man.

'You want bhang? Ah, ha, ha, ha, very good, very good.' He slapped me between the shoulder blades and winked enthusiastically. 'You can see signs for bhang shops all over Rajasthan. Good if you drink bhang lassi anywhere in India. Only first check and confirm that is it government-approved shop or not.'

'Is it legal, then?' Not that I didn't trust my children, but I was, shall we say, a little concerned after some of their past choices.

'Oh, madam, we in India are believe that bhang is a Brahmin drug.'

'What does it do? I mean, what are the effects?'

'We feel toxicated, of course, but it is not like drunken. Our saints used it for doing the meditations and we use it for our betterment. It can help you if you have serious matters in your mind. If you are sad and you are drinking the bhang, you will be more and more sad, and if you are happy, after drinking it you will start laughing and singing.'

'What happens if you drink too much of it? Do you get a hangover, like with beer?'

'The hangover for alcoholic drink depends on how much is consumed. Generally, bhang drink will give you good sleep and, when you wake up, you will feel fresh. But if for you odd or not practice, there is possibility of vomiting and hangover. You can wake up with bad head. The bhang taken with milk will give you different kind of toxication. You do things very amusing and onlookers enjoy watching you do funny things—like you cry non-stop; you laugh non-stop; you jump around while walking for no reason; you feel that you are flying and shout for help, et cetera, et cetera. But there is no hangover when you take bhang.'

'What is it made of?'

'Lassi always made of yoghurt, madam. Traditional lassi is yoghurt drink with spices such as ginger and cumin, and sometimes fruit like mango. The special ingredient in bhang lassi is marijuana. And we have also remedy for removing the toxication of bhang. If you drink yoghurt after having bhang, it removes toxication very fast. Try it and enjoy it laughing, but not if you are in sad mood, otherwise you should start weeping.'

'Okaay, thank you. You are very helpful.'

'Not at all, madam. It is my great pleasure to service you.'

What could I do but agree?

***

Mount Abu

The following day we were on the move again. No flies on me: keep moving, no thinking. We were headed for the World Spiritual University in Mount Abu, the last place on our itinerary. I had learned a meditation technique from a group in Guernsey, and Sara was keen to try. I wanted to recapture the calm and beauty of the jungle on our tiger tour, to leave India feeling positive, with my choices validated.

'They practise an open-eyed meditation there. We can visit the centre and learn about their teachings from one of the monks, according to a booklet I read. If we're lucky, we might be able to go into their meditation chamber. It'll be a positive, peaceful place, even if we don't learn anything.'

'What do you do? Sit cross-legged and chant?'

'Well, Conrad, when I did it we sat in a group and someone talked us through imagining we were on a journey, upwards, towards a light. We had to pretend we were in a very special place, where we felt safe and happy, and try to block out any worries or thoughts about day-to-day stuff. If nothing else, you come out of it feeling relaxed. The people there greet each other with "Om Shanti". It means "I am a peaceful soul". I learned that it's not that we have a soul, but that we *are* souls.'

'Arseholes, more like. And keep your mumbo-jumbo to yourself, you two. I don't want to hear it. I suppose you're gonna go floating through the streets waving your arms around and blessing everybody, bangin' on about how it's good for you, going into a trance and wearing long skirts. Spare me, eh? And what am I supposed to do while you are improving your karma?'

Hmm, okay, so he's in an aggressive mood today, I thought.

'I'm sure you'll find plenty of things to moan about. Tell you what, you can guard our bags while we go in, then we'll go hotel hunting.'

The visit to the centre was just as I'd expected: peaceful, interesting and uplifting. Sara and I emerged at dinner time, feeling full of love and forgiveness towards everybody.

Conrad was in a better mood after the beers he'd had while waiting for us outside the entrance. We walked to a nearby hotel named The Hilltone.

'I reckon they've called it that to confuse tourists. They reckon that once they get people booked in, they'll be too lazy to move,' I suggested.

'They'd have to be pretty daft to think it's a Hilton. One hundred rupees a night, in a piddly little town up in the hills!' Conrad said, disheartening me, as ever.

'We'd best make the most of it. It's our last night up here in Rajasthan.'

We ate a mediocre meal, chatting quietly, each of us thinking about the return journey to Mumbai ahead. A drunken man wobbled across to our table, banging into another on his way, sending cutlery to the floor, tea spilling into cracked white saucers.

'Keep silence, please!' he shouted.

Stunned, we ignored him and continued our conversation.

'I have told you to keep silence! You are not in your country now!' he shrieked.

The hotel manager appeared and had words with his unwelcome guest. A shouting match between them ensued, and ended with the drunk getting thrown out, still gesticulating angrily towards us.

'Thanks for the free cabaret, mate,' Conrad mumbled with a smirk on his face.

'How the hell did he get any alcohol when we can't get any?' I wondered. 'This was the first truly peaceful place we've been to, and we end up watching a fight!' I put down the napkin I'd been folding and unfolding, in the absence of a crisp packet to fiddle with. 'Come on, let's get going back to the hotel.'

Two days later, my son emerged, pale and exhausted, from his room after a horrific bout of diarrhoea.

'There wasn't even a toilet inside the room. I had to go across the corridor and sit there for bloody hours, staring at the dead insects on the concrete floor. You don't half choose some crappy dumps, Ma.'

I had no response. I'd passed him three toilet rolls in the two days, so I knew he wasn't exaggerating. Even the herbal medicine I'd bought in town only stayed in his system for a few minutes. My poor son. What on earth was I putting him through? And for what? So I could run away from something I didn't even acknowledge, in search of the adventure I'd always sought from childhood onwards? Were we having fun yet? The usual internal monologue repeated itself. Was this the adventure? What, exactly, was the point I was making? And for whose benefit?

The meditation at Mount Abu had been positive, but very short-lived. How much longer would it take to feel that I was achieving anything exceptional by this trip? So far, the light of new awareness hadn't exactly blinded me.

From now on, we would be on our way back to Mumbai. Feeling diminished and emotionally exhausted, I dumped my pack onto my narrow bed and lay down without undressing, the magic of the tigers forgotten.

***

'Good afternoon, ladies. Allow me to present myself. I am Pete Idle, but friends call me Piddle. How're you diddlin'?' The plummy Oxford accent belonged to a short, ginger-haired man, more wobbly than plump.

Sara screwed her eyes into a suspicious frown. We were enjoying a banana lassi on the hotel terrace, looking over Nakki Lake, named after the fingernails of the gods who apparently carved it out from the earth.

'Fine, thank you. Are you staying here?' Sara enquired.

He raised his bushy eyebrows and widened his eyes, an expression that elongated his numerous freckles so that they looked like a skin disease. He scratched under his armpit, raising it slightly to reveal a damp patch in his frayed, greyish T-shirt, worn over jeans which were tattered at the knees.

'Oh no, my dear, much too costly for the likes of me. I'm roughing it on the beach for a few days. You know, in amongst the cows. In my infinite wisdom, I decided that a trip to India would be good for my soul. Everyone warned me about the squalor. I, of course, knew better, and came anyway. But I find it all too much for little old me.'

'How did you travel here? By train?' Conrad strolled up to join us from wherever he'd been.

'I have absolutely no idea. Can't recall a bloody thing. Must have been the bottle of gin I very cunningly drank on my first night in Bombay. Ah, here he is! Do let me introduce my very dear friend Waffle.'

'Waffle?'

'Real name Will. William Offle, at your service. Does anyone know what I'm doing here?' He hummed a tune for a moment, then began making trumpeting noises with his mouth. He was wearing a suit jacket that had seen better days, shiny at the elbows, a collarless cheesecloth shirt bearing several telltale greasy marks and a few dark spots—which I recognised as old red wine stains—and jeans.

'You'll have to forgive him, he's completely potty. I do believe he took rather too many of those Ecstasy tablets one can acquire these days from certain quarters.'

'Stop fart-arsing around, Piddle, and let's get a move on. Did you get the tickets?'

Piddle's face fell. 'Nearly. A woman with a face like a monkfish informed me that I hadn't brought enough lolly with me, so I'm afraid we're here for the duration, old bean.'

'Can anyone tell me why I came here with him?'

By now, Conrad and Sara were enchanted. These two would be fun.

'Fancy a beer, mate?' Conrad winked at Piddle.

'D'you know, old chap, I don't mind if I do! How awfully civil of you!' I wanted to slope off. This conversation was not for me. An early night and a movie. Oops, no: not at home! A book and a backpack for a pillow would have to do. I settled down but couldn't sleep; I could hear their muffled voices.

'Tell me, my friend, why are you on this journey with your mother? And this charming young woman must be your sister. Am I right?'

'What do you mean?' Conrad prickled.

'It strikes me as odd, a young man like you travelling with his mother—and sister, come to that.'

'Don't people in your family go anywhere together?'

'Not really. Not unless they have to. You know, funerals and the like. To tell the truth, I don't have much of a family. Parents quit this mortal coil years ago. No siblings. I do have a charming cousin who tried marriage once but never produced any wriggly squirmers.'

'Pardon?'

'Babies, you know, offspring. Progeny. It must be hard for you being the only chap, surely?'

'Sometimes, yeah. But I'm alright, mate. Ta just the same.'

I imagined Conrad flinching inwardly. He didn't like discussing feelings; especially not feelings about his family. He was angry with David and me for splitting up, and for embarrassing him in front of his friends by our so-called polite behaviour. Why not just shout at each other and be honest, instead of pussyfooting about being "well-mannered"? He had been especially angry about a youth football match two weeks after the split when we both turned up to watch him play, something we'd rarely bothered to do when we were together. We'd stood side by side, pretending everything was normal, when the whole team knew that Conrad's parents weren't together anymore; that we were a failed family.

I kept thinking about them—Piddle the short, fat one; Waffle the tall, skinny one—and wondered if they were some kind of double act. I got up to visit the loo an hour—and I guessed several beers—later. It was as if I was invisible. None of them noticed me as I passed them sitting on the floor against the wall in the corridor, surrounded by empty cans.

'Piddle, you look a bit pale. Are you alright?' enquired Sara, absent-mindedly twisting a strand of her hair into a knot.

'Not three bad. I have, of course, seen better days, but that's life, isn't it? You are such a pretty young thing. Do you have someone to keep you warm at night?'

'No, not any more. I met this guy back home in Guernsey a couple of months ago, and I really liked him. He said he was coming back to the island for Christmas but he never showed up.'

'I do hope you haven't given up on love, my dear. We chaps are not awfully good at that sort of thing, you know. There is probably a good explanation.'

'Yeah, right. Like he got caught up in a war, or he lost his dialling finger in a fencing contest.'

'Do you really think so? How dreadful! Poor chap.'

'More likely he was actually a member of the Olympic bullshitting team.' She raised both hands to her hair to unravel the knot.

'Gosh, that's an awfully hard accusation to make.'

'Look, he didn't break my heart. I didn't know him long enough for that. But he certainly made an impression. And I feel stupid now, like I can't judge character anymore.'

'My word, it does sound as if you really rather liked him.'

'Yes. I did. But that's in the past. I'm living for the moment now.' She scratched her ear where a strand of fallen hair was tickling her. 'What happened, happened. It has nothing to do with my future. Nothing from my past life exists any more. My parents got divorced—the biggest shock of the century—my little sister is in Guernsey, and my so-called boyfriend disappeared. I don't care about any of it. Shall we have another drink?'

They drank into the night, my children and their strange companions, and when I woke next day, there was no sign of any of them. By two in the afternoon, I was worried, and asked at the bar if anyone had seen them.

'Oh yes, madam, on the shore of the lake. They were sleeping under the stars, and now they are sleeping under the sun. Mister Conrad, he is famous. He drove away an invader from his room in Udaipur. We all know about it here. He is a brave man, a hero to us.'

My God, I thought, *it's true. They really are batty.*

'No harm will come to him here,' he continued. 'He is protected. Don't worry, madam, your children are safe.'

It was then that my awareness expanded to accommodate a new possibility: I may have been looking for the meaning of life in all the wrong places, which was a pity, because I still didn't know where I should have been looking. But I had a sneaky feeling it might be within me, not outside. Not in the external world.

***

Ahmedabad

Late next morning, we gathered by the roadside to await the bus to Ahmedabad. Families rowed on the lake, overlooked by Toad Rock on the hill opposite.

'Bloody hell, they were well weird, those two...' Conrad rubbed his eyes.

'Yep, dunno what they were on, but they're fucked up, for sure. Reckon they'll be here another couple of days? What are they gonna live on? They're totally skint.'

I wondered why Sara seemed to be more concerned about their welfare than she had been about the girl who'd been sold. *Ha! But they've got this far*, I thought, *so I guess they'll survive.*

While we were waiting an enchanting, small boy with huge, ebony black eyes, dressed in rags, was busy making his living by cleaning shoes for the passengers waiting at the bus stop. A crust of dried snot covered his top lip.

'Scuse me, mate,' said Conrad. 'Good of you to clean my shoes, but they're open-toed sandals and you've just smeared black polish all over my feet.'

During the six-hour bus ride, I fell asleep by the open window, but woke when I felt moisture on my face. Not fully awake, I thought it must be raining. I jolted to awareness at an all-too-familiar sound: the woman in front of me was spitting out of the window and it was blowing back through my window and onto my face. Feeling instantly nauseous, shocked and disgusted, I bashed her across the back of the head. She turned to glower, but stopped spitting.

'I can't believe you did that, Mother. What happened to all your love and peace stuff?' asked Conrad. 'By the way, you've got a piece of tissue stuck to your face.'

'Naff off, Conrad.' I tugged at the offending tissue but it stuck firm. I had to scrape my fingers over my cheeks till I'd peeled it all away.

'Good afternoon, dear guests. Welcome to Relief Hotel. I show you now to your rooms.'

I had spent an hour using the Mount Abu hotel reception's phone late the night before, trying to find us a hotel near the station for our overnight stop here, and finally booked us in to spend the night in a hotel on Relief Road, Ahmedabad. It looked pretty grim but was all I could find in the guide book, and more to the point, the only one that had answered the phone.

'Must be called that because it's such a relief to get out of it, harr, harr.'

'Not funny, Mum.'

'Please may we have some clean sheets?' asked Sara a few minutes after depositing her bag in the room. She gnawed absent-mindedly at the skin by the side of her thumbnail. 'Yes, madam, I will bring replacements.'

The replacements were grease-stained, even filthier than the originals. I called in to see how Conrad was faring, and looked into Sara's room on the way back to see her standing on the bed, making a noose from which to hang her mosquito net.

'Don't do it, darling! Things aren't that bad!'

'Very funny, Mother.'

In the evening we walked along a road strewn with rubbish, looking for a restaurant. We almost had to wade through the piles of litter and rotting vegetables. Rats scurried in front of us. Suddenly a group of local lads began to hurl rocks and stones in our direction. No one had been this hostile before. Conrad chased them away, but after the meal we took a rickshaw back to the hotel.

'I had nightmares all night, Mum,' moaned Sara next morning. In our dark, damp, dingy, smelly rooms, cockroaches scurried up the walls, across the ceiling, and down the opposite side. Sitting on the toilet in the one-metre-square shower room required keeping your feet above floor level to avoid the creatures scrambling over your toes. I renamed it the "Cockroach Hotel".

'How come we managed to stay in one of the most polluted streets in the whole of India?'

'You know why. It was the only hotel with any room when I called around from Mount Abu at one o'clock in the morning! Apart from luxury hotels, of course, which you know very well we can't afford. We'll soon be out of here. Only a day or two till we get to Singapore!'

***

On the station platform next morning, Sara noticed something covered with a linen cloth and surrounded by a few incense sticks. No one appeared to be taking any notice.

'Oh my God! It's a body!' she cried.

'Yes, they just leave them there till someone's family notices a missing person and comes to claim them. I read that in the guide book.'

I turned to see a beggar on a trolley. He had no legs, but was towing beside him a West Highland terrier with a shiny new red collar and lead.

Standing on that platform, I had a rapid flashback to childhood:

I'm alone. My lungs caved in.

I'm lying on the lawn, stroking thick green velvety blades of grass. The baby has gone with Mummy. He's not my sister, he's not my sister. He's my brother; I must remember. I'll be a good girl. I'll take care of my brother from now on.

My promise to take care of my brother had, by adulthood, transformed into acknowledging my responsibility for my family's well-being, and I had failed miserably so far. I was not only divorced, I was hauling them around places where dead bodies lay unnoticed, where extreme poverty and physical deformities were commonplace, and where parents had to sell their children. What else might they yet have to deal with?

People huddled together on the platform floor, staring vacantly. Our train pulled in, grimy with the sweat of countless bodies, its windows smeared with a greasy layer which, from the interior, I later mistook for mist outside.

Once on board, after a scramble for seats, the countryside flashed past, changing from flat, suburban desolation, complete with the rusting remains of various vehicles, to slowly rising landscapes punctuated by scrubby trees and, finally, vast plains and hills. Against a background of continual babble in local dialects and the slightly odd sound of the English present continuous, a tea seller strolled nonchalantly up and down the aisle, calling, 'Chai! Chai!'

Fifteen people were crammed into our six-seat compartment. I had booked seats for the nine-hour journey but, squashed upright, I couldn't get any sleep. People were standing in the aisle, on top of our bags, even sitting on our knees. The luggage racks were simply seen as extra seating, so dusty feet dangled in front of our faces for the duration of the journey.

'What can you do? You can't make them stand for nine hours in the heat.'

Sara was beside herself with frustration. She felt helpless, frightened by all the strangeness. She pulled at her eyebrow hairs, despair showing around her mouth.

'When we wanted to sit together on the journey to Jodhpur, we were told we had to move because our seat bookings weren't correct. Now our seat reservations are right, and we have to have a dozen other people sitting on top of us!' she complained to the ticket collector. 'You can't treat us like this. In Britain, if you book seats you don't have to share them with a crowd of other people.'

'Madam, be quiet. You are in India now,' came the languid, disinterested reply.

Mumbai

By the time we arrived in Mumbai, we were covered with grime and dust. Our clothes were greyish brown, regardless of their original colour. Our bodies were sticky and hot. My trousers had disintegrated—worn through on the seat—and my far-from-attractive pants showed through. Our bottles of mineral water were too hot to drink. On the platform, the sun penetrated the gloom for a moment or two. My eyes hurt from squinting into the smog.

'Let's just go straight to the airport, Mum. We can sit in the restaurant for three and a half hours and have a meal until check-in at quarter past midnight.'

'Anywhere else in the world, they'd refuse to allow us in!' I removed my sunglasses to wipe dust from the corner of my eyes.

But they did, and we spent our last few hours in India in the airport café, feeling like a group of refugees—exhausted and traumatised. Hmm, that's another fine mess you've got us into, Rachael.

***

To: Wendy McKintock
From: Rachael Green
Subject: On the road again
Mar somethingth

Hi.

Just a quickie—at Mumbai airport en route to Singapore then Thailand.

When I set off, I had no doubt that it was the right thing to do. Now it feels like a huge error of judgement. What was I supposed to learn from this—traumatic overnight bus rides and being stoned in the street by angry lads?

I hope this trip will give me the answer to why I exist on this planet at all! I feel guilty that I have so much and I still moan about how I *feel*, for God's sake, when most of the people here scrabble around to stay alive.

Hope all okay with you. Miss your humour!

Cheers for now

x

PS By the way, it hasn't been all bad. We diverted to a National Park to see tigers, and the place was fab. Really peaceful.

***

South East Asia

Singapore

'Nice one, Ma!' My son howled with laughter at the sight of his mother face up on the floor, backpack underneath her, legs and arms waving in the air, like a giant upturned cockroach. I had tripped over my flowing long skirt at the end of the moving walkway at Changi Airport, causing great hilarity.

'I feel like the huge insect in Kafka's *Metamorphosis*,' I whimpered helplessly, smiling whilst fighting back tears of humiliation. 'Can you give me a hand?'

'You've got to be joking. Even two of us would never lift you and that whopping great pack. You'll just have to roll over, Ma.'

'I can't! I can't get enough momentum going.'

But, by now, a passer-by had placed his arms around me and, between the three of them, I was hauled up to my feet, wobbling precariously under the weight of my backpack.

'I'd advise you to post most of that stuff back home,' a kindly voice advised. 'It looks as if you've come away for a whole year.'

'Well, actually...' But he had already walked off, trailing an elegant, black leather trolley bag behind him.

A short taxi drive took us to Orchard Road. Up till then, I had never heard of it, but my kids had been looking forward to the elegant shops lining it. I loathe shopping and, as far as I could see, all this street had to offer was shop after shop after shop. There were no cafés, no sign of street life, no one walking around. Were they all inside, shopping? Everything was modern, clinical—and soulless.

'The city is known as a Fine City. Do you know why?' Gary, our chubby, cheerful and loquacious taxi driver asked, then continued without waiting for an answer. 'Because there are fines for just about every offence to public decency, such as eating in the street, chewing gum, smoking, and dropping litter.'

The result, I decided, was a squeaky clean environment from which every trace of history or culture seemed to have been erased.

Gary deposited us at Hotel 81, one of many of the same name.

'Have you noticed anything odd about this place, Mother?' my son asked with an enigmatic smile as we walked to our room.

'There are a lot of young girls dressed in tight skirts hanging around in the foyer.'

I peered at the room rate sign. Rooms by the hour. No wonder; that explained the girls. Our room was clearly functional: a double bed, one straight-backed modern chair. Characterless. The receptionist organised an extra bed so we could all fit into one room. The rate was extortionate by our recent standards.

When we went out to explore, we came across a shop window in the next block containing various scantily clad girls for rental. Each wore a label around her neck bearing a number.

'Clients choose a girl, then go to the office next door and book the number they want,' explained the receptionist in a matter-of-fact tone when we returned. 'This hotel is one of the places the couple might spend some time.'

Another of the classy places I take my kids to; all part of their education.

We spent the afternoon resting. For dinner, in one of the open-air restaurants, I tried "drunken prawns", a spicy local speciality. Later that night, I woke with severe stomach cramps. Medication had no effect. I was to spend the next thirty-six hours prone in bed.

The hotel management kindly offered me a local cure: a remedy comprising brown powder mixed with hot water, which caused me to retch before it even passed my lips.

'I'll just have to starve until the nasty little bug dies and leaves my intestines in peace,' I decided. 'You two go out and explore.'

'How was your night out?' I asked them next morning. My voice was weak from the effort of straining, and I was embarrassed by the noises my intestines were making and the horrible smell coming from the tiny adjacent bathroom.

'We had a burger and chips, and one beer between us. Guess how much?'

'No idea. I gave you fifty quid's worth of currency, so I hope you didn't spend it all.'

'The meal was forty quid. A mineral water was two pounds, and a packet of two digestive biscuits for lunch was one pound fifty.'

'Jesus, that means we've spent a hundred and thirty-five pounds a day here, compared with thirty-five in India. Let's get out of here, quick!'

I saw nothing more of Singapore. In the MRT station, I could barely stand, and rested against a spanking clean wall. I slid down the wall to my bottom, unsure if I'd ever get up again. 'Why did I get ill here? It's so bloody hygienic!'

'Maybe your system's got so used to shit, it can't cope with normal places.'

'Actually, you have a point there.' *Okay, on your feet, Rachael, let's get moving.*

'Oh wait! While we're at the airport, I'm going to try to call Guernsey. It's probably about the only place where it could work without mega hassles. We have an hour at least to kill before boarding. You coming?'

'Too right! Wouldn't miss the chance to speak to Sophie!' Conrad was unusually enthusiastic.

I could feel how much they both missed her. I wasn't the only one.

'Hello? Hello? Can you hear me? It's me, Rachael. We're at Singapore Airport—the most civilised place we've been so far. Is Sophie there?'

I turned to the others. 'Yes! We're in luck!'

'Put her on please, David. Much as I'd like to chat to you, I really don't have time and... Darling! How are you?'

After three minutes, I offered the handset to Sara, and turned away to let them talk in privacy. So, David had a new woman in his life. And Sophie was furious.

'So who's Dad's new bird then?' Conrad asked.

'I don't know. I've never heard of her. But Sophie hates her. Says she missed out on being with us 'cause she felt sorry for your dad, being on his own, and now he doesn't need her anymore.' Despite my initial anger at him, I could see how he didn't mean to hurt Sophie. He was just being a human, needing company. He would be suffering over his daughter's anger. For the first time, I was able to put myself where he was, instead of concentrating on my own story.

***

'G'day, ladies and gentlemen. Welcome aboard.'

The smooth, confident and reassuring sound of the Aussie accent immediately comforted me. Memories of civilisation slowly returned. We sat in silent reflection, Sara saddened by her helplessness—her inability to comfort her little sister—Conrad grateful to be comfortable again, and me disappointed not to have found my missing part.

We had survived India physically intact—if emotionally bruised. Before leaving for this journey, I thought I was merely curious about our planet. It was only once we'd spent some time away that my whole perception of reality began to change. I now had no choice but to embrace previously unimagined possibilities, and had to acknowledge the wisdom of spiritual rather than materialistic motives: the latter simply don't work there. I had been seeking a spiritual awakening, and India forced it onto me on her terms, not mine. Like a newborn thrown into the sea to swim, I had no time to contemplate, no time to work on myself: it just happened by dint of having to survive.

As a family, our time in India forced each of us to balance our development as individuals against our relationships, both with one another and with the people we met on the way. Sometimes, this had stretched us to our limits of patience and tolerance. On the occasions when we blew our tops, the practicality of being on the move forced a speedy reconciliation. We had to overcome our external prejudices and internal fears, and were just beginning to learn to welcome the challenges; to see them as opportunities to grow. We were moving away from being observers, and starting to participate in our own destinies. I felt comfortable with this idea and decided that, from now on, I would be calm—serene even—and observe life rather than try to control it. Our stopover in Singapore had been brief and expensive. The contrast between India and Singapore was so vast it was difficult to take in that the two places were on the same side of the world. Now it was time to move on again.

'Ready for Thailand, Sara?'

'Bring it on!'

'How about you, love?'

'Whatever…when do they serve the food?' ever-practical, ever-hungry Conrad replied.

***

To: Wendy McKintock
From: Rachael Green
Subject: Who am I, again?
Mar 15
Hi

At last, another internet café—few and far between in these parts. It's been a brilliant trip so far, despite my early doubts. Am so glad I'm doing it. No regrets—but I often feel I'm learning nothing new about myself. Still feeling like a freak of nature. Still lonely. No life-changing revelations. Maybe I should have gone to Damascus.

How does this work, then, this "finding yourself" lark? I'm not my body, that's for sure. I don't feel like a middle-aged woman; I feel more like a bloody adolescent. Especially when I want to shout, 'It's not fair!' This slightly plump, baggy body isn't me, surely?

Maybe I'm the sum of my experiences—all my thoughts, actions and feelings. Yippee. Get me a fancy hat, someone, I'm celebrating. Not. My experiences have been pretty limited up to now—I haven't exactly climbed Everest. And as for my thoughts… Bloody hell, move over, Einstein, my contribution to the world of intellectualism is about to stun the planet. Every thought, each and every one of them, has disappeared. They've churned around, milled about, tumbled over each other day after day, night after night, for forty-odd years, and it looks like another forty of the same. Christ, what a thought (there goes another one).

My feelings, well now, here we have hit the jackpot. Here we have a possibility. My feelings…could stun the world. Yep. How about abandoned (alone in the garden with my bee sting guilt, my mother no longer paying attention to me), useless (can't keep a husband of twenty-plus years; children forced to flee), separate, different, stupid, fragile, unlovable…? There's a list to encourage a body.

That leaves nothing. So I am nothing: no thing, no body, no one. We might be onto something here. Maybe I'm just an empty space. Hmm. An empty space…

Sorry about that—add self-indulgent to the list of my charms! Tell me what's happening in your life (or not, as the case may be…)

Om shanti, sister

R

x

***

Thailand

Bangkok
So this was Bangkok. It had sounded so exotic, but it was crazy. Traffic everywhere; streets heaving with people. The noise was deafening.

'Wouldn't mind having that place. What do you reckon?' Conrad stared at an exotic building.

'It's gorgeous—that golden thingy on the top is pretty cool. What is it, anyway, Mum?'

'The Royal Palace. There's an emerald Buddha inside that visitors go to see 'cause it's so amazing.'

'Yeah, well, count me out. I'd rather go on one of them klong thingies,' Conrad said.

'Me too!' Sara agreed.

'Well, so would I, as it happens. So let's head down to the canal to the floating market and see if we can find one.'

After an hour of belting along in a motorized canoe, I felt the need for dry land but, before we left for our hotel, I wanted to climb the Wat Arun pagoda.

'We're off for a beer while you climb up. Give us some dosh, please, Ma.'

As always, I handed it over without questions. Beers, I could afford. Comfortable hotels, not. Hmm...

I clambered slowly up as far as you're allowed to go. Feeling smug, I turned round to go down and...oops. I felt like a cat stuck up a tree. I had absolutely no idea how I was going to get my suddenly enormous-looking body down to ground level.

The steps were only about twenty centimetres wide, not as long as my feet, and the gradient—well, almost vertical. Oh dear. I could see eager faces coming up to the nearest platform so had to make a move or remain there as if frozen in stone forever. I shuffled round again to face the same way I'd come up. There was no way I could get down facing outwards. I inhaled, lowered my right foot gingerly down until I felt a step, and gently put my weight onto it. The process took twice as long as going up but, hey, I made it!

'You were gone for ages! We bought you a beer but it was going warm so we shared it.' Sara smiled at me.

'Well, it was fascinating up there. I wanted to savour every moment.'

'Yeah, right. We saw you.' Conrad winked.

'Ah.'

'You were so slow coming down a queue started to form; then half of them gave up and went home!' Sara threw her head back as she laughed. They were both enjoying themselves— albeit at my expense, as usual—and I experienced a deep sense of satisfaction. I felt validated. It was going to be alright; they were having fun, we were getting on well, nothing bad had happened to any of us. Yet.

***

Dear Sophie

Our hotel in Bangkok was luxurious by our recent standards. It even had a bath!! Indian horrors now seem past distant. Tomorrow, we are heading for the island of Koh Samui in South Thailand. The temperature here is 30 degrees, 28 at night. Last night, I watched Conrad and Sara out on our balcony, putting up one of her famous washing lines made out of old scarves, all knotted together at intervals. She was wearing her nightshirt; he was in his boxers. I could see planes landing every few seconds in the background. It looked very comical, a bit like a Chinese laundry. Bangkok Airport has a rail station linked by a bridge. I wondered how many backpackers have plodded across that bridge over the rails, down the steps to the station, to take the train into Bangkok, oriental setting, where the city don't know what the city is getting…da da dat—oh sorry! You probably don't know that song: 'One Night in Bangkok' – ask your dad to play it to you.

Next day. We are now well practised in causing chaos at international airports, and the flight to Koh Samui was no exception. Conrad very intelligently left his passport at the hotel. We telephoned them, and they kindly sent the passport in the airport courtesy coach. We just managed to board on time after an hour of nervous waiting.

Plus ça change, what! (ask Mademoiselle Dupres)
Love you darling xxxxxx

PS By the way, when you come out to Oz, you'll be what's called an UM—unaccompanied minor. You'll probably have a big label round your neck so the airline staff can identify you easily. You'll hate it but it will keep you safe. Just to warn you.

***

Koh Samui

A couple of days later, we flew down to Koh Samui. It wasn't my idea, but Sara and Conrad been right about Goa so, in my usual decisive fashion, I left it up to them.

The arrivals area was under thatch, formed from and supported by coconut palms. As we walked towards it from the aircraft, we passed rows of bright pink and orange hibiscus shrubs. An exotic scent teased my nostrils until my head began to reel.

Running the gauntlet of taxi drivers wasn't nearly as stressful here.

'Lamai beach, mate!' My son grinned at the driver as we climbed into a taxi. I could swear he gave Sara a wink as he said it. 'Do you know the Baan Lamai hostel? Take us there. Ta.'

Our driver nodded. His multi-coloured beach shirt was neatly pressed, his nails immaculately manicured, his leather sandals polished to a shine.

The road followed the curve of the bay, white sands visible between overhanging palms, vivid blue sea gleaming between coconut-thatched wooden huts. Buffalo ambled along narrow paths; wild boar snuffled in the undergrowth. We gasped at the bright turquoise oval jewels in the centre of arrogant peacocks' tails.

'How did you know about a place to stay here, Conrad?' I asked.

'Oh, you know me, got friends in high places, Ma. Quite a few of my mates have been out here and they said it's really cool there.'

At the hostel, a dozen or so wooden huts with terraces and high, pointed roofs were arranged around a garden of shrubs. The main building housed further rooms, each with an en suite shower, joined by a balcony and reached by steep stone steps. In the front garden stood a shrine—a square pillar, on top of which perched a miniature temple painted red, gold and white. Garlands of marigolds hung from the temple, and incense burned in tiny urns. A large wooden offerings bowl had been placed at the foot of the structure. Lying alongside it, a furry, fat dog lay scratching its belly.

'I think this will do very nicely. It's a bit more than I planned to spend, but well done.'

'Fair play to you, Mother,' replied Conrad, surveying the surroundings and casting his eyes towards the reception area decorated with gaudy Christmas tinsel.

'She must have found the secret of a happy life,' I commented. A very pretty girl sat behind the desk. She smiled continuously, but clearly didn't understand a word anyone said to her.

We had a little hut each, complete with terrace and bathroom. I got up for a swim early next day, followed by my new canine friend, had a manicure on the beach, then ambled back to a communal outdoor platform for breakfast of muesli, banana and pineapple with plain yoghurt.

Butterflies the size of my hand fluttered around my face. Surrounding hills were covered by tropical rainforest, and a scent of citrus blossom filled the air.

This was to become my daily routine while Conrad and Sara slept late—early swim, breakfast, then back to the beach. An unmade track lined with emerald green vegetation and an impenetrable forest of palms led down almost to the beach itself, where thick, juicy shrubs grew straight out of the sand. That first morning, I gasped at the sight, anticipating the hours of sensual joy to come. The sun would caress me, the lapping waves would refresh me without the usual fear of a coronary, and the sand— white talcum, of course—would warm me gently until I drifted into sweet oblivion. I couldn't wait. I hurled my backpack to my feet, and tossed my sarong carelessly aside.

There was no breeze. I lay in the sand and listened. *There's a first,* I thought. *I'm not talking, or thinking about talking. There's no inner voice whispering inside my head, making me feel nervous.* I heard the throaty song of fat toads, battling for noise supremacy with a chorus of chirping cicadas. Flying fish splashed as they leaped for sheer joy, glittering in the sun for a spectacular instant before breaking the crystalline surface of the water.

A fruit seller sat next to me. She wouldn't take no for an answer, and I tasted the bitter velvet of mango fruit, the sweet, sharp flavour of freshly cut pineapple, and the unmatchable bliss of a fresh coconut shake.

'Were you truly wafted here from Paradise?' I enquired of no one. The dog opened one watery eye in response.

Two hours later, my tanned back was decorated with what looked like the paleness of a recent slap from someone's hand, the result of falling asleep under the almost stationary leaves of a palm tree. It took me days of careful strategic repositioning to get rid of it.

That first day, I didn't see Conrad or Sara at all, and at eleven, I stumbled, skin tingling from the sun and the sea, into my bed. The whirring of the overhead fan lulled me to sleep within minutes.

I woke suddenly in the night and caught sight of a solitary bright star through the gap in my thin cotton curtains. I tried to meditate, to think positive, but I couldn't shake off the melancholy. I kept picturing the freckles which appeared across Sophie's nose and cheeks every summer.

'How could I have left her behind?' The whole adventure seemed completely unnatural; an anathema. I was in paradise with two of my children while the youngest was missing out on it all. I ached inside, just like I had in the marital bed, straining to hear the sound of his car, wrestling to hold on to my dignity. I still dreamed about him, often about the happy days—not regularly, but often enough to unsettle me. The emptiness I felt then settled into me again, this time not for David, but for my daughter.

Sleep was fitful after that. I was enclosed in darkness. Was I locked in a wardrobe? Crammed under a rock? I was filled with terror, alone, with no one to reassure me that I was still alive.

When I finally opened my eyes again, my sheets were tangled and damp with sweat.

***

'Bugger!' Conrad shouted.

'Not now, thanks. What's the matter?' I asked, trying to pick bits of breakfast orange pulp from between my teeth with my thumbnail.

'Do you have to do that?' He glared at me. 'Never mind. You know that Zippo lighter Sophie got me for my birthday? I lent it to some geezer and he's run off with it. She'd had it engraved and everything. Sneaky little git. He asked me for a light then legged it while I was talking to Sara.'

He looked crestfallen. He'd be annoyed with himself, I thought, for not being streetwise, and genuinely upset at losing a gift from his sister.

'Don't worry. You can buy stuff like that in Vietnam. They sell off old American bits and pieces left behind after the war. Push that knife over, please.'

'Yeah, but she's going to know it's not the same one, and she'll think I've just lost it.'

Ah, he was concerned about his sister's feelings. Not long ago, he would have dismissed any sign of hurt as pathetic. I worked at the intruding orange debris. The knife was reliably blunt, too wide for my teeth gaps.

'Guess what, Mum?' Sara beamed excitedly as she walked towards the breakfast table. 'You are never going to guess who I've just been speaking to!'

'Er, let me see now. Chairman Mao? Elvis?'

'Hilarious. It was Michael. I saw him last night. He's back here in Thailand. You know he's been here before. He found out from one of Conrad's mates that we were here, got the name of the island from Sophie, and tracked me down! It's a bit like

133

Guernsey here—everyone knows everyone, and strangers get talked about.'

'Well, well, that's devotion for you. How long is he staying?' I was still angry with him for letting her down, especially since I felt responsible for getting them together.

'Er, I wanted to have a chat with you about that. He says he wants to travel with us for a while. Is that okay with you? 'Cause if not, I'll tell him he'll have to make his own way and meet up in various places as we go along.'

Despite his traditional upbringing, and although he still got on well with his parents, Michael found them staid, dull and obdurate. I had been his tutor and general studies teacher. During discussions, I encouraged the group to question everything. Although he still had respect for authority, I remember telling him it was important to respect the person, not the rank or title. When he left school, he thanked me for that insight. I was duly flattered.

'Yes, of course he can, darling. Why ever not? As long as he pays his way, that is. I can't afford to support him as well.'

I never was one for thinking things through before opening my mouth. I didn't give a single thought to the logistics of travel and accommodation, nor to the new composition of the party and how this would affect the family dynamics.

'Oh, Mum, he must really like me to come back out here, don't you think?'

'Has he explained why he didn't bother to contact you before Christmas?' Was this man going to break my daughter's heart? Learning from experience is a bit tricky when you're under twenty.

'Well, sort of. I told you, his parents wanted him to go home for the holiday. He didn't want to upset me so he just stayed away. He thought I'd be angry.'

'Hmm, okay.' I thought better of saying any more. Like "cowardly little creep".

'He's waiting at the bar for your decision. Can I call him over now?'

'Oh, go on then, why not? It's okay with me, of course it is.'

I'd been his teacher five years ago. How embarrassing that I now looked so scruffy, compared to before. I never used to look shabby in those days—just the opposite: smart, and much slimmer. I'd definitely let myself go since David had left.

At the age of fourteen, it was clear to his parents that he was bright. It was not that he was academically inspired, but he was hard-working, and smart enough to memorize important facts and ideas and reproduce them in the right place at the right time. He learned how to please. Once, as a child, he'd been asked by an aged auntie if he liked the gift she had bought him. Having been brought up to tell the truth, he had said no, for which he was punished by his parents. Right then, he learned that it was better to lie, to tell people what they wanted to hear, than to tell the truth. So when, at fourteen, his parents had asked if he wanted to go a boarding school, he had told them yes, knowing that his father wanted to be able to boast about it.

Sara almost skipped away to find him. No matter how hard she tried to hide her excitement, she was clearly overjoyed.

Michael strolled over and extended a bronzed hand. 'Thank you so much. Sara's just told me you've agreed to let me travel with you. I hope I don't get in the way too much. I really wanted to be with Sara, and it seemed stupid for me to do my own thing when she's out here. I promise I won't get in the way or cause any hassle. I've got six hundred pounds, and I'll go along with whatever you decide.'

After five minutes, he'd won me over. Easily done, I admit. He had grown into a rather gorgeous young man: strong and witty, and appeared to be considerate. As I watched them stroll off hand in hand, my son turned to me, face like stone.

'What! What the hell are you playing at? How's that going to work, then? They go off all lovey-dovey and "together" while I play gooseberry. It won't make any difference to you. You'll keep banging around your old temples and I'll be lumbered with them, or stuck on my own. Thanks a lot. And what happens when they have a row? Which they will, for sure. Are you going to keep out of it? I don't think so! You may as well send me home. The rest of this trip is going to be shit.'

I felt wretched. I fretted. Conrad was right. What kind of a holiday was he going to have with his mother, sister and sister's boyfriend? Time for a drink or three.

I lay across my bed that night, wallowing in alcohol-induced generosity. I could fix this. All it needed was money, and I was well practised in throwing that at my problems.

'Conrad, of all your friends, who would you most like to be here with you?' I couldn't wait to ask him next morning.

'Dunno. Gecko, I suppose. Why?'

'Well, how would you like him to come and join us for a while?'

'Like he can afford to...'

'Look, I want you to have a good time. If I pay for him, he could maybe pay me back part of the money next year.'

'You don't think he'd really pay you back, do you? He already owes hundreds to his mum.'

'Maybe, but I'm willing to give him a chance, if you'd like him here.'

'I'm not taking any responsibility for him paying you back 'cause I don't think he will. But, yeah, that would be cool.'

***

Gecko, whose real name was Jez—well, Jeremy, but not even his parents called him that—was angry with the world. Stocky, square-jawed, with a muscular physique, he attracted girls easily. He had a magnetism which drew you to him, and a sinister force which repelled you almost as quickly. His suppressed fury with life seemed to fire his survival, and the energy it created powered him like an invisible engine. According to him, everything about his life was unfair—his birth, the climate, the traffic on the roads. Humdrum events like shopping or being offered a journey around the world conspired to thwart him. He didn't have a clue what he was missing whilst he was being forced to deal with everyday life, but he was sure as hell bitter about missing it.

'You have got an up-to-date passport, haven't you?' I asked him when I called him next day. 'I can only afford for you to come out for a few weeks, Jez—er, sorry, Gecko—and you'd have to pay me back.' God knows how he had acquired his nickname. Something to do with his surname being Stonewall, Conrad once said. He and his friends had a habit of giving each other weird nicknames.

'And you'll need to get some vaccinations, er, what shall I call you, Jeremy, or Jez? Or Gecko? Well, we can sort that out later, don't want to waste money on long phone calls, ha ha...so it'll be at least a week or so before you can fly out. I'll book and pay for your ticket, and get the travel agency to phone you when you can pick it up.'

Conrad shook his head slowly and sighed. 'You've screwed this up, haven't you, Ma?'

'Listen to me, Conrad. "For sure I'll repay you, I promise," is what he said.'

'Yeah, right, and you believe him.'

I called the airline, gave them my card details, and that was it. In two or three weeks, Conrad would have some company. But where would that leave me?

***

Namuang Waterfall was neither grand nor spectacular. I walked from the road for about twenty minutes. There were hardly any other tourists. This was one of those enchanting places which have an almost fragile specialness. It was as if an ancient spell had silently surrounded me and, by osmosis, entered me and held me transfixed. All sense of past and future disappeared. I put down my feral yearnings to the primordial scent of the rocks. I was convinced that, at any moment, Pan would rise from the earth and bring that same magic experienced by Ratty, Mole and me when I was six.

There was no animal god, but a flying squirrel startled me, missing my face by only thirty centimetres. Seated on a flat, sloping rock at the base of the fall, I watched as the channels eroded into the rock face by the tumbling stream formed a mesmerizing pattern. Hundreds of aquatic ribbons shaded green, brown, orange and ochre began as separate strands, then wove together to form an ever-changing flow, only to be engulfed by the icy waters below. A metaphor for the human race, perhaps. Energized by this revelation, I set off in search of beer.

***

A week or so later, on a day trip to Ang Thong National Park, Sara and I climbed up onto the top of the hill on Mother Island, from where we could see the other islands glimmering on the horizon like a string of pearls beyond the glistening waters of Emerald Lake, which was trapped by a hollow in the landscape directly below us. The water of the lake—also known as Talay Nai—reminded me of dew trapped in a flower petal. Greenery came right down to its edge.

A makeshift platform had been erected at the end of a series of wooden pathways and bridges. We made our way to a hut at the top, wondering how much weight the platform could hold. We stopped to watch the others playing in the water. Conrad and Gecko, tanned and laughing, were sharing a joke, while Michael swam nearby.

Snorkelling over the coral earlier, hand in hand with my children, I felt I had achieved everything I had ever wanted. I was completely content, in a gorgeous setting. There had been no arguments for days. The two new arrivals were fitting in well, and all was well in my world.

The protected island is home to rare species of birds, fish and plants. Long, silvery fish had slipped in and out of our legs as we swam. There were also tiny, golden yellow butterfly fish, blue and pink parrot fish, bright orange and white striped angelfish, and shimmering swordfish. Their colours seemed to burst from all directions; it was like swimming among floating gemstones.

'The three lads have snorkelled off around the corner. I guess they're exploring a new set of rocks.' I turned to Sara, looking stunning in her emerald bikini, glowing with obvious happiness.

'Oh my God! Look, Mum! I think they must have seen a shark!'

All three lads were swimming a very fast crawl back towards the shore. We made our way down to investigate.

'You should have seen it. We were all shitting ourselves. There was this huge jellyfish. It started to chase Conrad.' Michael was grinning.

'Hilarious. Remind me not to go anywhere near there,' I replied.

I did set out for a walk, though, in the jungle bordering the beach. As I approached the vegetation, a python whipped round at my feet and slithered quickly away. Time to go back: that was enough exploration for me.

As I panted towards the beach, I came across a National Park notice declaring certain rules:

Letting off firearm or explosive - 500 baht fine (about £12, I calculated quickly)
Removing pebbles from the beach 5–10 years imprisonment

Different priorities here, then.

On the boat home, I watched Conrad and Gecko, bare-chested, leaning over the rail on the top deck of the boat, looking down into the sunlit sea, and felt gratified. I had made a good decision. Conrad was already tanned from the preceding weeks, and Gecko was turning pink, his skin and eyes clear and healthy.

'Been a good day, eh, boys?' I said as I approached them.

'Yeah, not bad, not bad...'

'Thanks for climbing up to the lake with me, Sara!' I shouted above the engine noise.

'No prob. We got a good view of the great jellyfish chase!'

The red taxi bus—more of converted pickup truck—hurtled its way back to Lamai. It had been adapted to hold passengers: two long bench seats stretching along each side and a rail for mad people to hang onto outside the back. We heard it approach, the driver sounding the horn loudly, and, as it slowed, it rattled to a halt, displacing clouds of sand. We clambered on quickly.

'So much for peace and tranquility!' I laughed.

I sat next to a tall, casually elegant Frenchman.

'What are you doing here in Samui?' he asked.

'Good question. You should ask my children. They suggested it. But I'm very glad we came. It's heavenly.'

I outlined our travel plans for the year. Visibly impressed, he stood to get off the taxi and looked at me intently, full of admiration.

'*Ça, c'est la vie!*' He smiled, nodding in appreciation. At last I felt validated. This was, indeed, living.

As he jumped into the road, an English-speaking couple got on board.

'Ton Yang Resort, please, driver.'

'Er, I don't think you get to choose the route. He just follows the same road a dozen times a day. Oh, and it's obligatory to drive as fast you can along the narrow lanes,' Michael informed them.

'So, you guys are from England, then?' I asked. I soon regretted it.

'Correcto. Epsom, actually. What about you dear people?'

They were obviously desperate for the company of others, and tried making loud, witty remarks in an attempt to draw us into conversation. Poor choice; we were all tired out.

As the bus lurched to a halt, the woman turned to me. I noticed her knuckles were gnarled, her fists clenched, belying her over-cheerful manner. 'Hey, this is where we get out. We're renting a hut here. We're the only people on this stretch of beach. Come and join us for nude bathing. Let it all hang out!'

Horrible images of wrinkled wobbly bits, burnt flabby skin and drooping flaps-that-should-never-be-exposed flashed before me. But, polite as ever, I said, 'Oh, we'd love to, but we have to get back, sorry.'

'Yeah, come on, Ma, let it all hang at Ton Yang!' Conrad grinned, putting the fear of God into me. Surely he wasn't serious? 'But I'll pass, ta, all the same.'

'I wouldn't be a pretty sight,' said Michael. His legs were already covered in lumpy, itchy scars from fly bites.

I decided he was rather a vain young man. We never saw him in the football shirts Conrad wore, and he was clearly embarrassed when I appeared in my comfy silk trousers with their elasticated waist and my loose, long-sleeved tops to protect me from the mozzies. Wearing the turban outfit I had bought in Udaipur, I thought I looked like an Indian princess.

'You remind me of a misshapen piece of Turkish delight,' commented my daughter's new-found lover boy when he first saw it. Bloody cheek, It cost me a fortune. Well, an Indian fortune—about two quid.

Today was magic, I decided as I climbed into bed, swatting absent-mindedly at something barely visible at the corner of my eye.

'A tiny fly flew right into my mouth last night,' I informed everyone next morning.

'It was attracted by all the shit you talk, Mother.'

***

I could hear them all giggling when I strolled past their door on my way out. I was alone now for much of the day, and feeling isolated. I had rarely seen my son and daughter in the evenings before the arrival of Michael and Gecko, but now my days, too, were lonely. *I must think positive. I'll have more time to read and think.*

The day in Ang Thong had reminded me of family holidays camping in France. Kayaking down the Ardèches River, topless, the children squealing at each mini rapid—this had been a time free of cares, of sun and laughter and well-being. I'd been enthralled by the scenery along the banks of the river, especially a Roman aqueduct where we stopped to picnic on the shore. Today, the family group was smaller, missing two members— Dad and little sister. What happened? How had I come to be here in this faraway country, surrounded by people but lonely as hell? The place was gorgeous but, inside, I was still the same scared little girl who felt she didn't fit in anywhere.

'It's all kicking off at the shrine, Ma. The priests are getting lairy.' Conrad grinned.

'Ignore him, Mum. Some kids were shouting. They were baby-faced monks. I think it was some kind of debate or something.' She turned to her brother. 'Shut up, you idiot. If she finds out you were winding them up, she'll go ape.'

'Look, kids, I've had a long day. I'm just off out for a meal. Remember those girls I met on the boat? They invited me out. I've left money in my pack secret pocket for your dinner. I don't want to hear you two arguing, and I don't want to know if you've been causing any trouble. Only involve me if you get married or arrested. Deal?'

Conrad squinted at me for a second then broke into a grin. 'Cool.'

On the boat to the AngThong islands, I'd met two American girls who invited me to join them for dinner. Strolling to the resort next door for the rendezvous, I realized they were accompanied by two European men, who turned out to be French.

Oh God, I thought I'd be having a night out, and I'm just going to be playing gooseberry. Might as well have stayed in my room. I always was good at self-pity.

'Oh wow, cool, Rachael, so glad you came!' drawled Katy from California. She was the stereotypical clean, fresh, blonde American gal from Sunshine County, with the conversational skills to match. Bethany from New Jersey was at least capable of maintaining a four-sentence exchange, so long as it was about family, friends or movies. By now, I was dreading the evening ahead. *Why did I accept their invitation?*

Slightly pissed in a bar in Chaweng, wishing I had the guts to get up and dance alone to the live rock music, I tried to concentrate on the conversation. One of the Frenchmen was talking about his travels through Vietnam, whilst gazing distractedly, with the sparkling eyes of a man in *lerve*, at Katy. His words filled me with enthusiasm for the next part of our journey through Indochina.

In particular, he rhapsodized about Halong Bay, which he described as unmissable. 'Aah...'Along Bay...zee most bee-oo-tifool pless on zee ers...' He sighed. 'You must go zair. Eet eez a mairvay—'ow do you say?—mairvayooss...'

'Oh. Yes, I will. Thank you.'

I made an effort to focus my thoughts on our journey, to avoid staring at several couples dancing close as the music slowed.

After an hour or two I left the loving foursome to party on and returned to the hotel, hoping to settle down for a good night's sleep. Too tired to go to bed, however, I sat in the bar to write to Sophie and ended up watching not one but two gruesome movies. I was unable to follow the minimal plots. I headed back to my room where I pulled my pyjamas out of my daypack, which I had suspended from the door handle, and crawled into my single bed, feeling diminished.

Everyone else seems to have someone who adores them. What's so wrong with me?

I realized that this was one of the things I'd been telling myself all my life. *There's something wrong with me* had been the voice inside my head for as long as I could remember. *I'm not like everyone else. I'm weird.*

***

Dear Sophie/UM

I had a wonderful day today. I went to fax Kim Café in Saigon to enquire about a van with driver to take us from Saigon north to Hanoi. I felt very excited about faxing Vietnam, which was a war-torn country on the other side of the world when I was your age. I also had my hair cut, very well, for the equivalent of £2.00! Sara and I strolled along the beach to the next village, stopping for swims when we felt like it, and had lunch of barbecued corn on the cob and chicken, both served on a stick. We stopped at a beach bar for Bacardi and Coke. Dire Straits music was playing: "Sultans of Swing". There are several bars and restaurants tucked away under the palm trees, but you can't see them from the beach. Sitting in the shade listening to good music with a cool drink watching the waves and surf...what more could I ask?

Now I'm in a restaurant waiting for a movie to start: "Usual Suspects"—have you heard of it? Restaurant owners here attract custom by putting a large-screen television in the bar and showing free videos. People choose their restaurant not for what they want to eat, but what they want to watch. And, guess what, tonight I had "cow pat"!! It's Thai for fried rice, and "moo" is pork!

Not long now! I can't wait to see you!!

Your suntanned and happy mother

xxxxxxxxxxxxxxxxxxxxxxxxxxxxxxxxxxxxx

***

I could hear laughter coming from the hut next door. *Nothing to lose,* I thought. *I may as well join them. I can't sleep anyway.* I had been grabbed for a moment by self-pity, so I employed one of my favourite survival tricks: I took refuge in being different. I'd be smart, I'd be cool. I would join the younger generation in the middle of the night.

They were sitting on the floor in Conrad and Gecko's room with the shutters closed, listening to a compilation of trance music scraping from tiny Walkman speakers. Far from being horrified at my sudden appearance, they were completely unfazed by it.

'Hey, Mum, I've been remembering stuff from my childhood,' announced Sara, grinning. 'Do you know what I feel like now? Some of grandma's treacle pie.'

Gecko looked as if he was drooling. His jaw stuck out, and his bottom lip covered his top lip. 'Home-made soup, mmm,' he mumbled. 'A rare treat. At home it was usually made from powder out of a catering pack.'

Michael mumbled inanely about sticky toffee pudding, and Conrad went doe-eyed over buttered-egg-in-a-cup. That was a teatime treat passed down through generations of my family—hard-boiled egg cut up in a teacup, served with lashings of butter.

The music went on, and as the sun sought its way into the room through slats in the shutters, it illuminated dust particles and cast eerie, elongated shadows across their faces, spotlighting their features, sculpting exaggerated expressions as they smoked, chatted and laughed until dawn. They were having a ball. I crept out, almost unnoticed, at five in the morning. Once again I felt alone, but I'd had a rare insight into their lives.

***

I couldn't believe how quickly Sara was growing in self-confidence. She prattled on excitedly, 'We were playing snooker in the resort with Benny, Mum—after we'd just got to know him. He's Thai, but streetwise and westernized. He loves to attract attention. He's got long, curly hair flowing down his back—always bare, bronzed and muscular—as far as his buttocks which are squeezed together in tight jeans. Mmm, lovely! He could be quite tasty if he was normal. He's got a nose like a hawk, all proud and defiant, but he speaks like a girl. Not only has he got a squeaky voice and a Thai accent but he's got a speech defect and he can't pronounce hard "c"s or "g"s. They sound like "t"s and "d"s, so when he says "comical" it comes out as "tomital", and so on. It's hilarious, Mum, he's sooo weird.'

'Maybe the voice is down to the tight jeans?'

'Hah! Maybe. When we got here, he promised Conrad, "I tan show you where to doh. You don' wanna bother with the bars, they are too 'spensive. I tan show you where to buy beer an' dood stuff an' we tan det cheap dirls to tiss and tuddle, and maybe if we are lutty, to fut, ha ha!" Mum, you can just picture Conrad's face—it was so funny. He was stupefied. We just couldn't figure out if this guy was for real. So Conrad said, "You're funny, yeah. A bit of a dit, in fat." We all fell about— Conrad's so quick, and poor Benny took ages to figure out what we were laughing about. He just didn't get that we were taking the piss out of him. But we got on okay and had quite a laugh with him and his mates. Michael gets on well with everyone, though. He's brilliant.'

'Good, that's good, darling. By the way, you did a great impersonation. You should be a mimic!'

'Are you okay, Mum?' I knew she felt a bit sorry for me. I was on my own most of the time now.

Hoping I might get to spend some time with my family, I proposed a final outing before we left Koh Samui. 'Don't suppose any of you want to come to Big Buddha beach before we set off?'

'Nah, while you're out looking at shrines and stuff we can relax in our room.'

I wondered how they could spend so much time sitting around doing nothing. All night, yes, but all day too? Did I do that at their age?

So I set off, alone again, to see the giant Buddha, and browse the street market at his feet. A few days before, I had bought a fan made from peacock tail feathers. I just had to have the glorious turquoise and emerald colours on a wall back at home. The fact that I didn't have a wall, or a back home, momentarily eluded me. The postage cost five times as much as the fan, but I knew Sophie would take care of it for me.

When I returned from my last outing, flustered and breathless, the others were waiting for me on the track, Michael making impatient clicking noises.

'Bloody typical!' I grumbled.

I'd had a row with the taxi driver. When I got back to Lamai after a cursory look at Big Buddha, I threw his fare into the road in a fit of temper so he would have to get out and grovel in the dust for it.

He'd deliberately driven really slowly when he found out I was in a hurry, because I'd refused to give him an "extra tip"—meaning pay twice as much for the fare as I had on the way there.

'Hey, you! Where is my money?' he shouted as I clambered down from his vehicle.

'Where you should be, in the dirt!' I screamed back. So much for the serene new me.

We hurried to the end of the lane for the bus to the ferry to Surat Thani where we were to pick up an overnight train back to Bangkok.

'So, you guys, what have you been up to?' I pretended to be cheerful.

'Norralot,' Sara told me as Gecko started to sing, 'There was an old lady who swallowed a fly,' with a glazed look in his eyes. I reckon it was around then he'd started on the pills. I knew all of them smoked a bit of weed now and again—I wasn't about to be disapproving, being a child of the Sixties—but he seemed to need something more. And he was always the first to start and the last to stop drinking. Where Conrad, Michael and Sara would spend just a few baht, he used up all the money I gave him for his meals. He asked for three courses at dinnertime and, at first, I just thought he had a big appetite. He did, it seems, but maybe not for food.

***

Dear UM, (hee hee)

We are sitting on a train in Surat Thani station. It is 7.40pm and the train was due to depart at 5.50pm! The train is quite comfortable and clean compared to Indian trains BUT there are hundreds of big black bugs. We keep stamping on them, only to reveal even more! The engine has broken down and it might be at least another hour before we set off for Bangkok. Still, we have until 7.40pm tomorrow to get on our train to Chiang Mai and it's a twelve-hour journey, so we should make it. Got your fax today, thanks. It was great just to see your handwriting. I sent a fan made out of peacock feathers home to Grandpa's—the postage cost less than I feared, only £5.90, but still more than the fan cost!

After a nasty scene with a taxi driver who tried to overcharge me, we were late setting off and I ended up having to pay even more than he originally wanted in order to get to the ferry on time! Ironic, since we got to the train with only ten minutes to spare, having travelled for many hours, and we've been sitting in the station ever since!! Another eventful day in the travels of our clan...

Oh, by the way, for Mother's Day, Conrad ceremoniously presented me with a toilet roll and a bottle of water! He quite rightly pointed out that, in our situation, they are extremely useful gifts! Sara gave me a mini sundress. I would never have thought I could wear something like that, but here I swear I look ten years younger, and we've all lost weight, so it actually looks quite good!

A really cute, dinky little Thai boy has just come round selling face wipes for five baht. We all bought one just to please him. Vendors keep coming up and down the train selling spicy barbecued chicken, fresh pineapple, water and beer, but we are getting short of baht so we are sharing everything. Gecko and I got off the train about thirty minutes ago, and he ran to a money exchange while I kept an eye on the train. I suppose I'd have tried to stop the train if it had begun to pull out! It was a risk but we had no change at all. And we are still sitting here! Gecko and Conrad have just eaten something they are convinced is not chicken; maybe it's snake or dog...

It's now 8.15 and we still haven't moved. A friend of Gecko and Conrad we met in Samui has just popped his head in the *doorway to say goodbye. He was getting a later train than us but he is going first. Aargh, these bugs are crawling all over me...*

Okay, bye for now darling. We finally got to Bangkok so I'll post this now...love you forever, xxxx

***

Chang Mai

Chang Mai was bustling with tourists. It was Song Kran, the water festival. Thousands of people lined the streets, hurling buckets of water at each other and laughing hysterically. Some revellers doused passing cars with hoses; others had what looked like white powder stains on their clinging clothes.

'Flour,' explained my companion, an Antipodean by accent. I'd met him in some sleazy bar or other, as you do. We'd had a beer and got on well, despite his being about twenty years younger than me. 'That's the only really annoying thing, because it doesn't come off by hand washing.'

'Oi! You little devil!' A little kiddie carrying a water pistol twice his size shrieked as he caught me off guard.

I set off on my own to explore the market. I wanted padlocks for Gecko's and Michael's bags whilst we were on a three-day trek in the hills. We would leave our big bags at our hotel and carry day sacks.

'This place is so different from Samui,' Michael commented when I got back. 'It's weird being in a big town with cars and noise, but the atmosphere here is fantastic. I like it.'

I felt proud that I'd accepted him into our family group: he was clearly enjoying himself, and that, in turn, would make Sara happy. I was hungry after my shopping trip.

'Let's order some food now. Have a decent meal; we don't know what the food's going to be like over the next few days. We'll have guides with us and they'll provide all our meals, but who knows what they'll bring. We'd better get an early night. We set off at eight tomorrow. For once you'll have to sleep when normal people do, not from five in the morning till midday!'

149

'If wit were shit, Ma, you'd be constipated.'

I didn't get their constant need for sleep. In trains, I would be eagerly staring out of the window, consuming the view, feasting my eyes on the scenery, while they all slept soundly, waking only for food.

Amid groans, I explained our schedule. 'We have to take a four-wheel drive out of the city for three or four hours; we start walking there, then after an hour or so we're going to stop for supplies and a swim in a waterfall. We'll have lunch there then start walking again after lunch. We walk for three hours and get to the village by late afternoon. Next day, we trek for five or six hours until we reach the elephant camp. We eat there and spend the afternoon on the elephants. That night, we sleep with a different hill tribe, and start building our raft early next morning. On the last day, we'll go downriver on the bamboo raft, stop for lunch, and come back here in the four-wheel drive. How does that sound?'

'Riveting,' Conrad said.

'Knackering,' Sara said.

'Hot,' Gecko said.

'Lovely,' Michael said.

'Our guide is called Ya. His brother and sister, Yam and Yut, will be accompanying him, to cook for us and help with making the raft.'

'Ya, Yam and Yut,' was all Sara needed to say, her face full of mirth.

Next morning it was hot—around thirty-five degrees—and humid. Before we had even got into the vehicle, Conrad and Sara were complaining.

'How the hell are we supposed to trek in this heat?' Sara pleaded.

'Drink plenty of water. I told you to bring water bottles. You'll need at least two litres for the morning, once we start walking.'

'Why are we doing this, Mum? Why couldn't we just stay at the hotel and wait for you?'

150

'Because it'll be an experience you'll never forget, trust me. You want to ride elephants, don't you? And go rafting? The scenery is fantastic. You'll love it.'

Long faces betrayed their reaction.

'Um, I'm looking forward to it,' Michael proffered.

'Creep,' said Sara, smiling.

'Actually, so am I,' said Gecko. 'I've never done anything like this in my life.'

Gecko was the son of hoteliers. No one knew the word "holiday" in his family. His father was a drunk who rarely communicated with him, and his mother was a workaholic who also loved to party when she had the time, which was not often. She preferred to party without her husband, though, who inevitably let her down after his first bottle of vodka. The idea of actually going away anywhere was completely alien to them. Gecko was expected to help in the hotel in his free time, which he begrudgingly did, in order to earn a meagre allowance. Meals were always in the hotel restaurant; invariably what the residents hadn't chosen. There were no family outings, there was little laughter, and he was always embarrassed by his father's ravings about "the old days". He was fond of telling Gecko that he needed "cutting down to size".

Conrad told me Gecko had once answered, 'The same size as you, Dad?' swerving to avoid the slap.

'Last time Dad lost a bet,' Gecko told me, 'a regular ended up calling the police. Dad informed everyone at the bar that the local bookie was a criminal, that he slept with fifteen-year-old girls and that he was just waiting for a chance to punch him. He was so pissed he hadn't noticed that the bookie's wife and daughter were in the bar. Of course, there was a shouting match. Dad bellowed, then cried and fell over, breaking his arm as he crashed down, holding up his half-empty glass that had a mixture of brandy and fag ash in it. "Pass me my drink" were his last words before passing out.

'I can't just forgive and forget,' he confided, as we all bounced around in the back of the four-wheel drive. 'They've got hearts of gold, though. I suppose they're doing their best. They just don't know how to lead a different life. I've been desperate to get away from it. When you called, I felt my life was just starting. I'll never forget this, Rachael. I promise I'll pay you back.'

Something about the way he said it made me feel that he didn't mean a single word. It wasn't his language. It felt liked he'd rehearsed it.

The vehicle came to a stop and we clambered out.

'Welcome!' Three eager faces grinned at us: our guides. 'Here, here, follow. Happy! Follow!' They were dressed almost identically: shorts, T-shirts and flip-flops. They set off uphill together at a worryingly fast pace, turning back to give us occasional encouraging nods.

'Jeez, this is only the first hour,' mumbled Sara when we took our first rest. Red-faced, hair plastered around her temples and brow, she was panting, her mascara was smudged, and her cheeks were smeared with marks where her grubby hands had wiped away perspiration.

We continued up a narrow path until we reached an ice-cold pool where a small waterfall splashed over smooth rocks. Within seconds, we had peeled off and dived in in our underwear, too hot to care who saw us.

Phew! This is just the beginning, I thought. *I've dragged them all here. I hope I can keep up with the pace.*

It was peaceful. There were no other tourists on the path or at the waterfall. Amid the bamboos, butterflies brushed our noses; the song of cicadas was almost deafening. The dirt path wound through a forest of mixed deciduous trees and shrubs. The air was sweet and fresh. Our three guides sang and whistled the latest Thai hit.

'What's that tune, Yut?' I asked. 'I've heard it lots of times.'

'It is Dai Rue Plao. Band is new, all young. They called La-On.'

'It's very…unusual. It grows on you.' Michael looked puzzled. 'I mean, I like it now that I know the tune.'

'They are really content, aren't they, Mum? And they have next to nothing,' Sara said.

'Unless, of course, you count the trees, flowers, streams, rivers, birds, rice, chickens, clear water, fruit...'

'Okay, okay, Mum, I get the idea!'

'What tribe do you belong to, Ya?' Michael asked.

'We are all Karen tribe. Tonight we stay in Karen village. You will meet some of my family. Tomorrow, we will be at Lahu village. They are not so nice peoples as Karen peoples, but still very nice. You will like, I think.'

Yam squatted at the edge of a boiling spring, suspending a makeshift straw basket over the steam, boiling eggs for lunch. Her hair was pulled back into a long ponytail away from her tightly drawn face.

She gave a coy smile as Gecko approached. 'You like trekking?' she enquired sweetly.

'Haven't really tried it yet, this is my first time, but I like you,' he beamed.

She looked up at him and giggled coyly. 'These sparrow eggs, very good. I make you good lunch, don' worry.' She smiled. 'You will have plen'y strong for walking walking! Much walking, plen'y food, make strong.'

'I'm going to enjoy this trek!' Gecko responded with a cheeky grin.

We ate a lunch of rice, the eggs, and vegetables, then set off in earnest for the first part of the walk. I found my pace by counting in time with each breath, and after a few minutes I was comfortable. I'd taken a long-sleeved shirt to protect me from biting insects and the sun, and zip-off trousers. Sara seemed contented in her strappy top and shorts, but Michael looked hot and bothered in a smart fitted shirt, fine for a dinner party but quite unsuitable for these conditions. Still, he was smiling as he plodded on upwards.

'How much more uphill, Ya?' Sara felt sure we had climbed for hours.

'Only another hour or two.'

153

'Only?' came her response, through gritted teeth.

'You want to rest? We can stop in ten minutes.'

'I need some water. And a pee.'

'Here we have luxury toilet, in the nature!' Yut laughed from behind.

'I find it isn't so hot here under the trees,' remarked Gecko, determined to be positive despite looking worn out and sweaty. I figured he was trying to please, in case I changed my mind and sent him home.

Three hours slipped past, listening to our guides' singing as we breathed laboriously, wiped dripping brows, swigged lukewarm water, and climbed steadily.

At length, Ya called out, 'We are nearly there! Here is my uncle coming to meet us.'

A wiry, middle-aged man sprinted towards us, oblivious to the damp heat.

Ya translated for us, 'He say "Welcome, welcome. Come, have some fruit".' The man led us to a wooden shelter, where he extended a plate piled with orange segments and sliced mangoes.

'These are delicious. I hope dinner's ready. I'm ravenous.' Michael said.

'No ta, I'm okay for mangoes today.' Ya's uncle looked puzzled at Conrad's response.

'My son means he doesn't want any, thank you.'

'Ah. Okay. There, there, you sleep and eat in there. That for you. Okay?' He gestured towards a large wooden construction. 'Toilet at back.'

Our hut was on stilts. In the space beneath the floor, chickens pecked around in the dirt amid bags of grain, and pigs and dogs lay in a mutually comforting heap. A smaller hut reached by wooden steps served as the kitchen, from which steam was swirling. A propitious start.

In the sleeping area of our hut there were two large rooms, divided by hanging curtains. The windows were bare, providing easy access for mosquitoes. Ya still looked fresh and clean in his

Tiger Beer T-shirt and shorts, and he'd put on clean new trainers for the evening. Yut jostled with Gecko outside whilst Ya's uncle and aunt prepared the evening meal in the kitchen.

'Let me show you to your bedroom,' said Ya. On bare floorboards, five mosquito nets suspended from the wooden ceiling brushed flower-patterned sheets laid out neatly in a row. They looked like huge spider webs.

'I'll never sleep on a bare wooden floor, Mum. There aren't even any pillows,' moaned Sara, licking and sucking at the remains of the fruit on her forefinger.

'I bet you'll be asleep within minutes after your efforts today. Well done, all of you. Shall we play cards on the table outside?'

'Yeah, let's play slave,' Conrad suggested. 'And I'll show Michael some of my card tricks.'

It was five o'clock. By six-thirty, after a meal of fish and rice served in tin bowls on the floor, we were all sound asleep, fully clothed. We hadn't even had the energy to use the toilet; we'd just peed outside the hut as we'd noticed the family doing.

'Bloody cockerel, I'll wring its neck.' I squinted at my watch in the dark; it was three in the morning. 'Doesn't it know it's supposed to wait till dawn before it starts crowing?'

'Thai cockerels are very prompt.' Yut chuckled from his sleeping place on the floor below. At four, I heard a loud, rhythmic grinding.

'What the fuck is that?' shouted Conrad.

'Ya is grinding corn to make maize flour for the bread for your breakfast.' Yut again replied from below.

'Oh great, nice one. Look forward to that, when I wake up.'

The sound of a long fart vibrated around the room.

'Oh, that's gross!' Conrad yelled. 'What the hell have you been eating?'

'Sorry,' Gecko mumbled.

I couldn't breathe in. I lay still, perspiring in the clammy heat, waiting for the smell to subside.

An hour later, we could stand the noise no longer. By now, cries, chatter and laughter prevented any further sleep. Pigs were grunting, chickens squawking, children squealing, and the grinding had started again. Beneath us, someone began to hum contentedly. Pots and pans crashed, dogs yelped. Daily life in a Karen village had clearly begun, and preparations for our safari were under way.

'Have you found the post office yet, Mother?' said Conrad, not without irony.

From where we slept we could see straight out and down to the surrounding countryside. I peered out from under my sheet.

Michael was standing outside the toilet shed, waiting for his turn. Down on a meadow below, someone had erected two tall bamboo poles and strung a piece of home-made flax rope between them to make a goal. 'Let's challenge the villagers to five-a-side,' he suggested.

Ya and Yut smiled their approval as they both emerged from the toilet at the same time.

Conrad and Gecko sat up and eyed Michael disparagingly.

'Maybe later,' Gecko replied. He laid down again and turned over under his mosquito net.

I stretched, yawned and rolled over, my limbs sore from the bare wooden floor. *No use—I have to use the loo now.*

The rectangular shed stood some ten metres from the main hut. It was constructed from planks made of thin bamboo bound together by vine rope, and protected by a corrugated iron roof. It tilted at an alarming angle, the door hanging awkwardly from its hinge. I ventured inside, dreading what I might find in there; all sorts of creatures could have crawled in overnight.

Peering into the gloom, I made out a roll of tissue hanging from a piece of string. No sign of a toilet bowl.

Please don't let this be a hole in the ground. Sara will freak. What if there are spiders or snakes in here? Sara did not want to be an intrepid adventurer. She wanted to be a cosseted, fluffy white kitten.

A rusty bucket caused me a moment's alarm. Then I spotted the brown-streaked, white porcelain throne itself, raised on a wooden dais, like a giant molar in need of a filling. Sara went in after me. I watched and waited for my daughter's reaction, but when she emerged, dust swirling around her, she was smiling.

'What are you beaming about?' asked Michael.

'I tried to imagine I was in a comfortable hotel bathroom. Then I felt a mosquito bite my throat. I was about to burst into tears when I remembered Mum squatting in the grass in India, when she nearly toppled over trying to pee under the weight of her backpack.'

'I heard that,' I said.

The boys were already sweaty when we gathered to leave. After a breakfast of newly baked bread rolls and fresh fruit juice we collected our gear together.

The football game had been a success. Several local kids had suddenly appeared from the bushes to join in, and their squeals of triumph or wails of disappointment rang out into the morning as the sun rose above the trees, casting a warm yellow glow over the scene.

'Okay, okay, we go!' was our call to action. It was a short walk to our destination.

The elephant camp was on the shore of a fast-flowing, sepia-coloured river. Young boys were throwing buckets of water over the parched backs of five sun-cracked, desert-grey elephants whose trunks were swaying rhythmically in unison.

We didn't bother to change, and flopped fully dressed into the river. We moved towards the animals after a swim, or rather, a splash: the water was shallow.

'Please, please, please can I sit on his neck?' Sara asked in an ingratiating tone.

After being pushed and heaved up onto the animal's back—a rather humiliating experience—it was impossible not to relax, lean back and be soothed by the warmth, the silence—apart from the swishing of tails—and the rocking sensation.

'This is sound,' commented Conrad, his elbows propped behind him regally on the back of the semi-circular wooden howdah.

After the first hour, Sara complained 'Ouch! My thighs are sore!' Although a blanket had been placed over the elephant's neck, it was rough, and the back of her knees were rubbing against the animal's hide. 'But I don't mind,' she added, ''cause this is amazing, Mum!'

We waded upriver towards an open space where piles of logs lay on the pebbly shores.

'Okay, we dismount here,' said Ya. 'Stop for rest, stop for pee, drink water, eat biscuits, ha ha!'

Auntie's biscuits were delicious; a crunchy peanut flavour and just what we needed to restore our heat-sapped energy.

'Before lunch elephants wash, okay?' Yut said, smiling cheekily.

'What? We wash the elephants? What are you on about, Yut?' Sara looked horrified.

'Don' worry, very good, elephants helping!'

It was one of the funniest experiences of our lives. We remounted, and within seconds the elephants dipped their trunks into the river and raised them up again, spraying water all over us, until we were completely drenched. I laughed till my sides ached. This was an unexpected highlight.

'Ha ha, elephants wash you, not you wash elephants!' Yut was delighted with himself for tricking us.

'You wait, we'll get you back, you little rascal!' shouted Conrad, river weed clinging to his forehead.

As we lay in the sun afterwards, Michael stomped towards me in his boots and grinned. 'Just admiring the assortment of hats: you in your intrepid adventurer hat, Conrad in a sun visor, Gecko in a crocheted skull cap, and Sara in a floppy straw boater. Then there's Ya sporting a baseball cap, Yut a red bandana, Yam bare-headed. My knees are red from sunburn, and my feet damp from sweat. I reckon I've got trench foot. But I'm having a ball!'

'Ah, bless,' Sara sighed.

'Jeez.' Conrad did not appear to be impressed by his sister's comment.

Lunch was served on a checkered tablecloth spread out over the pebbles. An orange-coloured plastic salad bowl wobbled every time any of us changed position. It was impossible to get comfortable and eat, but the food was fabulous. We all ate straight from the bowl, using spoons and forks. Warm river fish, baby sweet corn, spring onions and noodles, mixed together and flavoured with spices, lemongrass and tamarind.

We spent the rest of the afternoon relaxing, watching the heat haze rising from the river, mosquitoes swirling and buzzing, turquoise dragonflies hovering and darting.

Next morning, Conrad and Gecko were eagerly assembling the bamboo raft which would carry us all downstream and back to civilization.

'We need to bind twenty poles together with vine, and knot them firmly,' explained Ya. 'We put a tripod of smaller poles in the middle of the raft to use as a hanging area for day packs and water bottles. The water is so shallow we might have to get out and walk along the banks, and probably push the raft.'

'There aren't any rapids, are there?' I asked, feeling nervous. We had just finished tying the last poles together, and were stepping gingerly onto the bobbing craft.

'Oh yes! We will have much fun!' Yut cackled like a demented chicken.

Sure enough, within minutes, the raft began to swerve ominously, large rocks loomed, and the water bubbled and churned, gathering momentum. Ya and Yut began shouting instructions to one another, Yam grabbed a pole, and all three skilfully manoeuvred the raft through a stretch of noisy cascading falls, inches from slippery, jagged rocks. The raft seemed to be planing of its own accord, yet one glance at the crew and it was obvious they were in full control, despite their maniacal laughter. I thought my heart would never stop pounding. Sara was screaming hysterically.

'We'll have to get off!' I shouted.

'No way! Why?' Sara screeched. 'It's brilliant!'

As the morning wore on, the raft became so submerged that we all had wet bottoms, but none of us cared. I had adjusted to the adrenaline coursing through my veins.

Gecko was ecstatic. 'I've never had so much fun in my life,' he said. 'I don't know how I can ever thank you for this trip. It's changed my life.'

'And you didn't even need to take anything,' Michael whispered.

***

Later, in Chiang Mai, we experienced the dubious benefits of a Thai massage, as our backs were being pummelled and our limbs bent backwards like pieces of putty.

Michael seemed concerned. 'Will I ever play football again?'

'Do you realize that apart from the villagers, we didn't see any other people during the whole trek? It was great not to have to bother what I looked like!' Sara said.

'You've gone from glamour puss to jungle woman, and I like it!' Michael beamed as he kissed my daughter's forehead.

Creepy twit, I thought.

I had booked a two-day course at Chiang Mai Cookery School for Sara and me. I thought it would be a good mother and daughter bonding exercise, seeing as how I'd never taught her anything about household stuff like cooking and cleaning. On arrival, we were each given a crisp blue apron, a ceramic pestle and mortar, and a bowl containing pieces of peeled ginger, chillies, lemongrass, coriander stems, shallots and various other ingredients.

'Okaaay—what do we do with these?' I asked no one in particular, adding as an aside to Sara, 'Looks like debris from someone's garden.'

'Ah, you mix together with equipment.' We took this to mean the pestle and mortar. A charming, smiling girl led us to a large rug on which ten other students were already kneeling, hard at work grinding the ingredients together. After half an hour, my paste was still lumpy despite a visibly increased bicep on my right arm.

'My wrist hurts, Mum, doesn't yours?'

'Hmm. This better be worth it. I don't think I'll be able to get up: my knees are numb.'

When everyone was ready, we all moved over to individual cooking stations where the equipment was explained: one wooden-handled steel wok each, plus a couple of spatulas; a murderous-looking implement whose use was not explained but which I'm convinced was for the punishment of students if the food was not up to scratch; a small bowl of oil; likewise of water; and a cloth for spillages. Bowls of chopped uncooked chicken and fish were passed around, and off we went, stir-frying amidst clouds of spicy-scented steam which brought water to the nostrils and tears to the eyes. The cooking took minutes only and we were soon tucking in, with cooked rice and cold drinks provided by the establishment.

'I'm going to buy one of their cookbooks, Mum, so when we get back we can have Thai evenings at my place.'

'Wonderful food. Hard work though. Give me a food processor any day.'

'Don't be such a wimp, Mama. It tastes much better after all the labour. Tomorrow we do puds: mango with sticky rice, water chestnuts in coconut milk, black rice pudding, and steamed banana cake. Yummy!'

I guessed two days wasn't going to give her a great repertoire of dinner party dishes, but it was a start.

***

Our time in Thailand was up. We hadn't had the full backpacker experience—we hadn't bedded down with hippies on Khao San

Road—but we'd had a taste and, at that time, it was enough for me.

'You know what? I feel like doing a side trip,' I announced.

'What? Where to?' Conrad and Sara replied in unison.

'Well, we are quite close to the border with Laos. We have the time. It'd mean less time in Hong Kong, but we'd see a really unusual country. Not that many people have been there. It only opened to tourists very recently.'

'If you say so. You're the boss. Well, the one who's paying, anyway,' Conrad said.

Wow, no moans. Things are looking up.

***

Laos

After a few enquiries at a nearby travel agent, we made our way to Chiang Khong, a border town on the River Mekong. We stopped for lunch in Chiang Rai, at a restaurant called Cabbages and Condoms. I had hired a guide called Tong at an agency. He met us at the restaurant and plied us with Lao Lao hooch.

We boarded a riverboat to take us across into Laos, which beckoned on the far shore. Once over the river, we jumped ashore, landing in thick mud. After a police check, we struggled up the slippery slope of the river bank to Pakbeng, passing a wat temple on the way, where monks were chanting like humming bees. I began to feel claustrophobic among all the skinny bodies, brown smiling faces and outstretched arms. Scrawny dogs, bony cows and emaciated donkeys ambled along the red sand, past squalid groups of houses. The streets smelled of animal dung and incense.

After the barren desert soil of India, the lushness of rich vegetation in this part of the world was overwhelming. Woodsmoke spiralled into columns among the fields, rising lazily to join low-lying cloud, adding to the oppressive heat.

Tong led us to the village, where he had booked us into accommodation which included breakfast. The guest house was cramped and there was no electricity. We had to share a room with four strangers, and I was eaten alive by mosquitoes. Our bunk beds were hard, rickety and smelled of mothballs—or whatever the Laotion equivalent was.

I had a nightmare: Sophie lying in a hospital bed, tubes down her throat, unconscious, monitors bleeping at the side of her bed. I woke up, disorientated, bewildered, before sobbing myself quietly back to sleep.

'Back downhill for breakfast, apparently!' I tried to stir my kids without waking the other comatose travellers.

Sara and Conrad were too tired to complain as Tong stepped cheerily out in front, whistling and greeting the villagers we passed on our way down to the river. We sat on stone benches and dipped warm rice bread into bowls of thick, sweet condensed milk. Once back on board our boat, we settled into hammocks for a lazy ride downstream.

***

Dear Sophie

We're in Laos. It's sort of in between Thailand and Vietnam. I probably won't post this letter from here as we won't be here long. I had to change money into the local currency which took ages, and I have no idea how much we've got left!

We got here by boat and we're going south on it, down the River Mekong. Ask your dad to show you where it is. We had a rough night last night in a poky guest house place, and I've been dozing in a hammock today with my book. I've read loads since we've been away. It helps me stop missing you.

Anyway, after about an hour's reading, I looked up to see a couple of fellow passengers nudging each other and pointing down at the water. They waved at me to go over to them. I extricated myself from the hammock (impossible to do that elegantly!) and joined them. By this time, whatever they'd been looking at had moved a few metres away, but I could still see it closely enough to recognize a body, bloated and discoloured, floating past. I wondered who it had been, and if anyone had noticed their disappearance. The captain stopped the engine and hopped ashore to buy fish from a riverside stall. I prayed it wasn't for today's lunch!

We moored beneath a cave called Pak Ou, where the Mekong joins with the Nam Ou River, and clambered uphill to look in it. Hundreds of wooden Buddha statues filled the cave. It was weird. Each one was in a different position—meditating, teaching, reclining. It was dead dark in there; just a few candles around. A bit ghostly, really.

I'd better go, we're about to get off. I think we've arrived at the town we're staying at next.

Love you darling, massive big hugs
xx

***

'That cave was weird, but amazing,' Sara said, tugging at her knotted hair. 'It's a shame so many of them were broken.'

'I bet when more tourists come they'll be restored,' Michael commented. 'It's too good a tourist attraction to leave as it is.'

After our visit to Pak Ou cave we were heading for Luang Prabang. Our guest house comprised separate huts, big enough for three or four people, arranged around a central garden area. It was about two kilometres from the town centre, easily walkable.

'There's a festival here, so there will be dancing in the streets tonight,' Tong informed us.

'Hey, this is an unexpected bonus. They're in costume. Don't they look gorgeous?' Sara smiled as we strolled along the main street later.

'Don't be up too late, folks, if you want to feed the monks in the morning.' As I spoke I had a flashback to school night warnings and smiled to myself. 'Feed the monks' had replaced 'finish your homework'.

Monk "feeding" meant squatting at the side of the road before dawn. As hundreds of monks strode past in silence, each alms giver stretched up and placed a ball of sticky rice into a passing monk's bowl. The only sounds were the pacing of their bare feet and the swishing of their orange robes, barely visible in the early morning light. Participating in the ritual filled me with awe: a simple action, but humbling. The monks' eyes never left the road, no one spoke, and I felt honoured to witness and contribute.

Sara broke the peaceful atmosphere with a piercing scream. 'Aargh! A huge cricket's just jumped in between my boobs! Get it out, Mum, quick!'

Dozens of curious heads turned, some of them smiling. The biggest grins were on the faces of the monks who appeared to be delighted at this interruption to their morning routine.

We didn't have long in Luang Prabang, but I was determined to return one day for a proper visit. There was so much we hadn't seen.

Once in the capital Vientiane, we managed a glimpse of the Golden Stupa before setting off again for a home stay in Hinboun. We were welcomed by a charming family who bowed and smiled as if we were royalty.

'Don't forget not to point your feet at anyone here. It's really rude,' I reminded them as we entered our hosts' wood and stone built home.

'Sure thing, Rachael. The smell of mine will scare off intruders, so we're quite safe.'

'Just as well, Michael. There's no doors, let alone locks.'

After we had settled in, Tong said, 'I have arranged a special outing for you, madam. Come with me please.'

'Are you sure this is safe, Tong?' Michael yelled. We were all sitting in a boat made from a B52 bomber fuel tank. Tong had assured us that this was a popular tourist attraction. Among Lao people, perhaps, but it didn't look very attractive to me.

'Don' worry. It will not rain.' Our guide nodded slowly as he tried to reassure us.

'That's not what I meant!'

Just then there was a loud crack, and lightning filled the sky.

'Aha. We better go ashore now, sorry.' Tong looked sheepish.

Michael explained about lightning striking the metal "boat" in the middle of a river. I had been oblivious to the danger.

Once we were safely back on land, Gecko said,

'Look, mate, there's some kids playing football. Come on. Let's show them how it's done.'

Conrad and Gecko ran towards a group of small boys playing in the road. They had only played for a couple of minutes when a shriek rang out, shattering the calm of the rural scene. There was a shout, and suddenly an angry man was running towards us.

'Stay still, don' run. Let me handle this,' said Tong. We waited, subdued, by the edge of the road.

'I didn't mean it. Obviously I didn't do it deliberately.' Gecko looked mortified.

'Uh oh, Tong's coming back. Let's hope he's been able to pacify them.'

'What happened, Tong? Why are they all shouting, and that man waving his arms around like a banshee?'

'The football hit his three-year-old son right in the face, Ma. The kid's screaming his head off. Sounds like a cat being skinned.'

'Oh, how awful! Poor little boy. Gecko, couldn't you have been more careful?'

'It's football, Rachael. You just kick.'

'Not hard! Not when there's little kids about!' I screamed at him.

'Well, it's done now. I'll go over and say sorry.' Gecko took a few steps towards the gathering crowd.

'Oh, no. That not enough. You must pay compensation to father,' Tong said.

'What? How much?' I panicked.

'You must pay for son's treatment at hospital. Also wife cannot work; must care after boy.'

'Hospital?! He's only got a bruised cheek, surely?' I asked, anxious.

'Village elder come to us at house tonight. He decide how much you pay.'

I couldn't eat for worrying. What if he demanded more money than I had? I had visions of being clapped into a Laotian jail, to waste away the rest of my days.

At nine o'clock, the elder arrived with his entourage of a dozen men and women. He wore a stern expression, and bore himself with the dignity befitting his position. Tong showed them into our hosts' main room, where they all sat on the floor, cross-legged.

He and Tong bent their heads and spoke in low tones for what seemed like ages.

'He say three chicken. I say one chicken. We have agreed two chicken.'

'Conrad, stop it. Stop laughing. I've got to take this seriously. I don't want to be the cause of an international incident. What? What are you laughing at now? Why is that funny?' But, by now, I was fighting to suppress my own laughter. I turned to face Tong. 'So I pay two chicken? I mean, chickens? How do I do that?'

'Come with me to market at morning. We buy, we break neck, we take to family. They forgive. All finish. You go home. We go home.'

'And what about the supposed hospital bill?' I asked.

'Don't try to be smart. We'd best get out of here, Ma. Quit while we're ahead.'

'I quite agree. We haven't any time left in Laos anyway. We've seen everything that's worth seeing and we need to get back to Bangkok.'

'You being childish, or what? Sounds like you're sulking, mother!'

'No, I'm not. Childish, moi? How dare you, young whippersnappers?' I grinned.

So that's what we did. Tong drove us back to Vientiane, a short flight away from Bangkok. He deposited us outside Departures after passing me our tickets, bought with the money I'd handed him when I settled his payment. I started to thank him but he turned away before I could say goodbye, got back into the car we'd hired, and drove off, seemingly unconcerned.

'Ouch! What the hell was that?' My toe throbbed with pain. Whatever had just bitten me must have had really strong jaws. 'I think I need to see a doctor. This is more than a normal bite.'

I hobbled into the airport and asked for the medical centre, where I was informed in a mixture of French and broken English that I had stepped on a fire ant. Extremely painful, but harmless.

'That's your comeuppance for being snide to Tong, Mother,' Conrad quipped.

'Oh really? Of course. Thank you for sharing that with me.'

Flight QF200 departed on time from Bangkok to Ho Chi Minh City.

Leaning back in my seat, I re-read the message handed to me at the check-in desk:

Hi Rachael

I have left Andrew. I decided it would be good for me to join you, so I am booking on a flight to meet you in Saigon. I will leave a message at the Qantas desk when I arrive to let you know what hotel I'm in. Please leave me a message at my hotel reception when you arrive and I'll come and meet you wherever you're staying.

Lots of love
Louise

My sister-in-law was joining our party.

Vietnam

Ho Chi Minh City
Louise had survived an unhappy marriage by pretending that nothing was happening, which was how she coped with any crisis.

I could picture her talking to her son, my nephew Solomon. I was sure it would have been he who suggested she join us, and she would have responded 'yes' quite coolly, with no thought for the implications, nor for my reaction. Sara watched me refold the note.

'Mum, your face has clouded over. Don't look so gloomy! What's in that note?'

I shut my eyes to give myself time to think. They loved their aunt, but how would they feel about having her as a travelling companion? Then again, Louise would be company for me, and it would make rooming easier if we were an even number.

She had married my brother twenty years before. At first, she enjoyed the stability he offered: serious job, careful financial planning, provision for the future. With the communication skills of a stone, he spent his evenings watching television and went to bed nice and early to get his "beauty sleep"—the same joke every night as he mounted the stairs, leaving her to sit with a glass of wine, listening to her favourite music. She had loved him for the comfort he provided. Yet, as she grew older, she longed for excitement, and Andrew was not of that ilk. Solid, dependable, he was. Alluring, enticing, he was not. But he was my brother, and I loved him. How dare she hurt him? *I'm a rubbish sister,* I thought. *Have been since he was three months old. I didn't speak up for him, never supported him when she complained that he was dull. I've let him down again. I didn't even protest when she glibly told me she wanted to leave him. I am the three-year-old*

169

version of myself, back in the garden, hiding while he howled. But what can I do?

'Oh, to hell with it, it's too late now. She'll be there already. I can hardly ignore the note and leave her stranded in Saigon. God knows what she'd end up doing,' I muttered to myself.

'What? What are you talking about, Ma?' asked Conrad as he passed me in the aisle.

'Well, see here, your Aunt Louise...'

Like me, she was small but, unlike me, she had a flair for dressing herself, using accessories and fabric combinations to produce a Fifties' starlet look.

Would she bring many clothes, I wondered. How would she carry all her suede bags, silk scarves, woollen hats, fake fur stoles?

After a lonely childhood dominated by a fear of school, Louise had yearned for security. She had been afraid for as long as she could remember—afraid that her homework was poor; that she would be asked something incomprehensible in front of the whole class; that she would fail all her exams; that she would be cast off by the rest of the human race as worthless and stupid. She always felt as if she had merely skimmed the surface of any topic, never sure she really understood. From adolescence, she had known that she was a bit different, and had developed her own quirky personality. She could be naïve, a quality she could also fake when it suited her.

'Aunt Louise? She's barking. She'll drive us nuts. Still, I s'pose you'll make a fine pair, the two of you.' Despite his scathing comment, he adored his aunt who had looked after him frequently before he started school. She always took the time to play with him—unlike me who only played for a few minutes before getting bored, pretending I had some job to do or someone to phone. Aunt Louise's house was crammed with objets d'art, antiques and plaster cats. Her garden held secrets that only the two of them shared—the tortoise's house, the worm burrow, the dog's grave, birds' nests, statutes of nymphs, hidden, overgrown ponds—a treasury of adventure for a young boy.

Entering her house, a winding, narrow stone staircase straight opposite led up to the first floor. The kitchen, to the right of the arched entrance, had a low, beamed ceiling, from which pots, pans and dried herbs were suspended, a traditional AGA stove warming the whole house. The debris of previous cooking sessions lay scattered over every work surface—peelings, crusts, empty glasses—but it did not look dirty, merely disordered.

Soft, rhythmic music would be playing from a distant music system, hidden within the depths of the sitting room. This was like a den, an oval oak table laden with art books and unread newspapers, exposing half-completed crosswords and margin doodles. A tall, fat Buddha statue beamed beatifically from one corner, whilst a semi-collapsed settee held pride of place in the centre, in front of the fire set in a baker's oven with a forged iron doorway. An illuminated alcove displayed a miniature inlaid Chinese cabinet.

The witches' stairwell, attached to the rear exterior of the building, wound to the first floor, to a golden yellow bathroom of minimum comfort, past a store room crammed with pre-recorded videos, the floor strewn with magazines, to the master bedroom. This was like a sultan's harem—the lighting was subtly romantic, and oriental patterned, chimney-style fabric shades covering orange-toned lights hung low over the king-size bed, burgundy and purple linen draped over its edges. A dozen or so sepia photographs with curled edges lay on top of a small mahogany bedside chest, and empty wine glasses lay at various angles on the polished wooden floor. Beyond the bedroom was an ultra-modern office containing not one, but two computers, a compact disc player, radio, and a knot of wires and cables. In front of the largest screen, Louise would sit on a huge black leather swivel chair, designed more for sleeping than for working. In every room, incense burned, day and night, competing with the scent of fresh flowers, even though these were not often visible.

It was not the home of a traditional married couple, more like that of a single, free-spirited artist. Aunt Louise was eccentric, but fun. She was an excellent raconteur. Her stories of "the old days" made Conrad laugh—stories of batty uncles who kept geese as pets; of intellectually challenged (as she put it) village children where she grew up, that she and her brother used to tease with sarcastic remarks.

Best of all, she was always laughing. People often had no idea what she was finding amusing, but her happy countenance cheered her family and friends who often found themselves laughing alongside her with shrugged shoulders and an expression of bewilderment.

Louise had an aristocratic accent, almost nasal. She said "hice" instead of "house". She also had a habit of sprinkling her sentences with the word "remarkable". She had overcome her earlier feelings of inadequacy by creating for herself a quirky identity, which sat with her comfortably enough. We'd both felt isolated as children, but dealt with it in completely different ways.

As I anticipated her arrival, I couldn't help feeling that this journey was now running itself; that I had lost all control over it. Just one second, I thought, in which I cast my eyes over a brief note, and the rest of the trip has now changed. It's as if all our futures are subject to random fortuity; as if each instant in our lives is like a developing snapshot, somewhere between a negative and a print; each thought an impulse yet to be calibrated. With each new moment, a new future, a new universe is born. It seems like it's pure chance which future takes form and becomes real.

***

To: Wendy McKintock
From: Rachael Green
Subject: Damascus
April 20??…30?? (I have no idea…)
Hi
Well, I still haven't had any Damascus moments, but am definitely learning a lot—have been able to read and think—generally contemplate life. I've had the time, a luxury I didn't have

when I was working, and I bet you haven't much time for yourself, either. What's it like teaching in an American uni? (They don't call them universities over there tho', do they?) Any road up, I'm finding out more about the world from this trip than I did as a student. Mostly about myself, but I guess that's okay. Own house in order first, as they say.

We've had a few tense moments—well, okay hours, days even—but on the whole it's worked okay. My sis-in-law is travelling with us for a while. Remember a student called Michael Le Cheminant? In my tutor group at college. Quiet kid then; still is. He's out here too. Came to see Sara in Thailand and stayed! Haven't made up my mind about him; doesn't say much. But Sara is really happy. Must be good with his willy. And to complete the set a friend of Conrad's (Jez, don't think you met him) came out a few weeks ago, too. So we're quite a mixed bunch!

Gotta go, bye hun

R

x

***

'Saigon. N-n-n-n-n-nineteen,' I sang to myself on the flight, trying to picture the city. I imagined bicycles and pushbike taxis, weaving slowly along, passengers sitting in a large basket-like structure in the front. People wearing coolie hats would be walking in the middle of the road, some carrying baskets on each end of poles. *Goooooood morning, killing fields. What will the people be like? Will it smell different from India or Thailand? What does Vietnamese sound like? How will it feel?*

I tried to doze. I'd read Greene's "The Quiet American" set mainly in Saigon, and pictured the "shabby chic" of the French colonial buildings. I could almost feel the tension of troubled times.

'Come on, let's get a drink somewhere,' I said after we'd picked up our bags from the luggage carousel and exited the arrivals terminal. 'That looks like a café over the road.'

173

'I'll be with you in a minute. Get me a coke please, Ma. People to see, places to go...' Conrad said, striding away from us.

'He's always off somewhere. How does he get to know so many people?' Michael asked.

'You know Conrad,' I answered, 'He makes friends wherever he goes.'

'So why does he hang around with Gecko? They didn't even go to school together,' Michael continued.

'No, but they both play football. That's why they make so many friends. Wherever you go in the world, you can find people willing to kick a ball around. And even Ya, Yam and Yut had heard of British footballers.' I turned towards Sara. 'By the way, I just want to tell you I think you were very brave on the river trip, darling. I never thought you had it in you—you were always such a city girl. More Dior than daring, you know...'

'Back in a sec.' Michael got up and followed Conrad.

Sara nudged me. 'Oh, Mum, leave it out, please! You manage to convey disapproval even when you're trying to show support. You blather about "real" travel, hold forth about theories of time not existing and other stuff you've just read in a book, but you never ask if I'm coping with life. You just assume everyone else copes like you do. I'd love to talk to you about Michael but, if I give away any hint of concern, you'll turn it into a counselling session and make a big issue of it. I'm fed up with being given advice about how to act the part of a proper traveller.'

'It's a skill you acquire, darling. You learn how to locate quickly things like "way out" signs, metro station names and lines, without looking like a tourist. You have to trust other people and the information they give you.'

'You're doing it again! Mum, get this: you don't listen. And you always take on responsibility for the rest of us, stopping us from finding things out for ourselves. You might be a teacher but you're a lousy listener.' She tapped her fingers nervously on the Formica-topped table. 'Still, I love you anyway.'

Where did all that come from? I was lost for words. Sara had never spoken to me like that before. Was this Michael's influence?

'Alright, Ma? Acquired any more travelling skills today? Where's my Coke?" My son was back, Michael trailing behind.

'Whatever were you doing?' I asked.

'Keep your wig on, Ma,' Conrad grinned. 'Just went to buy some fags.'

My expectations of Ho Chi Minh city were far from the reality. The streets were full of scooters, cars, bicycles, boxcarts, taxis, lorries, buses, pedestrians and animals, interweaving, hooting, just missing each other. It was a kaleidoscope of movement, perpetual motion working in a rhythm, like threads woven into a tapestry of locomotion against a soundtrack of blaring horns, shouts and ringing bells.

'Here we stop, madam.' The taxi driver almost whispered. When he turned to face me I was surprised to see that he was plump. Most of the people I had seen in the streets were slight. This chap looked well fed, almost sturdy. His tone of voice was deferential, as if he was scared of me, or of upsetting me.

Sara, Michael and I toppled out under the weight of our packs, too big to fit into the taxi's small boot. Conrad and Gecko's taxi pulled up behind us, horn still resounding. Louise had picked a genteel hotel, its faded elegance reminiscent of British Empire days.

'Is Mrs Louise Green here yet, please?' I enquired when we reached the reception desk

'Wha'?'

'We - are - meeting - a - Miss-us - Green.' I reverted to my dad's "talk loudly and slowly to foreigners" communication technique.

'Ah yeh. She hee-ah. Rum numba won oh won. Hee-ah you key.'

'Thank - you.'

'Well, well, and what may you be doing in this part of the world, pray?'

175

A familiar voice called to my back in the foyer. Swerving round, I walloped a passing businessman with my oversized backpack. Louise was trailing a smart, hard-sided wheelie bag, and a soft brown leather handbag hung from her shoulder. She looked as if she expected a porter to relieve her of these at any moment.

We hugged and retired to her room, where she explained her last-minute decision to fly out to meet us instead of going to friends in Devon.

'Seemed a little more adventurous, you know. One has to keep up with one's sister-in-law. Mustn't let the side down, what!'

Her only defence for running off and leaving her husband, my brother, was, 'Sorry about…you know…about Andrew. Had to be done, just had to be done, you know.'

No, I didn't 'know'. But I hugged my ex-sister-in-law again as the kids hovered around the doorway.

'Oh, I didn't get you a room.' She addressed the young people. 'I wasn't sure if you'd be staying in this hotel. But I'm sure they'll have plenty. It's not exactly crowded. I've hardly seen another living soul here.'

'You didn't tell me she was blind,' muttered Michael.

'Aunt Louise, there's millions of people out in the street!' Sara exclaimed.

'That's as maybe, but I wasn't about to go out there till I had some back-up. I've been waiting for you to arrive.'

The look Sara gave me was scary. I glanced at Conrad. His was even scarier. 'I'll go down now and sort it,' I said.

'Did it all go smoothly at the airport? They still had my note at Qantas?'

'What do you think? Give you three guesses.'

'Eh? Oh, yes, I see. How silly of me!' She tutted. 'When you come back up, Rachael, could you do me a favour and bring me up a cup of tea? I can't make that girl understand.'

Oh God, give me patience.

I got a family room which would have been called a suite back home. It had two double beds and a third single, a bathroom and separate shower, and a sitting area overlooking the busy boulevard below. Noisy but spacious, and the street view made it really special. For a moment, I felt envious; then remembered these were my children, and whatever good stuff they had, I kind of had, in a way. I would double up with Louise from now on.

Louise had never before been on a long-haul flight, and had spent the last two days recovering. Delicate little flower. So she had nothing to tell us about Saigon, but plenty of anecdotes about the hassles and discomfort of air travel. By dinnertime, I was almost sore from laughing. Her mix of genuine and feigned naivety entertained me, just as it had in the dinner party days before she and my brother began to drift apart.

'So, how did you find this hotel, Louise?'

'Oh, I just did some research in the Lonely Planet book. It was only a few million dingdongs—or whatever they're called—a night. Quite remarkable.'

I couldn't hate her for hurting Andrew, despite feeling that by accepting her into our group, I was somehow letting him down. Face to face with her now, I realized that, just as I couldn't stop the bee from stinging him, I couldn't stop life from hurting him. Slowly, I was beginning to forgive myself for being a lousy mother and a lousy sister. Maybe I could now forgive David, too? Had I perhaps been a lousy wife also? I decided not to dwell on that line of thinking, and got into bed.

By the side of my bed was a tourist magazine. A feature on Cambodia, adjacent to Vietnam, caught my eye, and I read it eagerly. At breakfast next morning, I announced, 'It's no good. I know it seems like I'm spoiling us, but while we're here I'm going to find out if we can get into Kampuchea to see Angkor Wat. I've always wanted to go there, and we might never get the chance again. What do you think, guys?'

'Never heard of it. What is it, Ma?' Conrad asked.

'Would you believe, a massive complex of ancient temples, some of them still half-buried.'

The groans were thinly disguised.

'Nah, thanks. I'll pass on that.'

'Oh, Mum,' Sara groaned. 'Didn't you see enough temples in India?'

'These are really special, believe me. I won't know until I get prices and stuff, though. I'm off to the hotel foyer to talk with the official tour organizer.'

'I'm afraid you'll have to count me out, too. I'm not ready for another foreign flight yet. Still haven't recovered from the last one.' Louise added her response.

'But it's only a couple of hours away, if that.' I felt nervous about going on my own. 'It's up to you, though. I wouldn't want to drag anybody anywhere.'

'You what?' Conrad and Sara cried in unison. 'Since when? You've done nothing but drag us around for the last three months!'

'That's different. You're my kids. And I'm paying for you. Louise is paying her own way.'

'Oh really? I thought you'd be treating me.' She grinned, trying to look innocent.

'Not funny, Aunt Louise.' Sara turned to me. 'Just because you're...'

'Okay, that's enough! I get it.' Ever since Michael had arrived, my daughter was becoming more and more difficult. Truculent; critical; righteous; a pain in the arse.

It struck me suddenly that I was actually angry with Louise. She'd just assumed I would be quite happy about her joining us. Leaving her here to look after my kids could be a form of subtle revenge.

'By the way, why were you trailing your wheelie bag around when we met you in the foyer?'

'Ah, that's a long story. You see, when we landed, I was chatting to a charming man sitting the other side of the aisle. He was interested in hearing about Guernsey. Had never heard of it, of course. Nobody ever has. Well, except people in the UK, and not many of them...'

'Get on with it, love.' Oh dear. I had weeks, possibly months, of her long winded stories ahead.

'Well, you see, I got so absorbed in our conversation, I completely forgot to take my hand luggage out of the overhead locker thingy before getting off the plane. We talked all the way to the luggage carousel, then all the way through Customs and Immigration, till we got to the taxi rank where I thought we'd be going separate ways. But it turned out he was going into the city too, so we shared a cab. Then, after he'd got out, I realized about my bag. By then, we'd pulled up outside this hotel, so I just got out and checked in. I had all my documents in my handbag, you see. The receptionist very kindly called the airline and told me to go back, that they'd taken it off the plane and it was waiting for me at the airline baggage enquiries desk. I left it till just before you arrived to go back to the airport. I was hoping I might see you arrive.'

I thought about the rest of our travels. In just a few weeks the whole balance had changed. No longer was I the one adult; the leader. With the arrival of Michael, Gecko and Louise, we were suddenly like a tour group. I still held the purse strings for my own family and Gecko, but both Louise and Michael were independent of me, and I felt threatened by this. What if my kids wanted to do their own thing now that they had the back up of others their age? Would that lead to more arguments?

It didn't take long for me to find out.

***

Kampuchea

'It won't be easy, madam. This country is still not properly open to visitors. I will see what I can do.' Our hotel's receptionist had directed me to a luxury hotel nearby, which had its own tour desk. I waited an hour in the elegant foyer, reading my battered paperback, until the uniformed desk clerk called me over to hand me a ticket and several flimsy sheets of what looked like rice paper, on which an itinerary had been Gestetnered in pale lilac ink. The original characters had been poorly translated into English for me to read. I thanked him for his consideration.

'Oh I like speak English!' he informed me with pride, his chest swelling visibly.

The Royal Air Cambodge ATR 72-200 rose noisily above geometrically-shaped fields and shiny ribbons of rivers, up into fluffy, snow-like clouds, After what felt like only minutes, it began to descend into the capital.

I was met by Kun, my guide, who was to accompany me throughout the three-day tour I'd booked from Saigon. He had limited English and a poor accent, but he was my only hope of finding my way around in the time I had. I was very lucky to have been able to get a visa at such short notice. There was no way all of us could have gone, so it was just as well we didn't try. So I left them at the hotel to entertain themselves, and rushed by taxi back to the airport for the flight to Phnom Penh, where I stayed at a fairly expensive tourist hotel.

Sitting in the bar of the Foreign Correspondents' Club, I felt exhilarated. This was my own adventure. I was free from the responsibility of keeping everyone else happy. Large fans swirled slowly overhead as I people-watched from a battered, leather-upholstered armchair, sipping a gin and tonic. The French windows opposite were all open, and drinkers were gathered on the balcony overlooking the Mekong River, looking down at the street below, teeming with life. The mellow, languid milieu, with its timeless French flavour, evoked a not-too-recent past. I could picture journalists gathering here, smoking, drinking and telling jokes. In the streets, cows caused traffic jams, and potholes made any kind of transport both uncomfortable and dangerous, as no road etiquette was observed. There were vacant, rubble-filled lots all over the city where bombs had devastated formerly elegant buildings.

Kun drove me first to Tuol Sleng Genocide Museum, a former school, which was used as a prison camp and torture chamber during the Pol Pot regime. Twenty thousand or so men, women and children were processed here, and the photographs taken of them on their arrival cover the walls of the old classrooms. On some of the photographs, families have written the names of the victims. This is now forbidden, according to a notice.

'Think, come here, find photo your dear relative, know they bin tortured most cruel then killed by execution at Killing Fields,' Kun said.

Subdued, I stared in silence at the instruments of torture, the cells in which they were used, and the rusty manacles used to restrain detainees. A whole generation of Kampucheans was wiped out: three million either killed or fled, a total of one third of the population.

'Intellectuals first, in case ask questions.'

I stood before a photograph of a pretty young girl, no more than six years old, moments away from death. I will never, ever forget the look of sheer terror in that child's eyes.

'Please take me away now, Kun. I've seen enough. I can't bear it.'

But worse was to follow. When the rains wash away the top layer of soil at Choeung Ek, new bones are sometimes exposed, as well as torn pieces of clothing belonging to the eighteen thousand corpses. Among the frangipani trees lie piles of clothes, bones and teeth, including those of children.

'You see nails on tree?' Kun pointed. 'That where they tied children and beat to death in front of parents.'

'Oh no. Oh no. How could they beat children? What could the children possibly have done wrong?'

'Sometimes just tied people up and buried alive. They took spikes from trees, slice throats, save bullets. And babies— soldiers toss into air and catch on bayonet as fall down. They compete, like people shoot game in your country.'

'Jesus, they'll be lying just a few feet beneath where I'm standing.'

The unspeakable horror of a glass tower full of skulls brought streams of tears. But the sight of these craters, these mass graves, would be what haunted me most. There was no wind, no birdsong, only a hint of the odour of evil, as if the earth were digesting their bodies, salivating some kind of poisonous enzyme which would break down their tissues into pulp, discarding only the unfamiliar cloth of their garments. I imagined their eyes, bulging from fear, from the horror of knowing evil, staring out into blackness under the mud, a rotting compost of human flesh. I could not speak for several minutes, only to ask, as we drove away from the site, the name of a solitary flower at the roadside.

'Morning Glory,' Kun replied.

***

I stayed in my room that night, unable to eat. I felt that in some way I had to atone for being part of the human race; for being one of a species capable of so much cruelty.

Someone—Kun, I guessed—pushed a note under my door: "Tomorrow we fly to Siem Reap. Please be ready at six to go to airport. Tomorrow will be happier day."

It didn't start well. Breakfast was on the ground floor, my room on the fifth. Immediately after I entered the lift, it was plunged into blackness and came to an abrupt halt.

Power cut, I suppose.

Several minutes later, I heard the adjoining lift moving.

Don't panic, press the emergency button. But as there was no electricity in my lift, the button didn't function. Long moments passed.

Breathe deeply and slowly. Someone will do something soon.

I tapped the door, knocked on the walls, banged the emergency button. Nothing. Suddenly the lift jolted into action, dropping quickly to the third floor, where it stopped again.

Oh, God, this is it. I'm going to die in everyone's worst nightmare: a plummeting lift.

Perspiration tickled my hairline; my heart pounded. Come what may, I'd said, come what may. The words echoed in my mind, taunting me.

'Help! Help, please!' *No, try to keep calm. Getting all panicky won't change anything. If you're going to die, just be serene. Oh God, the kids, what about my kids? They don't even know where I am.*

Tears welled and my knees gave way. I sank against the lift wall. Then it jolted again, this time descending even more rapidly—so it seemed—to the first floor. Another minute passed and it dropped again. The doors slid open and a young man grinned at me widely, his arms outstretched.

'Stop laughing!' I shrieked. 'It's not funny! Tell him to stop laughing at me!' I screamed at the reception staff. 'How dare he? I was terrified and he thinks it's funny! Can't he see how distressed I am? Get him out of here!'

The young man sidled away with a bewildered expression. I turned to face the reception desk again.

'Madam, the young man was the one who brought you down, floor by floor. He pressed the buttons one at a time so as not to scare you. He was not laughing. He was smiling, happy that he had rescued you.'

Suddenly I was sobbing with humiliation. 'How can I apologize?'

'It doesn't matter, madam. He is off-duty now.'

So much for my diplomacy skills.

By ten, Kun and I were walking towards Banteay Srei, to see the intricate carvings in the temple.

'There is a whole world here on the walls: entire armies, dancers, goddesses and workers, marching in procession around the temple walls, carrying food, small animals and gifts,' Kun explained.

Later, we climbed to the highest point of Angkor Wat. I caressed the stone, wondering who had carved that section, what his life was like, what he was thinking as he worked. From the distance, the complex looks like a giant crown, its bulb-shaped towers reaching skywards. As we approached, the detail of the bas-relief was revealed. It could have been built by beings from another planet. I drew my fingertips along every one of the row of Buddhas, decapitated by the Khmer Rouge.

'Is beautiful, yes?'

'It defies description, and it's huge. You can see that the whole area must be covered in more temples.'

'Yes, there were lakes, channels and irrigation canals, which helped the Khmer Empire to flourish. The kings built palaces, monuments, mausoleums and temples, linked by a system of roads.'

My body ached from clambering over stone blocks, but I ate heartily that night and slept soundly, dreaming of ancient kings and stonemasons.

Next morning, I rode an elephant up to the Bayon Temple at the heart of the royal city of Angkor Thom. Fifty-four towers bear the image of King Jayavarman, god-king, earthly representative of Shiva, Lord of the World, smiling mysteriously, his eyes closed.

Just when I thought I had seen the best, Angkor Thom was equalled by Ta Phrom, the famous ruined temple, deliberately left unrestored to capture the moment when Henri Mouhot first discovered it in 1858. Trees grew up through the crumbling walls, great carved blocks were strewn across the ground, lichen spread across the columns, and vines crept their sinewy way around them.

Huge tree roots looked as if they had not grown upwards towards the light, but downwards, descended from the sky like giant birds, to grip the walls and tear them away in their monstrous claws.

Kun watched in disbelief as I pretended to be Lara Croft for a few minutes of fantasy. I couldn't quite manage the famous leap, but I did use a "bum-slide" technique to descend from the top. A bewildered monk eyed me curiously as I attempted to regain my dignity and walk with my head held high towards the car.

Ho Chi Minh City
On the flight back to Saigon, I sighed happily. *I'm so glad I've seen these magnificent sights,* I thought. *I could so easily have missed out on them. From now on, I'm going to make sure I do what I came for. Otherwise I'll never figure out the meaning of life!*

Back at the hotel, Sara gave me a broad smile. 'We've had a brilliant time, Mum. You should go off and do your own thing more often! I've been window shopping, and Conrad and the boys have played loads of pool and won beers for us all each night. The barman even fed us 'cause we entertained his customers so much he wanted us to go back the next night.'

'Did you do anything during the day?'

'Not much. We, er, chilled out,' Michael replied with a despairing look.

'Did nothing except lie in bed, you mean?'

'It's hard work being us, keeping everybody happy round here.' Conrad squinted.

I decided against asking any more questions. Instead, I insisted we all took taxis to see Cholon, the Chinese quarter, and the famous Chinese pagoda, where a beautiful young man followed me with his eyes until my knees went weak, my body aching with lust. How long had it been? I couldn't remember. I viewed the pagoda through dazed eyes with flushed cheeks, and I couldn't remember anything about it afterwards; only the thrill of being attractive and attracted to someone. After weeks of eating mostly oriental food, I'd lost weight and was beginning to look human-shaped again.

Ambling through the streets that night in the haze of diminishing light, I saw two cyclos—bicycle taxis—silhouetted in the orange glow from the street lamps, bearing the familiar grinning faces of my son and Gecko. With a cheery wave, they pedalled on past. Yet again, they had made local friends. This time they'd been given a free ride.

'Watcha, Ma! Hello!'

'How do you get away with it?' I called after them.

'They got cheek! Ha ha!' replied one of the drivers.

***

It was time for me to get into action. I'd had enough of the city. 'I'm just off to a travel agency to find out about the cost of getting north.'

When I returned, Conrad and Michael were deep in conversation, both looking tense. They stiffened visibly when I approached.

'Where's Gecko? What have you done with him?'

'You don't want to know, Ma. Really, you don't. How about buying us a beer?'

'Okay, sounds good to me. Louise is still flat out on her bed, apparently still recovering from her flight. Can't believe she's so feeble!' I wondered about her stamina. Was she going to be like this every time we flew a long way? I wondered about Gecko, too. Where could he have gone, and why? But I hadn't been watching any of them all day every day, so why start worrying now?

Within an hour, a slight young man wearing a "Kim Café" T-shirt approached me while I sipped a "33 Export" beer.

'We have a proposition for you. Please come to see me when you have finished your drink.' Result. It looked like my enquiries had paid off.

***

'We'll have to call it the "Nam Van". Ten days in a van in Vietnam,' Sara sang with an appropriate American drawl.

I planned to hire a van and driver to take us north towards Hanoi. Louise and I had been looking forward to the train, but Sara and Conrad would hate the discomfort, and a van gave us flexibility.

186

'She's obsessed with post offices, you know, Aunt Louise. We are quite worried about her. Are you sure you don't want to change your mind about coming with us?'

'Sara, behave!' I whispered.

***

Dear Sophie,

Saigon, Vietnam. The temperature is 84 degrees, with 58 per cent humidity. We all have headaches.

After the usual argument at the airport with a taxi driver who wanted to take us to a hotel where he would be paid commission, we got to our hotel, booked by guess who—Aunt Louise! She told us you and your dad knew she was coming. It was quite a surprise for us, I can tell you! Say no more! Anyway I went off to find Kim Café, a well-known meeting place for travellers, according to the guide book, and they are sorting out suggestions for how we can see as much of the country as possible in a couple of weeks.

The currency here is called dong and there are 18,600 to the pound, so we need a calculator every time we pay for anything! It felt weird paying for a round of beers and cheeseburgers at 137,000 dong!! A beer is only 7,000 dong, under 50p, so we're happy about that. I took out 2,600,000 dong at the airport so I'm a dong millionairess. Saigon, now called Ho Chi Minh City, is very exciting. It has all the atmosphere of a truly foreign city but without the filth of Mumbai. People get pushed along in a contraption called a cyclo (which I thought was called a "sitlo" because you are sitting low down!). They cost about 20p for half an hour. The noise here is startling—bikes, cassette players, café radios, car horns all competing with each other. This of course adds to the headache syndrome!

They eat a lot of something called pho, which I think is noodle soup. I expect we will all be able to manage to eat that, if nothing else! I hope we don't get ill. You can't put toilet paper into the toilet here. You have to put it into a little basket by the side of the seat. It takes a while to remember but, if you forget, you have to call someone to come and unblock the mess you cause.

Don't forget to reconfirm your flight to Sydney 72 hours beforehand. By the time you get this letter, there will only be three and a half weeks to go!!!

All my love, my darling girl,

Mum

xxxxxxxxxxxxxxxx

***

'This feels familiar. Like our first night in Goa,' I surmised.

'That was like a lifetime ago. We were so naïve then!' Sara said.

'It's a bit sad. We've got more cynical now.'

'Or realistic, you mean.' Conrad was not one for melancholy.

'Well, it's back to our usual level of accommodation, I'm afraid. No more of the posh hotel. One night round here and then we're off. Fancy yet another banana pancake, anyone?'

By now we'd all decamped to Kim Café, our bags piled up on the pavement. I couldn't afford for us to stay another night in the hotel Louise had found. Besides, we had an early start and I wanted us to stay close to the café, from where I figured we'd be setting off. Gecko looked awful; pale and drawn.

'Are you alright?' I asked him.

'Yeah, sure, just a bit tired.'

Conrad and Sara exchanged a knowing look.

'Brought on by anything in particular, d'you reckon?' Conrad asked.

Gecko's response was a silent lowering of the head.

After the ubiquitous and somewhat tasteless pancakes, I went into the café and confirmed the hire of a minibus with driver for three hundred and eighty pounds from the café owner's brother, next door. A driver would arrive to meet us next morning.

'You must pay first, before he drive,' I was informed. That meant me getting up really early to get cash out of a bank, using my card, and I would have to go to the financial district.

When the negotiations were over, we checked into a hotel right opposite the café. Functional and characterless, but clean and budget-priced. In the foyer, I turned to look outside.

Dried, flattened squid were on sale at a street food stall. Children were selling books of postcards, cigarettes and sweets from trays suspended by straps from around their necks. No matter how I tried, I couldn't see anything any of us could possibly want to buy from these adorable-looking children, so I just went out and handed over some notes. Their total value was about one British pound.

Next morning, alarmingly early, I took a cyclo to Sacombank to draw cash out but, to my horror, for the first time my card was refused.

'Very sorry, card not accept.'

'There has to be some kind of mistake!' I couldn't take in the difficulty of being stranded in Vietnam on a Saturday with no cash.

'There are plenty of funds in my account.' I sounded like I was wheedling.

The teller twittered sweetly while I went off to find our driver guide, who was waiting for me outside our hotel, to translate. After all, without cash I couldn't pay him.

'It is a problem with the system, not with your card. Try another bank.'

We drove between scooters moving six to eight abreast to Vietcombank where, to my relief, the transaction went through without a hitch.

My God, I have been stupid, I thought, *coming away with only one card. What if the system hadn't accepted it?*

I was ready to move on. We'd "done" Saigon, and the rest of the country awaited.

'Okay, guys, stack your backpacks into the Nam Van. It's after ten. We're leaving in fifteen minutes.'

A shy, drawn face turned towards us. I introduced our driver.

'This is our driver, Mr Phuc,' I announced, my face rigid to avoid giggling like an adolescent, 'and he has a son called Wee. Isn't that nice?'

'Right, okay, Mister Fuk.' Sara smiled.

'Alright, mate?' Conrad kept a straight face.

'How lovely! How old is your son, Mister...Phuc?' Sara tried to look genuinely interested, but it sounded false.

'He can't hear you over the engine noise up here in the front.' I turned to face them. 'Just as well!'

Gecko and Michael couldn't speak, but their shaking shoulders betrayed their mirth.

***

'Here we are—the Cu Chi tunnels. The Viet Cong used to hide in them. There are four hundred kilometres of them, maybe more.' Mr Phuc beamed with pride. This was our first stop after leaving the big city. I'd read that the tunnels were well worth the forty kilometre drive.

'They must have been skinny little bastards then—the entrance holes are minute.' Conrad looked bored already.

'You could be standing on top of one without realizing. Entrance holes, I mean, not Viet Cong. Although...' Sara mused.

'I bet the American soldiers got really frustrated. They wouldn't be able to follow them down, fat gits.'

'I don't think they were that fat in those days, Gecko,' I countered.

'Didn't McDonald's exist in them days?'

'They have made tunnels wider now, for foreign visitors,' Mr Phuc said.

'Thank you very much!' Louise lifted her chin, closed her eyes and turned away, looking slighted.

Inside, the tunnel was hot, dank and dark, and you had to crawl on your belly in order to move along.

'Blimey! These are the widened versions?' I was astounded. To Mr Phuc, who was wiry and muscular for his race, we must have looked like giants.

In the distance, we could hear the sound of gunfire: tourists practising shooting at a target, paying a dollar a bullet for the chance to fire an AK-47.

'Quite remarkable.' Louise tutted loudly to express her disapproval, obviously still offended.

Three hours' drive later, we boarded a boat on the shores of the Mekong. Mr Phuc had recommended a delta boat trip, for a 'glimpse of river life'.

I was sickened by the sights at the market we passed as we walked down to the boat. Fat toads, turtles, fish, chickens and snakes were tied together, alive but dying, wriggling or twitching depending on the time they had left to live. Vendors sang to advertise their "wares", their voices ringing in our ears as we boarded.

Skinny children splashed in the brown water. A small girl in a thin cotton dress sat at one end of a long boat, partially hidden by overhanging bushes in an inlet, surrounded by lilac water hyacinths. A woman showered under a hosepipe at the rear of her craft.

'Wow! So this is the famous Mekong Delta?' asked Louise.

'Named after the emperor from Flash Gordon, right?' I answered.

'You're funny, Ma—not.'

The first stop ashore was a "garden centre" where a Mister Tiger served lethal rice wine, no doubt to dull the senses for the singing and music to follow.

We ate sumptuously, enjoying huge prawns and fresh fruit, drinking tea to counteract the dehydrating effect of the rice wine.

'Oh God, that's disgusting!' Sara caught sight of a bear in a tiny cage, kept so that its spleen could be drained. I had read that local people believe this cures many illnesses, but the sight of it was shocking. Louise, in tears, pleaded with the owner to release it, offering him money. He smiled indulgently at her incomprehensible behaviour.

Five minutes later, she had a python around her neck, and the locals were clapping, smiling and nodding at her "bravery". In the "girls' dorm" that night, complete with tattered mosquito nets, Sara and I giggled as Louise gave a rendering of "mares eat oats and does eat oats and little lambs eat ivy."

After a sticky, itchy night we set off towards the north from the Saigon area along National Highway Twenty. After leaving the city, where the usual bicycles, scooters and box carts wove in and out of a slow-moving line of lorries, we emerged onto the open road. It looked like an ugly scar on a defenceless landscape.

Images flashed past, of baskets suspended from shoulder poles, water buffalo gently swishing their tails in muddy rivers, field workers in conical hats bent low as they toiled. In the villages, barefoot, skinny children played in rubbish-strewn streets. We stopped for lunch by a small lake near Dambri Falls, where monkeys approached lopsidedly to steal bananas from our hands, whilst macaws screeched in protest at our presence.

Laundry was laid out on grass and draped over bushes. It hadn't yet rained on this day, but we could see that every night a downpour hammered the flowers flat and left thick ochre mud, where tyre ruts hardened and dried into tracks, and previously squelchy footprints resembled large ammonites.

Across a remote lagoon, fishing nets stretched among oyster beds trembled in the soft light, like delicate webs sprinkled with dew. On Langa Lake, thatched houses floated in the haze, resembling upside down rectangular baskets. Small platforms between them acted as wharves for the people to tie up their boats. They were very low in the water, as if sinking. Bamboo bridges joined haphazard groups of two or three. These were just some of the sights we saw as we made our way north, and I knew they would stay with me forever, that I would recall them for the rest of my life.

Dalat

As our van climbed into the hills, the air began to cool. En route to Dalat hill station, we stopped for a cold drink at a roadside café near Bao Loc, sitting on tiny, very low chairs under the shade of a tree.

'I can only fit one buttock onto these seats,' remarked Louise cheerfully.

A radio crackled in the kitchen. 'On a dark desert highway...' I recognized "Hotel California". 'Oh, please turn it up! Full!'

We sang along at the top of our voices, watched by the bemused café owners who kept the radio on loud, perhaps hoping for another impromptu cabaret.

'At least that song's in English,' said Sara. 'Most of the stuff you like is in some weird language, like Moroccan, native Indian chants and Deep Forest.'

'And your point is...?' I said, raising an eyebrow.

When we reached the town, high in the hills, the driver took us straight to the "Crazy House" as the locals call it. Hang Nga guest house was designed by the daughter of Truong Chinh, Ho's successor. She went to Moscow University to study architecture and developed her own bizarre style—not unlike Gaudí in Barcelona—finally designing a Walt Disney house in Dalat. Before tourists were allowed in Vietnam, hers was the only hotel in the town permitted to accept foreigners.

'There's a grizzly bear in our room, Mum!' announced Sara.

In response to my wide eyes, she added, 'I promise we haven't been taking anything, honest!'

Hang Nga comprised three huge concrete "tree houses", a grand giraffe with a tea room inside its belly, and big wire cobwebs outside in the garden. Each room was furnished strangely. Sara and Michael's had a life-sized model bear, mirrors on every wall and ceiling, and oddly shaped furniture, with curtains to divide the different areas of the bedroom and bathroom.

The dining room was filled with bric-a-brac, reminiscent of a Victorian room, with brown-tinged photographs, ornaments, candles, and paintings in tattered frames. The lady herself flitted about, dressed like a hippy. The place was a delight, and pushed back the limits of disbelief, as if she had created the world's first theme park, here in the hills of Indochina.

I had always considered a hill station a slightly romantic title, without knowing why. I had visions of a community somehow separated from the rest of humanity, living aloft on a "rolling hill", receiving communications from the outside world at rare intervals, excitedly. The guidebooks said that Dalat was set in parkland, with streams, waterfalls, lakes, and rubber or coffee plantations. I had been expecting to see baskets full of mulberries, or field workers in conical hats tapping rubber from the trees, or working on silk farms.

Yet the architecture belied the books' descriptions. Most of the buildings had flat or low roofs. The streets were cobbled, and there were some pretty churches, but a lot of the architecture was forlorn and functional. The market, Cho Da Lat, made of reinforced concrete, was ugly. Near the Summer Palace, however, a scent of pine teased my nostrils into accepting the cool mountain climate, and I found the tranquility of Xuan Huong Lake in the centre of the town comforting.

There seemed to be a refreshing lack of tourist amenities, but this included a lack of shops.

'There's nothing remotely picnic-like to eat for lunch,' Sara sighed.

'You mean apart from fruit—limes, nectarines, greengages, lemons, satsumas, apples, pomegranates, melons, grapes? Isn't that enough? What else could you want?' I asked.

'Er, meat? How about meat? You know, that stuff we used to eat, like they do in the rest of the world?' Conrad added.

'They don't have that here. And, if they did, it would probably be rat meat or dog or something,' I replied.

We ended up with only bananas and bread—much to Conrad and Gecko's consternation—the only things we could all agree on.

Mr Phuc was disappointed. Dalat had not made much of an impression on us, apart from the French Quarter, which reminded me of colonial times. The Pasteur Institute was a surprise. I had always thought that the couple who had made such important scientific discoveries "belonged" to Western civilization, and didn't know that they had lived in this part of the world.

I was beginning to realize how little I knew of this country. What I thought I knew was gleaned only from one or two books and movies: the usual war films, and "The Lover" and "L'Indochine". I'd definitely been guilty of stereotyping.

What I thought was naïvety, I now realized, was stoicism, optimism and tenacity. The Vietnamese seemed to have retained a happy disposition despite the turmoil of wars, adversity, and the spoiling of their land.

Worst of all for a people who worship their forefathers was surely the destruction of tombs, shrines and graves. They like to be near their deceased ancestors, and it is tragic for them to have to relocate. For the Vietnamese, life after death extends into the present, into the now, as they believe that "dead" souls are close, around us.

Do they feel this in their hearts or souls, or do they know it in their minds? In fact, are all our perceptions internal or external, or a mixture of both? When we construct meaning, do we think it internally or could we be sensing it, feeling it, from an external source? Are our thoughts all the product of deductive processes in our brains, or are some of them the likes of race memories, predictions, glimpses into other realities?

***

'Cam on em.' Louise carefully enunciated her thanks to a young woman. 'You'd do well to learn a few phrases, Rachael. For a young man, you say "cam on ang", to an older man "cam on ong", and to an older woman "cam on ba", always with a big smile and a nod.'

Who does she think she is? I'm the linguist around here. She was getting on my nerves big time. Apart from her irritating mannerisms, she was continually the target for bloodthirsty mosquitoes, and kept scratching and picking at the scabs on her ankles until they were raw and bleeding. This was not a pretty sight, especially at mealtimes.

In the morning, Mr Phuc drove us to Lam Ty Ni Pagoda to meet the Zen Buddhist monk Vien Thuc. He was also a poet and painter, and had his work exhibited in Paris. The locals called him "the Mad Monk". He lived at the back of the pagoda in a ramshackle workshop, crammed full of his work. When we visited him, the studio was a series of makeshift lean-to huts, the garden in disarray.

Louise had recently lost her dog, so bought a sketch entitled "My Beautiful Dog Awaits Me" with a drawing of the sky. She declared it remarkable. Surprise, surprise.

After talking with Vien Thuc, I felt myself growing spiritually. Confidence in the future was beginning to spread through me, filling me with warmth and happiness. 'Live for the now,' I repeated to myself, 'live for the now.'

'We are going to visit a village known as "Chicken Village",' explained Mr Phuc as we set off again.

Approaching the village, salt patches lined the dirt road. In the rice fields and coffee bushes, rising from the centre of a group of mud huts, there came into view a five-metre high concrete statue. Of a chicken. And I hadn't been smoking anything.

'There is a legend about this statue. A young bride went off into the mountains to fetch a nine-toed chicken to please her future in-laws, who were not satisfied with her. But this was an impossible task and, unable to complete her quest, she died of a broken heart alone up there in the mist-clad rises, rather than admit defeat. The villagers erected the statue in her memory, according to the story. But nobody believes this, so no one knows why the statue is there.' Mr Phuc didn't say much, but when he did, in his lilting sing-song voice, he entranced us all.

I set off to explore and, before long, came across a villager working on his house. As I approached, he looked up briefly but didn't acknowledge my presence. Squatting, he continued to mould reddish-brown clay into a brick. The slapping noises reminded me of baby's bath days. His opaque thighbones lay beneath a layer of drum tight, transparent skin, which his knees seemed to be striving to pierce.

He was making mud bricks for a wall of his hut. He repeatedly walked to a well, took water in a pot over to the soil, trampled fully clothed in the resulting mud, patted it into brick shapes, set these aside, and left them to dry. He was building a home. Love and determination in equal portions shone from the half-finished wall on which he was toiling under a sluggish sky.

A few moments earlier, I had disturbed the reverie of a montagnard, a highlander, bare-chested and barefoot, clad only in baseball cap and shorts, striding downhill, carrying a stick and a tin kettle, on one of his infrequent sorties from the nearby hills. The villagers were in awe of him, eager to explain to us that the mountain dwellers had only recently begun to descend, now that the government had ceased to deny their culture. He didn't speak to anyone, but strode purposefully past us all.

The villagers were very hospitable. Sitting on a tiny stool, Sara and Michael politely sipped a cup of tea.

'This is the most disgusting tea I've ever tasted,' Sara whispered, unwilling to offend, and listened patiently once again to the tale of the tragic bride who had gone off into the hills in search of a now three-toed chicken in order to impress her antagonistic in-laws. It must have lost six toes since they last counted.

Sara bought a fabric bag from one of the women. We had watched it being finished off. I knew that, from now on, every time my daughter opened its drawstring fastening she would picture an anxious little boy, holding his hands behind his head, his flip-flop sandals on the wrong feet, in tie-dyed T-shirt and cotton trousers, leaning against the plank wall of his home, watching his mother work. I wondered what the future held for him. Had we improved his fate by spending cash in his village, or had we taken away the dignity which was his birthright?

Whilst other villagers were laying out coffee beans to dry at the side of the paths, Conrad and Gecko played football with the local children. Once we got back to the van, Sara and I gave a demonstration of disco dancing which caused hilarity. The children clapped and copied us, giggling.

'Obviously what is now an extremely poor village will one day be firmly established on the tourist route, I bet you,' Michael declared with too much cynicism for my liking.

We had dinner in a Chinese restaurant recommended by Mr Phuc. It was decorated with the usual red embossed wallpaper and gilt lanterns, a bit like a London Chinese restaurant; certainly incongruous in this country.

'I'm sorry, I don't feel well. Just off to the Ladies.' Sara looked pale. She'd managed only a mouthful of egg fried rice. She'd been dogged by discomfort of some sort or another for days, and felt queasy in the van. I didn't see her again that night.

***

Nha Trang

After descending from the hills, we left the evergreen forests and flower gardens of the highlands to join Highway One, the coast road. Nha Trang, our next destination, was apparently a favourite tourist resort for the locals, and was famous for its eight-kilometre beach.

We rested after three hours, among banana trees and paddy fields. Baskets of limes and papaya lined the road.

Sara confessed to still feeling unwell. 'What if I'm pregnant? How do you think Michael will react?'

Oh, sweet Jesus, how can a daughter of mine even allow that to be possible?

'Don't worry, love. It's most likely just a traveller's bug.'

'Oh God, can't we listen to something else?' Louise complained. Prince, followed by the Fugees and Bob Marley, had been playing on the van's tinny cassette player. Music was essential to drown the sound of continuous car horns.

Next up was thirty minutes of rap: "I'm not a motherfucker, I'm a motherfucker's son…"

'I insist we change the cassette!'

'Louise doesn't much like our choice of music,' I explained to Mr Phuc. 'Do you have any of your own?'

He looked delighted; had obviously hated our choices. So we endured three hours of shrill Vietnamese singing.

'We need to buy fruit. Can we stop at a market?' Louise asked.

'We don't want more bloody fruit! We want crisps! You said we could have what we want to eat,' Conrad shouted.

'Here's a load of dong. Go and find a crisp shop, then. See you back here in half an hour.'

I must have sounded irritated, because Louise said, 'They're not going to change their eating habits now, Rachael. You shouldn't have let them eat that rubbish when they were younger.' I opened my mouth to protest, but thought better of it. *Bite your lip, Rachael, bite your lip.*

It was muggy, stifling, and Louise and I joined the vendor women sitting on the floor, using umbrellas as sunshades, feeding their babies while they worked. This was the only way of doing business. Otherwise, our attempts at making a purchase were ignored. It was essential to sit at their level and look as if we were taking part in the conversation before anyone acknowledged our presence.

'Can you imagine having to squat down like this at home before being able to buy a cabbage?' Louise asked.

'I can't even remember what home is like,' I said. 'And I don't think I ever went to the real market; just supermarkets. My mum used to get up early on Saturdays to go for fresh fish, but I was always recovering from Friday night excesses. Seeing this crowd here, it makes me wonder what I missed out on.'

'What, like contact with other people?'

'Yeah, I guess so. I don't know anyone in my circle of friends who'd spend time just chatting. None of us had time for that. You'd have to book each other up weeks in advance for a dinner or drinks party, or you never got to see each other. What a weird world we lived in. And we thought we had it better than the rest of the world. Ha!'

'We'd best get back to the van,' Louise said. 'The others are there. Looks like they've found some salty, greasy polystyrene muck to eat.' *Say no more.*

***

Dear Sophie

It is very peaceful here in Vietnam. Funny, for a country known to us because of a war. People work quietly in the fields wearing conical hats which act as both a sunshade and an umbrella. There seems to be no sign of change for at least a hundred years. They still use hand- or bullock-drawn ploughs. They plant and transplant individually, by hand, with sacks balancing on the ends of poles across their shoulders. They weed and pick, sometimes transporting the sacks across the back wheel of a bicycle. You also see animals tied onto bikes here. They move water around in baskets which look like upturned hats. Salt and beans are laid out along the roadside to dry. Occasionally, we pass square, concrete family tombs. The road is full of potholes, or shell holes from the war. As we drive along, I keep picturing scenes from the war: bombs exploding, people scattering. Then I see a couple of buffalo ambling along or being ridden by skinny children with no shoes, or wallowing in the water in groups, obviously enjoying themselves, and I am brought back into the Nineties.

We saw some towers called Po Klong Garai Cham, but they were in ruins, on top of a brick platform. The style is very ornate and reminded me of India. Women stooped at the river edge using open-weave wicker baskets to submerge vegetables into the water for washing. The boats looked like baskets, too, made of woven bamboo covered with pitch, and used like dinghies. Honestly, Sophie, it is really special, the best country I've visited so far.

Lotsandlotsandlotsoflove
Mum
xxxxx

***

It was hot and sultry, and our bottoms were getting sticky on the plastic seats. Mr Phuc suggested a rest stop. On a silent, decadent-looking beach, empty canvas deckchairs with fringed canopies serving as fixed parasols were lined up alongside wicker bath chairs, imitating a row of sentinels. The heat shimmered only millimetres above the sand, the distant sea a mirage of enticing coolness. The scene could have been from a French film, or an Impressionist painting. I expected to see Aschenbach from "Death in Venice" sitting in one of the deckchairs in a cream linen suit. Mr Phuc had pointed out the famous China Beach, where the US soldiers went for R and R, but it wasn't nearly as impressive as this one.

We had lunch at a seafood restaurant on stilts, one metre above the South China Sea, and looked down through slats in the floor to watch fish swimming below.

'Ooh look, lov-er-ly. On the menu there is "fried jumping sea snail". Must try that.' I enjoyed winding my children up.

'I, for one, decline, thank you.'

'Oh, Louise, get you! You've picked up the locals' way of talking to us,' Sara commented.

***

'We're passing Danang. Remember "Danang me, Danang me, *something, something, something* and hang me"? From the movie?' I chirped.

'Er, no,' replied Conrad, Gecko, Sara and Michael in unison, even though I knew my two did: I used to watch that movie over and over.

'Don't pretend you don't remember Robin Williams in "Good Morning, Vietnam", because I know damn well you do,' I smiled. Their only response was the usual blank stare. *What have I done now? I wondered. What's their agenda? Or is it me? Have I invented my own version of the past?*

'Until recently,' said Mr Phuc, 'police used to stop travellers here and fine them for a trumped-up offence. You will be alright as long as you are not conspicuous.' This was his polite—and surprisingly well-articulated—way of warning us not to draw attention to ourselves.

'What's that?' Louise pointed to a huge white Buddha seated on a lotus flower, watching over Nha Trang from a hillock about fourteen metres high.

'That is Long Son Pagoda,' Mr Phuc replied.' We will visit it now.'

'Look, they remind me of the little Vauxbelets chapel back home,' Louise continued, indicating mosaic dragons made of glass and ceramics at the entrance.

***

Our Nha Trang hotel was more comfortable than some of our recent accommodation; in fact it looked quite luxurious from the outside. Once indoors, however, it could best be described as shabby minus chic.

We had three rooms: a double and two twins. They smelled musty and damp but had air conditioning and hot water. Outside the window, rusty barbed wire left over from the war lined the top of an adjoining wall.

Dinner for the four youngsters was a plateful of enormous prawns.

'It's a hard life, eh, Ma?' laughed Conrad.

Afterwards, they hired push bikes and set out to find alcohol.

Louise and I retired early, as we had arranged an excursion the next day.

'I want to go to Mieu Island,' I had said to her. 'It's well known for its open-air aquarium. Giant turtles approach you to be stroked and fed. I'm really looking forward to seeing one close up,' I explained. 'I can't quite believe you can get so close to a creature like that. The others aren't interested, of course.'

In the morning, after a short boat trip, I was staring into a pair of primordial eyes and holding a flipper, as the creature imbued me with its wisdom.

'They are so beautiful,' I told Sara later. 'I stroked one and held its flipper for ages. You would have loved it. They have lovely faces, wise and peaceful, as if they have accumulated billions of years of knowledge. I gazed into his eyes; he was like a prehistoric creature. I wonder what his version of reality is. What does he see that we can't? Because we cannot see his world, it doesn't mean it doesn't exist. So why should we rely so much on what we see? Our encounter with the "mad monk" was like a window into a world of endless possibilities. Maybe the people we call mad, or mentally sick, actually do live in another universe, and that's why they don't relate to ours. How do we measure sanity, anyway?'

'Well, in some cases, lovely Mum, that would be quite a challenge.'

'Very funny, lovely daughter.'

After Mieu Island, the captain of our hired boat took us on to another island for a swim. On the way, he tapped Louise on the shoulder, pointed out to sea and yelled, 'La baleine!' We looked at each other in bewilderment.

'Must be some kind of local custom,' I said.

Once moored, Louise and I sat on the island's beach. There was a lot of noise coming from another passenger boat moored not far from ours in the bay. I squinted, and was able to make out the name. Behind the wheelhouse of the "Love Boat", a spread of exotic food was laid out: avocados, pineapples, prawns, watermelon. A smell of marijuana drifted over to us.

Soon we were summoned back to our boat for the third stage of the day's excursion: a visit to another island to see a fishing village. The party-goers gave cheery drunken waves as we putt-putted away.

***

Later, we visited the fishing village island. Boats can't get right into the shoreline so there is a system of floats to hop over. These are built for Vietnamese, not hulking great westerners, so rather than entertain the locals with a dunking, we opted for the alternative transport, and were sculled ashore in a precariously wobbly coracle steered by excited girls who decided to have a race to the shore. Convinced we would tip over, I clung on to the edge of the boat nervously, trying to maintain a confident, friendly smile.

Once ashore, I felt disorientated. We were miles from anything familiar. The village was small, just a row of huts made from concrete and thatch. There seemed to be no boundary between homes. They all opened onto common dirt land which directly bordered the seashore. A puppy grovelled at Louise's feet as she stepped ashore and picked her way around the huts, not sure in which direction to walk, but curious to see more. Before long, I felt like an intruder. This was obviously not meant for tourists' eyes.

'There's hardly anyone around, but I sense we're being observed from some of the huts. It doesn't feel hostile, but I want to get away. How about you?'

'Hmm, yes, it does feel a bit strange. How come we don't see any fishing boats, do you think? It's meant to be a fishing village,' Louise responded.

'They must be out at sea. The only indication that it's a fishing village is the smell,' I replied.

I felt deeply sad, out of place, and guilty for allowing my curiosity to overcome basic good manners: at home, I would never have gone trudging across other people's properties.

We strolled back along the beach, as far as a small harbour where we found the fishing fleet moored. Long, wide boats with a spatula-shaped stern carried small shelters woven from bamboo. There was a pungent smell from the dried fish on the quayside—cuttlefish, tuna, shrimps and lobsters.

When we got back to our hotel, Louise announced, 'Phew, I'm boiling. It's been a long, hot day. I'm really sticky.' As she tried to fill the basin, water spilled straight through onto the floor. 'Oh, just great. Not only is there no shower, but the plumbing isn't even connected. '

'Ah look, house guests.' I indicated two three-centimetre long cockroaches skittering around the pedestal base to escape the water flow.

'Another spray?' Louise suggested. 'Soon we'll stink of repellent, seeing as we can't wash properly,' she laughed.

Better than your BO, I thought. 'Here, Louise, have a face wipe.'

We met the others at Nha Trang Sailing Club for a dinner of spaghetti and pizzas. Good traditional Vietnamese fare.

'Food, glorious food...' Louise warbled. 'I could eat a horse.' She wrinkled her face into an inane grin.

'I've been reading up on the religion here. One of them is Cao Daoism. Apparently, its followers worship great people like Pasteur, Shakespeare, Joan of Arc and Churchill. They receive messages from these ancestral heroes using a kind of Ouija board,' I said, in another attempt to educate my kids about the culture of places we were visiting.

'Oh right, they talk to the dead. Weirdos. Ask them to find out a few tips for making loads of dosh. Oh wait—they only talk to the dead. Not much use really, if you're actually still alive.' Sara quickly dismissed the religion of millions.

'Don't be so cynical. Not everything in life is black or white, you know,' said Michael.

Sara's face fell at this first criticism from Michael, but she quickly retaliated. 'I'm not perfect. So crucify me!'

'It's like believing in humanity as a whole, my dear, a collective soul, the force of love. In Cao Dao there is only one law—love—and they don't believe in nations or races. It's really quite easy to understand; quite remarkable.'

'Oh, for God's sake, Aunt Louise! I do understand it. I was just trying to be funny.'

'Please don't speak to me like that, young lady.'

The already flushed cheeks on my daughter's face deepened to pink. Uh-oh, here comes the inevitable moment of uncomfortable silence.

'What's that mountain, then?' asked Michael. 'Come on, Mrs Guidebook, tell us all.'

Thank God Gecko spoke up. 'Apparently that's Fairy Mountain on the horizon, named after a lady who grieved so much for her husband lost at sea that she lay down and turned to stone. It says here, if you look carefully you can see that the mountain's shape reveals her face, breasts and legs. That one over there must be Turtle Island. No prizes for guessing how it got its name.'

I couldn't believe he had actually bothered to find out something about where we were. 'Well done, Gecko, for knowing that.'

'S'alright, all part of the service.' A nerve in his cheek twitched, like a tiny muscle spasm. I wondered what he was thinking; about me, about Louise, about our family. There was something in him that I couldn't trust, as if he was just tolerating us, and that hurt. I didn't want to think...*after all I've done for him*...but those words popped into my brain just the same.

Walking back through scrub and trees, we watched bathers in the sea, fully clothed, including hats—only their sandals had been left on the shore—wading up to the waist, giggling happily.

I wondered if the kids had been swimming.

'You've spent the day asleep? How could you just sleep when there's so much to do and see around here?'

'Only in the daytime,' Conrad said. 'We played pool yesterday evening.'

'We chatted to an American author last night,' Sara added.

'We drank beer,' Gecko smiled.

'We danced,' Michael continued.

'Alright, enough. I get it.'

'What's the problem anyway? We can't do much. You've got all the money,' Conrad said, but less aggressively than recently.

'Oh, and we met a really beautiful, effeminate man with a gorgeous figure,' Sara said. 'He was telling us about some towers; he reckoned you'd like to see them, Mum. It sounded as if they were crumbling brick, like the ones we passed.'

'You know, Louise, I'm sorry we haven't made more of an effort to sightsee here. The islands were nice, but we've missed out on more important sights.'

'Yes, but just being here we're learning about the country, without having to see everything. I think travel gives you a peek into other people's realities.' My sister-in-law rarely sounded philosophical; I wanted to respond carefully.

'Hmm, I know what you mean. But I think travellers are voyeurs. It's like promiscuity—you can have your fun then withdraw at any time without commitment.'

'Trust you to turn the conversation to sex!' she laughed.

***

Sophie darling

We're in Nha Trang, on the coast about halfway up. Just been out for a day sailing around some islands. Well, Louise and I did, the others stayed behind (as usual!)

When were out on the boat, the skipper suddenly yelled something out about a whale. We got all excited and looked eagerly, but saw nothing. Someone told me later that there are no whales in the region, so I don't know what he was on! When we got to the beach on the deserted-looking island, there was a small ferry boat moored alongside the jetty, crammed with young Americans who were having a "whale" of a party: dance music thumped, they danced on the deck,· on the jetty, on the beach and in the sea. We were quite jealous! One couple came over to where Louise and I had installed ourselves on the sand, where we were enjoying a pedicure. They told us the boat was called "Mama Hanh's Love Boat", and it cost five dollars for a whole day outing, including lunch!

It's really weird weather here. My clothes stick to me all the time, but the sun doesn't come out. There's always a kind of haze. It's muggy, you know, damp and close. We're all getting irritable and snap at each other. But it never gets nasty. It's like we're all in the same boat and we have to get on with it. Sometimes you can hear rumbling in the distance, as if a storm is brewing, but it never comes.

Love you darling. Massive big hugs,
Mama (not Hanh!)
XXXXXXXXXXXXXXXXXXXXXXXXXXXXXXXXXXXXXXXXXXXXXXXXXXXXXX
XXXXXXXXXXXX

***

Qui Nhon
Life in Vietnam seemed to revolve around the road. It was as if the entire population was trundling along, pushing bikes or carts, leading animals, sharing mopeds, carrying heavy baskets, or simply ambling, all in the same direction, across broken bridges, towards a mutual destination.

There were more people walking up and down than there were cars, pulling things behind them, including beds and wardrobes, burdens across their shoulders on poles or in baskets, or driving buffalo carts, or leading the creatures, moving them around to eat the grass, like living lawnmowers.

River sampans sunk low in the water passed by, laden with piles of sand or hay. Motorbike taxis held four people: the driver, one passenger behind, and the other two in baskets hanging off each side of the bike.

A ghostly, abandoned hotel stood just off the coast road to Qui Nhon, a depressing reminder of misplaced optimism. The town itself was rather shabby, with a modern, boring market, no good beaches and few decent eating places. Too tired to venture very far, we ate in a basic, tatty café. In the street outside, packets adorned with faded script were hanging from threads suspended from coat hangers, held aloft by small children.

'Look what's on the menu: "scainbled eggs", "put in over wrap beef in paper", "teared to pieces chicken" and "fin of fish and crap soup". Mmm, lovely, I don't know what to choose,' Sara read out, squashed into a nursery school-sized chair.

We tried Bo Gan—beef and peanuts on rice crackers. The waitresses sat at a nearby table, patiently waiting for us to finish. I ate slowly, distracted, wondering what those packets outside contained.

'They're watching our every mouthful. It's somewhat unnerving, isn't it?' Louise tried to whisper above the sound of cats involved in a yowling challenge in the doorway.

I rubbed my eyes. Children were playing football outside in the street, barefoot, among piles of rubbish. Fruit and vegetable peelings, fish and poultry carcasses, egg shells, paper, cardboard boxes, cigarette packets, toilet paper, prawn shells, cooked rice, lettuce leaves and packets of broken biscuits were all rotting down together like a compost heap.

Family living rooms were open to the street. Inside were motorbikes, televisions, plastic-covered eating tables, sewing machines and table football.

'Everyone here lives in full public view. It feels like we are spying into their private lives, but you can't help but see.' Sara sighed.

'What's up, sweetheart? You look perplexed.'

'Oh Mum, I don't understand why I feel so, I dunno, so...disorientated. I know we're a long way from home, of course, but it's more than that, like some greater truth keeps trying to reveal itself. And on top of that,' she whispered, ' I'm not sure about Michael's feelings. I just feel worried, but I don't know what about.'

Like mother, like daughter. I know all about that one.

'I know how that feels, sweetheart, believe me. Try not to think about it too much. You have a speck of mascara on your cheekbone, darling.'

She rubbed it but it spread across her eye socket till it looked like the trace of a black eye. I was reminded of how young she was, how vulnerable.

The hotel we stayed at had a big, wide staircase, with a huge stairwell decorated with flaky brown paint. It was dirty, dusty and unswept. It had obviously been a large residence once. The room doors were old partitions. In contrast to India and Thailand, there were no Westerners to be seen, only a few Vietnamese holidaymakers.

I went out for a walk, and after wandering the broken pavements, feeling vulnerably alone in a dark foreign town, found myself sipping a comforting hot chocolate in the only bar open at nine o'clock.

A young Vietnamese girl with a pretty, expectant face approached and asked deferentially, 'Essciuss, pliss ca' I tok wi' yeo?'

It was a gloomy night, the empty streets were despairingly grey, the buildings wet with drizzle. The poor street lighting merely highlighted the town's solitude, and I welcomed the company.

She was going to leave, she said, as soon as she could, to seek a better lifestyle. I nodded, lazily condoning the idea that the girl's life at home was somehow impaired. I imagined a broken-down house, a sorrowful family torn apart by war, struggling to exist from a devastated landscape.

'Your name?'

'Lam Kieu.'

'Lam Kyoo, you say? Oh, I will always remember that.' I pictured small sheep standing in a line.

210

'Yeo first English person I meet. I must to practise English.'

I was flattered by the girl's interest in my life. Her enthusiasm and innocence were enchanting. She was so keen to find out about Western fashions, fads and film stars. I contemplated disillusioning her but, sitting in that lugubrious café, I was too weary to change the world, so promised to write, paid my bill of three thousand dong—about twenty pence—and shuffled my way back to our shabby, brown-painted hotel.

What gave me the right to make those assumptions? How did I know what her home life was like? Like thousands of others, I had gazed at the haunting face of a naked burning girl fleeing along a highway, and had been thinking of that newspaper photo while I talked to the girl.

'You wan' massage?' a distant voice shouted.

In my slumber, I heard a door banging in the adjoining room—where Conrad and Gecko were—followed by raucous laughter. The partitions were wafer-thin.

'Yes, sure. I'm interested. But you'll have to go to the room next door and check with my mother. She's the one who's paying.'

'I can't do that!' A shriek, and the sound of a door slamming.

'I tell you what, the guy opposite will be interested,' shouted Conrad.

'He is with his wife.'

'No, no—that's not his wife. That's his…sister.'

Sara took weeks to forgive him.

***

'When we first met, your parents were running a hotel, weren't they?' Louise asked me as we walked towards the Nam Van for the next part of our journey from Qui Nhon to Hoi An.

'Yes, but it was nothing like this. It was a few years after we moved from Lincoln. My mum was bored out of her skull, and it was her salvation, really. In the university holidays, I used to go

211

back to Guernsey and work in the tourist office, finding accommodation for visitors who turned up on the ferry with nothing pre-booked. The idea was to earn enough to pay back the overdraft I started running up about three weeks into every term. My parents were of course expected to support me meanwhile. Anyway, years later my father reminded me that I had booked an unsuspecting family into our house for a holiday when there was no other accommodation available on the island. I just forgot to ask my parents first—a minor omission.'

'Why does that not surprise me? Typical of you!'

'The family turned up on our doorstep with a slip from the tourist office confirming their reservation for a two-week holiday and my parents let them in, bewildered, and waited until I got home for an explanation. I somehow managed to persuade them that it was a good idea. The family stayed, and my parents spent the next ten years running a guest house and loving it. Well, my mother did. My father would come home from his day job to face a pile of washing-up in the kitchen whilst Mum played hostess with the mostest, chatting to tourists in the dining room.'

'How could you have forgotten that you had booked people into your parents' house?'

'I just forgot. I guess that means I have absolutely no idea of who I am, because when I remember that story, it feels like I've been making all my life up as I've been going along. What a terrifying thought.'

'Do you think so? I think it's rather liberating, actually. Quite remarkable.'

We drove on northwards.

'This is just like being in a war movie,' said Louise.

Nguyen van Troi bridge was rusty, long and narrow, with a walkway each side of the road. As we drove across, rather tentatively, I remembered that millions of tons of bombs were dropped on this land. When we reached the other side, we stopped for Mr Phuc to have a break.

'Were you in the war, Mr Phuc?' I asked.

'Yes, of course.' He spoke slowly, drawing out every syllable. 'Here you can see my wounds.' He pointed to long scars around his thigh and knee. He seemed to be not at all bitter, and just shrugged in resignation. 'I am luckier than some.'

Not long after crossing the bridge I turned to face the others, seated behind me in the van.

'Mr Phuc says we can't miss a visit to Marble Mountains. The story is that a turtle god hatched a divine egg, and a nymph emerged. The shell cracked in five places, leaving five mountains, named after the elements of water, wood, earth, fire and gold.'

We pulled into a car park. Mr Phuc jumped out, waving his arms with enthusiasm.' Here divine egg hatch!' he shouted. 'Here one of sacred mountains!'

'I'll look forward to missing them,' Gecko muttered. He stamped off along a narrow, winding path. Once again I wondered where he could possibly be going.

Conrad and Michael headed for the gift shop while we "girls" trudged up the steps to a cave where the atmosphere was oppressive. When we came back down an hour later, the boys were sitting on low stools, observed by a standing Gecko.

'I bet you've been playing with that chess set for an hour,' I said, 'and you've got no intention of buying it. Don't you think that's a bit much?'

'We asked the owner of the shop. He doesn't mind at all.' Conrad took a gulp from his beer.

'Well, he hasn't got much choice, has he? You're so selfish.'

'Just shut up, Sara. What's it got to do with you, anyway?'

'Hey, there's no need to be like that. Your sister's just thinking of the owner. He must need the money. I bet he's hoping one of us will buy it,' Michael said.

'He'd be pretty stupid then, wouldn't he? He can see we're not Vietnamese. How many heavy marble chess sets does he sell to tourists?' Conrad retaliated.

'Okay, leave it out, you guys. Let's not fall out over it. I'll buy something else from him and hope that's enough to keep him happy. *Please don't fight over this*, I thought.

'Why do you always have to fix everything, Mum? Let's just go, get out of here.'

'Sara, I'm sick of all these petty squabbles. If we can't be nice to each other, we may as well pack up and go home.'

'Sounds like a good plan to me,' Conrad muttered.

By noon, we were crossing Hai Van—or Cloudy—Pass and were mobbed by a crowd of vendors of Coca-Cola and cigarettes. Although I insisted that we didn't want to buy, the vendors persisted in forcing things onto us, shoving things in through the van windows and demanding payment.

An ugly scene ensued. It began with pushing, when we got out to look at the view, and ended up as a brawl. Hair was pulled, faces were slapped, abuse was hurled from both sides, until, alarmed, we bundled ourselves back into the van and drove hastily away, all saddened at this first encounter in Vietnam with the unpleasant face of tourism.

'You must buy; all tourists must buy! We must have money for our family, you have money; you give us.' A surly youth pushed his face up towards my chin.

'Like I give a shit about your family, dick 'ead. You don't care about my family, do you?' Conrad's aggression was unnecessary.

Oh please, let's get out of here, I thought. *This has been a horrible day.*

'Come on, let's move,' I told Mr. Phuc.

Hai Van used to be a frontier between kingdoms, and remains of walls and fortresses can be seen from the road. The col is five hundred metres above sea level. It was spoiled by advertising hoardings and vendors, but the views are stunning—a sweep of beach stretching away to the north, and mountains to the south and west.

Remote lakes sparkled in the twilight as we drove on till late afternoon. Names like Buu Long Mountain and Dragon Lake whispered of history and romance.

In the van, however, the atmosphere was less ethereal when the music changed and we sang along to the Spice Girls. "Mama, I love you. Mama, I care. Mama, I love you. Mama, my friend..."

Tears wet my face. I pictured my own mum, lying in a hospital bed back home, crippled from a series of strokes which had left her with a balance problem. I forced it away with images of her baking cakes in a Fifties' apron when Andrew and I got home from school.

I looked at Louise, singing away happily.

How could you hurt my little brother? I thought. *He didn't change; you did. He didn't do anything wrong. What am I doing letting you travel with us? You didn't even damn well ask.*

I turned to look at Sara, seated behind me. I was amazed to see tears streaming down her cheeks, too.

'Oh, Mum, this reminds me of you,' she said. 'I do so love you!'

We continued to sob until the song ended.

'Christ,' whispered Michael to Conrad, dismayed at the sentimentality.

Gecko stared out of the window at the flat paddy fields flashing past. After Vietnam, it would be time for him to go home. I guessed he'd be in turmoil, a confusion of suppressed desires, secret resentments and hard anger revealing themselves in his face. He had spent so long getting high regularly that his mind could no longer function sequentially. This respite from the mediocrity of his real life had been short-lived, and his time would soon be up. I could almost feel his desperation.

'You okay, Gecko?'

'Never better, Rachael. Never better.'

***

Hoi An

Approaching Hoi An, girls dressed in ao dais pedalled along on "sit up and beg" bicycles. The full-length, side-split coat with high neck, worn over trousers, flattered everyone. The girls wore their black hair long, straight, usually tied back, with a conical hat dangling down their back. The whole ensemble, worn with flat shoes, enhanced their natural coyness.

'This road could be in France, dead straight and lined with tall trees,' Sara said.

'Not quite, though, love. This one's got borders of reeds, water hyacinths and bamboo cafés, and there's incense burning in little temples. Not like the France I remember from my teaching days.'

We checked in to a single-storey, functional hotel, and set off for a wander.

'Have you found the post office yet, Mum? We've been here for half an hour already.'

'Very funny, Sara. But, oh yes, our hotel is quite close to one, and there's a bank en route to the main shopping streets. I've checked.'

'Ha ha! I should have known!' Sara quipped.

In the hotel bar, Louise asked Mr Phuc about having ao dais made.

'One of my lady friends here is dressmaker. She is rival of tailor man opposite hotel. His name Hung Long.'

Conrad and Gecko nearly burst.

'Your lady friends? How many do you have?' I asked.

'Not so many. But I come here a lot.' He winked at Conrad.

'And the dressmaker? Is she a special friend?' I asked.

'Oh, she...er, she talk too much.'

'Looks like your sweet Mr Phuc is a really sly old dog, Ma. He's got a woman in every town. He's even offered to take us out to find girls, and he obviously knows where to go.'

'You be careful. You never know what you might pick up.'

'You don't think we'd be desperate enough to go with girls Mr Phuc procured for us, do you? We're not that stupid.'

I held my tongue.

***

After an initial exploration on foot, we went separate ways. Louise and I strolled back to the hotel to rest.

The lads returned from shopping after a couple of hours. Gecko had an intricately carved pipe made of buffalo bone that would not survive in his rucksack, and some packs of mock Marlborough cigarettes, and Conrad had a new Zippo.

'Hey, when we went in the shop, Gecko asked if they sold pipes. The shopkeeper answered, "I don't got pipe, but I got pong." This place is hilarious!'

'We've been everywhere looking for Rizla papers.'

I had long ago given up pretending that I didn't know what they wanted them for. Especially after I'd smoked a few with them. 'How come you can't find any? I should have thought they'd be easy to get.'

'None of them stick together enough to make a joint,' Gecko explained.

The four of them had been resorting to painstakingly emptying the tobacco from a filter cigarette by gently rolling it between their fingers until it all fell out. The tobacco was then replaced by ganja, which they had to push carefully down into the paper tube using a matchstick. The whole process took a frustrating thirty minutes, a preparation time which increased in relation to the number of joints they smoked.

Next to the hotel was a cycle and scooter hire shop. We hired Honda Om scooters to ride to the river for dinner. Groups on shared scooters smiled and waved.

'You must sample Cao Lau, it local speciality. Noodles, bean sprouts and pork. It only made with water from here. It real treat,' Mr. Phuc advised.

The café owner ambled towards us and we ordered drinks. After pouring water for me, she coughed, lifted my glass, and sipped my water. Shaking her head, she held up an index finger and wiggled it.

'If you wait, owner will bring you freezer.' Mr Phuc nodded conspiratorially, unaware of the bewildering effect of his announcement.

'Uh, huh,' replied Sara with a thinly disguised smirk.

A tinny radio played somewhere.

There appeared to be no fridges anywhere. Instead, café owners lugged around huge blocks of ice, which they attacked with a pickaxe whenever it was needed.

'Freezer, Vietnam style,' Conrad smiled as the proprietor shuffled back with a tray, on which lay a small axe and a big lump of ice. Her skin was olive, smooth and plump. She was short, squat, with rounded shoulders, almost hunchbacked, and she moved slowly, jerkily, like a robot. Her most prominent feature was her hooked nose, which honked like a horn when she blew it, frequently. We ordered drinks and a meal. As she placed our meals on the flimsy plastic table, our glasses wobbled and I thought our drinks would spill.

Throughout the journey, I had been frustrated by my kids' unwillingness to try new foods. They invariably chose the most Western-style dishes on menus, drank Coca-Cola, and grumbled if there was nothing they liked. Tonight, I was disappointed by my "real treat" meal, and was suddenly overwhelmed with an urge to complain. But I didn't want to tarnish the reputation of tourists, so I simply pushed the food to one side of my plate and said nothing.

'Wasting food, Mother?' commented Conrad.

'Who gives a flying fuck?' Tension had been building in my temples all evening.

'Okay, okay, keep your wig on.'

'Oo-er! Mummy! At last, you've learned that it's okay to leave food you don't like. What a breakthrough!' Sarcasm sounded alien in my daughter's voice.

I opened my lips to speak, but shut them immediately.

Like many a post-war baby, I had spent my life believing that it was somehow morally wrong to waste food, even though I knew that if my body didn't need it, it was still wasted. I couldn't shake off the conditioning of my childhood. My parents, like many deprived by the war years, had instilled a sense of outrage at leftover food. It had to be eaten, even if it was disgusting. Now, as I glared at the repulsive mixture on my plate, I felt liberated. In an instant, I had triumphantly joined the ranks of what I perceived to be the "affluent" young who did not put up with second-rate, having never endured rationing. Light-headed with new-found gastronomical freedom, I indulged in an ice cream, even though I hadn't finished my main course.

'I've learned how to waste, and I'm proud of myself. How has this happened?' I tried to be witty.

'You are so sad, Mother.' Conrad shook his head slowly. Michael coughed and stood, looking embarrassed.

'I think Michael's having some kind of crisis,' Sara whispered to me as her boyfriend moved away from the table. 'He says his whole life has been a scam, something about being absent inside himself, empty, and a bit scared. I don't know what to do. Do you think he's going to dump me?'

I too had noticed his strained expression. And I knew how random fears would be careering around in her brain, like particles in an accelerator. I've had that T-shirt in my collection for decades.

'He's just being a man. Aka, discontented. At least he's talking to you about it. If you were the problem, he'd just go. There's nothing forcing him to stay with us.'

I knew that wouldn't be any comfort, so I hugged her. 'Listen, love, there's nothing we can do to stop other people from suffering. If he's full of doubts about his own life, it doesn't mean he's gone off you. And, if he has, you'll meet someone else. Someone who is right for you.'

'But we got on so well. Still do...' She fiddled with her hair.

'Have you asked him? Whatever he says can't be as bad as worrying about something you don't even know is going to happen. That's just wasting your life—and making you miss out on this fabulous journey.'

'I'm sorry, Mum. I don't want to waste your money...'

'Well, stop bangin' on about Michael, then. Mum's right for once—just ask him and put us all out of our misery.'

'Leave her alone, Conrad. Where did you pop up from anyway? Have you been listening to our conversation?'

'Obviously I don't know him that well, but if he's fed up, I reckon Gecko and I would know about it. He wouldn't say anything to me of course, 'cause I'm your brother, but we'd know.'

I wanted to comfort her, but I didn't know how. I understood her fear. As well as my recent emotional turmoil over the divorce, I had vague memories of what I call the submarine dreams of my early childhood where, in the darkness, wavy tendrils swept around like tentacles, seeking me out to strangle me. Or else I lived on the bed of a profound ocean, hiding beneath an overhang, invisible, watching crustaceans scraping on the ocean floor, always alert, always aware that, somewhere in the dark depths, an unspeakable creature was lurking, its size and shape unknown to me; waiting for its moment to pull me down deeper until I was stifled. In my childhood I would wake up from these nightmares to the light of the day, bewildered, glad to be alive, safe in my warm bed, my mother stroking my face. Up until a few months ago, when I woke to an empty bed, and these nightmares stopped, replaced by a living one every day. I hoped Sara wasn't feeling afraid, alone, but I knew nothing I said would console her if she was.

And what about Sophie? Was Sophie having nightmares? Without me there to comfort her when she woke? I lowered my head. What kind of monster was I? My child could be suffering while I was away with the fairies, pondering metaphysics and playing at being adventurous. I'd been so engrossed in my own issues I was utterly useless to my kids. What damage had I done to them?

***

'Onwards and upwards, Carruthers!' Louise was in good spirits. Enjoying her liberation, she was feeling euphoric, rethinking her likes and dislikes, swept along on a tide of self discovery. We all plodded up the stairs, after a stroll along the water's edge, to retire for an early night after our Cao Lao experience. We would meet for breakfast, we agreed, in a tiny café just up the road, almost hidden from sight by a tall hedge. Those of us who made it would enjoy a Western meal, including fried eggs!

Our anticipation was misplaced. The "fried" eggs were baked, and rubbery.

Louise, Sara and I collected the ao dais we'd ordered from the dressmaker, and pedalled along the straight road to Cua Dai Beach, which was lined with deckchairs and crowded with fully-dressed people, some up to their waists in the waves.

'Blimey, almost a year ago I was paddling in the sea at Vazon Beac

h, in the warm sunshine, wondering why our beautiful island just wasn't enough; why I had to have more; why I couldn't be content to be in a place most people would be thrilled to live in.'

'You know now, though, don't you?' Louise smiled.

'I guess I do, yes. It's not that Guernsey lacks anything. It's that I want more.'

The boys met us in the hotel foyer at dinner time, and we set out together to find a restaurant.

'Clam soup, please.' I was feeling adventurous.

'Oh yuk, it looks like a pond! What's that slimy stuff at the bottom?' Gecko asked.

'I think I'm going to be sick.' I froze. *No, Sara, no.*

'Please tell me you're not pregnant.'

'Actually, I thought I might be. But no worries, Mum, I'm not. My period came this morning. So I feel like celebrating!'

Sweet relief. That would have been the end of her holiday. Back on the first plane to get proper medical care. Something else I'd not considered. We'd talked about protection, but who knew what the quality of condoms out here was like? And taking the pill was out of the question, with all the anti-malarial meds messing up her system. *Thank God I'm beyond all that*, I thought.

As the sun set, and twilight cast its hazy shadows, Louise and I watched as the others gathered on the beach for their last joint. They had been offered none in Vietnam, and no one had seemed to respond to their hints. Somehow they'd found some and, from the looks on their faces, it was good.

Eyes rolling, grinning inanely, Gecko slurred, 'Look, there'sh a couple having shex over there. He'sh taking her from behind.'

'Time for us to beat a retreat, Rachael. You coming?'

Later, at the hotel, their eyes watering, their tongues furry, their brains addled, the young people were howling with laughter. When the full moon had come out, it had illuminated the two bushes they had taken for a copulating couple.

Sara was happy again. No pregnancy to worry about, Michael's mood seemed to have improved, and she seemed to be feeling positive about their relationship. How he would have reacted to fatherhood she had no idea, she told me, but she felt comfortable with him, and a strong bond was forming between them.

I felt depressed as I laid out my clothes on the bed, to pack for the next day's travel.

'Tomorrow we move on again. Hoi An will be behind us, in space at least. I wonder which part of our time here we'll remember the most clearly. Why is it that some memories are no more than recollections and others feel as if the whole experience is being repeated? Is there a physical law which governs this selection?'

'Whatever, Ma.' Conrad pecked me on my cheek as he left for his and Gecko's room.

***

Dear Sophie,

It's great fun being pushed along in a cyclo—just like being a baby in a pram! We drove through some fantastic scenery today: salt fields, then a winding road high above the coast, following its line, looking down on fishing coves and long white sandy beaches. There were lakes where waterfowl with long necks and yellow beaks floated or picked a path among lotus flowers. Everyone is tiny. A man asked to try on my sandals and they were twice his size! The men here squat to pee in public. I remember how in our "civilized" society, when you were all babies, it was not considered appropriate to breastfeed in public. What a different world!

Mr Phuc likes to toot the van horn all the time, as do all the drivers here. They drive along with one hand permanently on the horn. He was a South Vietnamese soldier, and had his kneecap blown away and got shot in the arm. As we go further north, we see more and more war graves. There is a field near our hotel full of old tanks, guns, armoured cars, cannons and a missile launcher.

Before I forget, I found out that Ong Nam Hai, or Lord Fish (whale), is a god, and that's why the sailors shout to him to appear and help, or to protect their boat from harm at sea. When a whale dies in local waters, they wrap him in red silk and give him a respectful burial. When he is just bones, they take him out of the earth and to the temple. Once a year, the bones are removed from the temple during a three-day ceremony and taken out to sea. Well weird, as Conrad would say!

Everyone sends you loads of love…by the way Conrad and Sara say they posted a letter to you a few weeks ago—did you get it? Oh, you can't answer that, ha ha!

Your Mama

xxxxxxxxxxxxxx

***

Hue

'Rachael, let's take a "dragon boat" ride on the Perfumed River. We can go to Thien Mu Pagoda. It was built for the lady who helped found the city.' Louise showed me a postcard of an octagonal brick structure with porthole windows, about twenty metres high. There was also a picture of a huge marble turtle and an even huger bell, which apparently weighs over two thousand kilograms.

'Okay, why not? Let's go.'

A laughing bronze Buddha with a chubby face beamed at us in the languid atmosphere. His big, black eyes twinkled gleefully under bushy eyebrows, and his black beard and droopy moustache were neatly trimmed.

'He reminds me more of a favourite uncle than a religious icon. He's wearing damask pink, powder blue and yellow—mmm! He looks as if he's suppressing a smile after a joke, don't you think?'

It was our second day in Hue, and Louise and I had set off to sightsee, leaving the young ones in their rooms, yet again. I was glad to have her company; I would most likely have spent hours each day waiting around for the others to get up if she hadn't joined us.

We toured the Forbidden Purple City, the site of former royal palaces, much of it bombed or otherwise destroyed. The citadel was built to protect the emperor, his wives and concubines. I tried to imagine the hustle and bustle of activity in this now sad, abandoned place.

The dragon boat owner barely acknowledged us. After mooring, she ignored us and concentrated on listening to what sounded like pop music. She had sold me a "turtle man", for good luck, carved out of dark wood. The top part was a turtle shell but, when turned over, the belly revealed a man. The boat had a carved, painted dragon at the prow, a creature which plays a big part in local culture, both an enemy and a bringer of good fortune. We were free to roam around the site; there was no sign of guides.

'Whatever this turtle man thing is, it's kind of mysterious, just like the country. You feel as if you can only scratch the surface of its soul,' I said.

'I wonder if there's any toilets. My teeth are floating,' Louise responded.

'Thank you for sharing that, Louise,' I said.

Mr Phuc came to meet us from the boat. In the hotel later, he gave us a potted history of the city. 'Name Hue comes from word "hoa" which mean "peace". Here is famous for beautiful women.'

'No doubt you know a few of them, Mr Phuc! I bet you've got a little black book with women's names in,' Michael said.

Sure enough, he pulled one out of his pocket stuffed with cards bearing girls' names.

'Hey, hey, I knew it!' Michael was triumphant. The boys all laughed.

***

I glued the stamp on my latest missive to Sophie. There were no self- adhesive stamps in the post office. I was given a little pot of glue and a paintbrush.

'Have you ordered me a coffee?' I asked when I joined the others at a white-tiled café on the river bank.

'Yeah, but it's got a layer of condensed milk at the bottom of the glass, like the one you had the other day.'

'That's okay, Michael. It's 'cause they don't have fridges for fresh milk. It's the same with cold drinks. That's why the beer is lukewarm.'

'A banana pancake with honey, please,' I told the waitress.

'Me too,' Sara said.

'I'll have the same, without honey,' Louise added.

The pancakes arrived: one honey pancake with no banana, one plain pancake, and one banana and honey with no pancake.

'Remarkable.'

I had anticipated some language difficulties in Vietnam so, before coming away, I'd bought a little book called "The Travellers' Wordless Dictionary", containing little pictures which, in theory, you simply point at to show what you want. The theory was about to be tested, for Sara's benefit, in a local pharmacy.

'She needs some tampons,' I explained, pointing to a picture of a woman with sanitary towels alongside her. A clear request, I thought.

But the pharmacist started shrieking with hysterical laughter, showing the picture to her friends who were passing the time of day in the pharmacy, chatting. Long minutes passed, the group of women doubled over, tears coursing down their cheeks, before I got my book back. I took a closer look at the page, and realized I had been pointing at a picture of a man with a condom next to him. Evidently, the pharmacist thought I wanted condoms. Why that should cause such hilarity, I didn't know.

This was the second time we'd tried to use the book. Wanting to order duck in a restaurant, Sara had pointed to the relevant picture.

The waitress had nodded gleefully, a wide grin creasing her tiny features. 'Ah yes, dick.'

'I don't *think* so!' Sara looked suitably offended.

'Maybe the wee book was not quite such a good idea, after all, Rachael?' Louise suggested.

***

That night, Conrad asked, 'So what's the nightlife like here, Mr Phuc?'

'Oh, we can go to nightclub, if you like.'

At the door, the lads were asked if they wanted to pay for a girl to dance with. 'Five dollar each, but only kissing included in price. You also have to buy girl drink.'

'Nah, you're alright, mate,' said Conrad. 'I'm okay for women for now. Thanks anyway, though.'

'Wha' is your age?' a young girl asked Conrad.

226

'Eighteen.'

'No, tha' no' possible!' She and her friend giggled.

'Okay, I own up, you're right. I am really much older. This is my daughter.' He pointed to Louise.

'She look older than you.'

'Sure, she's had a hard life. I've been a rotten father.'

'Don't be mean, Conrad. They're innocent, don't take the piss.' Michael laughed.

After half an hour of Western music, the locals began ballroom dancing. Time to go: we'd had enough of Hue's high spot.

***

Dear Sophie

The streets here in Hue are wide and leafy. It is described in the guide book as "a tranquil culture centre, with a university". The Eiffel Bridge is built in Parisian style, complete with lamps. Lotus flowers float on the moat around the citadel. There's jasmine trees amid orange-painted houses with flat roofs, columns and arches. Communist troops used the citadel as a base during the war. Both the Americans and the South Vietnamese bombed the town, and there are bullet holes and shell marks in the walls. Roadside stalls sell water, biscuits, small packets of tissue, cigarettes and packs of playing cards, all equally tatty-looking and browned with age. That's your tourist guide extract of the day! There's a test when we get home.

We are getting along well together, with Michael, Gecko and Aunt Louise. We've had hardly any rows, and the boys are really good fun. I wish you were here with us. I miss you like mad. We're both missing out. You must think you're missing out on all the travel, but I'm missing out on seeing you grow up, which is irreplaceable. I made a big mistake thinking three months wouldn't matter. It was selfish of me to go ahead without you. It never occurred to me to postpone it. Everything had been set in motion: house sold, jobs ditched, belongings gone. Anyway there's no point in going on about it now, but I just want you to know that if I had known how much I'd miss you—how much we'd all miss you—I would have fought harder for you to come.

All my love, darling girl

Mum xxxxxxxxxxxxxxxxxxxx

***

Even as I posted the letter, I was beginning to question my motive for writing what I did. I was dumping my guilt; she didn't need to be feeling sorry for me! But it was done. Posted. No point in dwelling on my "bad mother" thoughts when there was now nothing I could do to change what was happening.

As the haze cleared during an early morning walk along the Perfumed River, I saw Michael and Sara by the river, sitting together watching long, narrow boats, piled high with vegetables stacked in large bamboo baskets, gradually being revealed from within a veil of mist, and bare-chested, wire-thin men emerging onto the decks of houseboats to stretch their arms and legs. Long narrow canoes were punted from a prow flattened like a tray. Shanty huts on stilts lined the banks, yet there was no sign of rubbish.

They didn't notice me approach from behind them.

'You know I'm going to have to go back home after this, don't you? My money's running out.'

'Don't. Don't say it. I can't bear it. We'll be away another nine months. Unless I come back with you?'

'You can't do that. Your mum would be gutted. And you'll probably never get another chance to see the world. You've still got Hong Kong, Australia, New Zealand...'

'LA and Mexico. But it's pretty pointless without you. If we get jobs in Oz, we could stay for a few more weeks.'

What did she mean: 'if'? She had to; they all had to. I didn't have the money to keep them all. I did a quick sum in my head. If we all kept going as planned, I wouldn't be able to afford a smaller house in Guernsey or Spain.

'Mum'll be travelling around with Sophie. We could work in Sydney, and go home after a couple of months. Both our tickets are paid for.'

I hadn't thought through what would happen after our adventure, just like I hadn't thought through the effect a year away would have had on Sophie. What did I intend to do afterwards? Keep travelling? Alone? Without my kids? My stomach flipped as panic rose.

For our last meal with Mr Phuc, and last night in Hue, we chose a restaurant I'd read about, run by deaf mutes who took orders and communicated with each other and the kitchen staff entirely in sign language, or by using hand signals. It was highly entertaining, like a cabaret, and they gave us a specially designed bottle opener as a gift—a piece of wood with a nail stuck through it. Demonstrating its use, the owner had a mad gleam in his eyes, smashing his hand down onto it with a flourish, to send the bottle top flying across the restaurant.

We ate shrimp, pork, and bean sprout and peanut pancakes served with sesame sauce, followed by banana doughnuts and coconut with pistachio ice cream, served with a bean and coconut drink.

'Mr Phuc, could you do me a favour? I've left a pair of sandals in the hotel in Hoi An. If I give you the postage money, could you post them to the Qantas desk at Sydney Airport?'

'Ah, Miss Louise, I do not know when I will be in Hoi An again. I have to go back to Saigon now.'

'Oh. Well, perhaps when you're next there? I will be in Australia for a long time, and I'm sure they'll keep them for me at the airport.'

Sara and I stared at each other in amazement.

'Does she really think that the ground staff at Qantas Sydney will actually keep a pair of tatty old sandals ad infinitum?' Sara quipped.

'Your Aunt Louise is a bit naïve, love, go easy on her,' I whispered.

Truth was, I was irritated too.

'Have you seen my scarf? Do you know where I put my brown socks? Now where did I pack my nail clippers?' At every departure, the same scene would unfold: Louise rummaging around in her pack, spilling the contents onto the floor, or wringing her hands in despair, spending up to thirty minutes each time looking for something she'd mislaid.

'Why don't you put everything in the same part of your pack each time? Then you'll always know where things are.' But she never did.

***

Hanoi

For the first time in nearly a month, we had to manhandle our packs. I dragged mine along the station platform to board the Reunification Express from Hue to Hanoi.

As we passed along the corridor, curious eyes followed us, some smiling, some curious, some cautious. The train was packed. We had to clamber over chickens squawking in baskets, squealing piglets, and children asleep, curled up at their mothers' feet. The Reunification Express travels so slowly it feels as if it would be quicker to walk, but we were comfortable in our compartment. I'd paid slightly more than the standard fare to avoid wooden seats.

We arrived in Hanoi late in the evening, and gave in to the temptation of a hotel located by a taxi driver.

Louise and I spent next day sightseeing, including the ever-so-serious Uncle Ho Mausoleum, where the queue wound slowly for over two hours, in silent respect, in front of the decaying corpse.

"No talking, no coughing, no smiling", a notice warned.

'No smiling?' Louise asked. 'Why would anyone want to smile?'

'Perhaps because he's dead,' I replied in a whisper, in case the policeman on duty was listening.

In the evening I decided to treat my family to a cultural experience.

230

'Oh my God! What's that horrible screeching?' Sara asked.

'What the hell is that?' Conrad yelled.

I had insisted we all went to a final, truly ethnic Vietnamese event. I hadn't reckoned on my not liking it. My not being able to bear it, in fact. The theatre was richly decorated in gold brocade, with heavy ruby-velvet curtains draped around a tiny booth. I felt as if I were about to watch a Punch and Judy show.

The puppets were cleverly made, and the performance highly skilled, but the high-pitched sing-song of the dialogue drove us to distraction. I still managed to fall asleep, my chin nodding its way slowly to my chest, until the fireworks at the end startled me awake. So much for one of Hanoi's not-to-be-missed experiences.

'Nothing like a bit of local culture, right? Okay, home for bed, early start again tomorrow.' I was hoping to draw attention away from the evening's failed cultural experience.

***

Crammed into the local chicken bus, we set off early next day for Halong Bay.

'Why do we have to go there?' asked Conrad. 'It's only going to be a load of islands, just like home.'

'Just wait and see, sunspot. And if you hate it, it's only for two nights.'

After we boarded the rib-sailed junk and had slipped away silently into the mists, we leaned over the wooden banister, captivated. Within an hour, the mist was replaced by an eerie clarity, a stillness, where nothing moved, and every karst islet was outlined in isolation. We swam off the side, in cold but clear water, to a peaceful lagoon echoing with bird calls, and caught sight of a kingfisher glistening at the water's edge.

I'd promised the Frenchman in Thailand we would come here, and I silently thanked him. I watched my children's rapt faces against the backdrop of emerald sea, jungle vegetation and limestone caves, heard the lapping of gentle waves against the wooden bow of our junk, and mentally wired those moments into my psyche.

***

'Only one more night in Vietnam after tonight. I'll have to say goodbye to Michael the day after tomorrow, Mum. Oh, what am I going to do? I'm going to miss him so much!'

I put my arms around her and tried to console her as she wept. There was nothing else for it; I could not let her lose a chance of happiness.

'Look, he's getting on with us all really well. If he wants to stay, I can pay for him as far as Australia, but he'll have to get a job- you all will- because you'll be keeping me for a couple of months when we get there. I can't get a working visa because of my great age. And, anyway, I'm going to take Sophie round Australia on one of those bus tour thingies. If Michael gets a job- and only if- I'll pay his way there. He'll have to save money for the rest of the journey if he wants to come with us when we move on.'

'Oh, Mummy, I do love you! Thank you, thank you, thank you!'

I had misgivings about this relationship. Michael was a fine enough young man, but I didn't like his hypocrisy. He would often nod and smile politely at one of Louise's remarks then turn to face the others with a glassy stare, which never failed to bring forth half-suppressed laughter.

'Alright, geezer?' Conrad approached me, grinning, not long after my conversation with Sara. 'What's this I hear about Michael staying on, then?'

'Do you mind? You've got Gecko with you and I thought...'

'No need to justify it to me, you make the decisions.'

***

We went out for our last dinner in Hanoi. Louise's eyes had lost their spark.

'Come on, what's up?' I asked.

'Oh, I don't know, just feel a bit down. I suppose I'm missing my mum. She would have been so proud of me.'

'Nil desperandum, Carruthers! She wouldn't want you to mope. She was a go-getter, and so are you. Look what you've done, launching yourself off on a trip like this. No wonder you're feeling a reaction. It all happened so quickly.'

'But Mum died years ago...'

'No, you dope! I don't mean a reaction to that. I mean a reaction to leaving your husband—my little brother, by the way. Come on, sing us one of your songs.'

'Oh, alright. "There was an old man called Michael Finnegan, he had whiskers on his chinegan"...'

Our fellow diners stared in bemused delight.

When the meals arrived, Sara enquired about a piece of gristle in her rice. 'What is that, please?'

'It is lickerman,' the waiter replied.

She paled, in puzzled silence. 'Mum? What did he say?'

'Ligament, darling. I'm not exactly sure what ligament is, but let's just say that I wouldn't eat it if I were you.'

'Gotcha, Mama, thanks for the warning.'

Bingo! No argument about food. Must be a first.

I sat on the low white wall outside the hotel early next morning, reading. I couldn't concentrate on my book. Sara and Michael were miserable, bickering in their room, the climate was stifling, and we all had slight headaches.

An echo of a bygone era, when this city was still elegant, rang for a second in my mind, and suddenly I didn't want to leave. I'd had what I came for: just a glimpse, a taste of the country.

I wished I'd had more time to absorb it, though; to just be there, without moving about. To sit like this and drift back and forward through time, to capture what was still eluding me. But it wasn't to be. Early next day we'd be in the air to Guangzhou, where another adventure awaited.

Please don't rush to leave, Lam Kieu. I wish I hadn't. If we ever meet again, I hope it will be in your own lovely country.

As a young woman, I had often lain awake, gazing at David, comforted by his presence and the knowledge that our three children were asleep in their rooms close by. I had feared that one day I would wake to find that it was all over—a past dream. It was unbearable, this gnawing doubt that all was not quite as well as I thought. I had tried to control my life—David called it manipulation—in an effort to ward off disaster. I even collected four-leaf clovers as an insurance against future lost luck.

I'd never felt really close to anyone, including my mum. I always felt there was something missing in me; something that other people had. I had to be some kind of freak. I was beginning to learn about myself only now, in middle age, with all this time to think. I had dreams about frantic attempts to clean a filthy room or, worse, nightmares when I would pick incessantly at the crumbling walls of a house, believing that once I had got rid of all the rot I could rebuild it, fresh and clean.

I looked at the flowers behind the wall, the crimson tenderness of their petals, the fragile, silken sheen of their stems, the intricacy of stamens. Suddenly everything now seemed new and fresh, like the first crocus bursting through the spring soil.

***

Next morning I looked for Conrad and Gecko, to give them an hour's notice of our departure from the hotel. I was surprised to discover that my son had slept in the same room as his sister and Michael.

From the state of his bed, I could tell that Gecko had not slept well. The sheet was pulled away from the edges of the bed, exposing the stained horsehair mattress, and the top coverlet

234

looked as if it had been through a prolonged tumble dryer programme. A cigarette was burning in the ashtray.

Gecko had slept with a hooker the night before, Conrad had informed me. They'd all tried to talk him out of it, but he was determined. Gecko was attempting to stuff his belongings into his pack when he saw me.

'You look like death on a plate, Jeremy.'

'Thanks, Rachael. Nice one.'

'I need to talk to you. I...'

'Shit, is this it, then? Is this when I go home?' he burst out. I couldn't bring myself to mention the hooker; he looked so crestfallen.

'It depends. What's that musty smell? Have you been doing bong hits in here?'

I know all the jargon, no flies on me.

He blinked at the sunlight blinding him through the open door. 'No, the people in the room next door were last night. I'm just getting ready to leave.'

'I want to talk to you about that, right enough.'

'I know, I have to go home now. I'll never forget what you've done for me.'

'Michael is staying on because he's promised to get a job in Australia. Can you promise me that you'll do the same?'

'For sure, yes, of course.'

In for a penny... 'Well, in that case I'll sub you till then. I won't buy you any fags or booze, or prostitutes, while we're at it! But I'll buy food and pay the rent for a flat in Cairns, where I think you should find jobs easily. You can get temporary working visas at your age. Is it a deal? If you don't get a job then I'll have to put you on a plane, because I won't be able to afford to keep you through the second part of the trip.' He looked up, with a stunned expression. 'No, don't say a word. Right now I'm angry with you for wasting my money and taking risks with your health. I promised your mum I'd look after you! So keep your mouth shut before I explode.'

'Hi Ma, all ready to be off?' Conrad smiled as he strode into the room.

Gecko slumped on his dishevelled bed and glowered at Conrad. 'Why did you let me do that? '

'We warned you, but you weren't having any of it. You were mad for it!'

'I'm gonna puke. That slag was disgusting. You didn't say anything; you're lying!'

'How about "She's bloody rough, look, she's got bruises, don't be a dick"? Or "It's not worth it, mate, you never know what you might pick up"?'

'I don't remember any of that!'

'That's because you were out of it. You're always out of it these days.'

I left them to it. Gecko had been acting oddly, probably drinking too much, I decided. I'd have to keep a closer eye on him, for his mum's sake, if not his own. I hoped that working would settle him down a bit and help him to grow up.

'It's remarkable, I can't find my lantipoons. I'm sure I put them with the rest of my underwear in that drawer.'

'Oh, Louise, you are surprised about this? Never a day goes by without you losing something!'

Stifling a yawn, Sara glanced up from her prone position on my bed.

'Perhaps they are in a parallel universe, eh, Mum? What's with the lantipoons anyway? What the hell are they?'

'Pantiloons, of course, my dear. Long johns, thermals, whatever you call them.'

'You've brought thermals to south-east Asia?' Sara looked horrified.

'Well, I didn't know what the climate would be like. In any event, it'll be winter when we get to Australia, so I'll probably need them.'

'I dread to think what else you've got in there. No wonder you can't find anything! Did you bring scarves, gloves and matching handbags?'

'Just watch it, young lady. Remember, I came out here in a rush. I didn't have time to think about what to bring, so I erred on the safe side.'

'On the heavy side, you mean.'

***

'Bargain!' Conrad held up his hand in a high five.

I had just offered the four youngsters the alternative of going on to Hong Kong together while Louise and I explored Yangshuo in Guangxi Province.

'I'll give you enough money for food and beers, and to pay for a cheap hotel, and we'll meet up in a week. Leave the name and address of the hotel at the Qantas desk at Kai Tak, like Louise did. Or you can email it to me.'

So it was goodbye to Vietnam; to the delicacy of the landscape and the dignity of the people. Nothing could have prepared me for the poignancy, purity and truth which rise from this land like an early morning mist, linger in patient faces, and sink again into the moist soil to rest with the ancestors until the next day. Nothing would erase from my mind its fragile, tender beauty, reflected forever in the eyes of its gentle people.

***

China

Guangzhou
The kids had gone ahead to Hong Kong. In Guangzhou, where we'd flown from Hanoi, we'd escorted them to the overnight ferry, after being driven to two incorrect terminals by a dozy taxi driver.

'This is beginning to feel like a plot. I'm getting paranoid,' Louise muttered. 'No one in this part of the world seems to know what they're doing.'

At the second terminal we had even disembarked, paid, and set off on foot to the ticket office, only to find we were on the wrong side of town. There was no one around, and I began to feel the by now familiar panic—lost in a strange, huge city without the language—but we hailed another taxi and eventually reached an insignificant building which looked more like a deserted yard than a ferry terminal.

I waved them goodbye. I tried to be positive. They would enjoy the freedom; the challenge. They'd complained about being shepherded around by me. They were together, four of them. Hong Kong was a civilized place. My friend Lyn lived there and they had her address. At the counter, I'd tried to ensure that the fare included cabin accommodation. I hugged them all and watched, trembling, as my children strolled away for a week in a setting as opposite to their home as could be imagined.

Please, universe, let them be safe. There will be no way of me finding out if they're okay. I fretted. Had I given them enough money? I had assumed Hong Kong would be cheap. What if I was wrong and they didn't have enough for a hotel and food? But then, Lyn would help if need be. Would they ask her, though? Another fine mess, perhaps?

All that was arranged was for them to leave a message at the airport once they had an address, and we chose a day, either side of which Louise and I would turn up at the address.

'Don't you worry, babe.' Michael had smiled at Sara. 'We're gonna have a ball in Hong Kong! I'll make sure we're alright, Rachael. I've been to Hong Kong before, with my parents. I know my way around a bit.'

***

Yangshuo, Guangxi Province, People's Republic of China (I like writing that!)
Dear Sophie

Although I was nervous about coming to China, I couldn't have been more wrong—the people are very helpful. We stayed in a fantastic hotel in Canton (Guangzhou in Chinese). It was supposed to be a budget hotel at £10 a night each, but it was one of the most luxurious hotels I've ever stayed in! Everything in Canton is HUGE, except the people. Our hotel foyer was the size of a leisure centre, with enormous chandeliers and marble floors. Outside is a lovely big fountain with all different colours of water sprays. Throughout Vietnam and here in Guangzhou, they still have Christmas decorations up; there is even a tree here! We had dinner at the China Hotel after seeing the others off onto the overnight ferry to Hong Kong. We ate in a "food street", like a mall of restaurants. They bring you a little bag containing a moist towel to wipe your fingers, probably because you make such a mess with the chopsticks. The food was magnificent and Chinese beer is really good, at 50p a pint. Some things are really expensive, though. In our hotel there is a row of food stalls and they were asking over £4.00 for two nectarines, so we put them back. We flew here to Guangzhou from Hanoi. When we landed, Louise went over to an ATM to get cash, and the machine ate her card! Fortunately, she has another one but if that happened to me, we'd all be sunk.

Not long now!
XXXXXXXXXXXXXXX
PS I was amazed how easy it was to find a post office here. In some places, it's taken me hours to find one (your brother and sister think I've developed an addiction to them) but in this village in the middle of China there is a huge one. Admittedly, you have to tie your letter up with string and it gets sealed with hot red wax, but at least you can't really miss the post office. I suppose it's because there's lots of tourists here.
Love love love love love, xxx

***

The Pearl River ferry from Guangzhou to Wuzhou had docked. From Wuzhou we would take a bus to Yangshuo. We boarded via a narrow gangplank.

'Good Lord, the weight of my pack is going to topple me into the river.' Louise sounded genuinely anxious.

Boarding the ferry was easy. We only needed the name of the village—Yangshuo—to achieve the linguistic task. We got to the top of the steps leading from the rusty embarkation deck up to the accommodation deck.

'You are not going to believe this, Louise. Look.'

I counted one hundred and thirty eight "bunk beds" on the floor of an open dormitory, aka the deck. Everyone would sleep about ten centimetres away from their neighbour. The divisions between the "beds"—which were either just the floorboards, or a wide shelf one metre above the deck floor—were upturned planks of fifteen centimetres high. At one end of the bed was a rolled up mat (there was no pillow) and a wood-framed sash porthole, so you could look out onto the river as the ferry sailed.

'Well, this has to be the most unusual accommodation I've ever had!' Louise took off her pretty straw hat, allowing her wavy hair to fall to her chin, the back layers still tied with a pale pink ribbon.

There was a row of unisex toilets lined up like sentinels on the deck below, which were continually flushed clean by running water. It was impossible to sit down as they were more like urinals, and there was no room between the swing door and the tiny bowl placed halfway up the wall. So we had to semi-squat, with slightly bent knees, and stare out at passers-by over the top of the half-sized stable door, our nether regions enjoying a cold wash from the running water 'This is, er, unusual, too.' We sat in the restaurant, not sure what we were eating.

'Let's just be grateful it's not poisoning us,' Louise said.

'Are you sure about that? We haven't digested it yet.' I tried to manipulate chopsticks to pick up great globs of greasy skin, bits of bone and slimy greens.

A hundred pairs of eyes were on us, observing our every gesture with blatant confusion.

An enormous television set at one end of the deck was the only piece of furniture other than the tables and chairs. I tried to avert my eyes to blot out the gruesome images on the screen, to prevent them from encouraging the churning in my intestines, but it was impossible. We watched swirling swords, and flying chopped limbs pumping blood, whilst the hero charged at full pelt, screaming and gesticulating wildly.

I opened my eyes in the early morning light and peeped out of my porthole. The river was grey and silent. Sampans, junks and barges slid past; the muddy shore was bare apart from an occasional bamboo shack or pagoda. I lay there, looking out at the scene, slightly in awe and inwardly thrilled that I was lying on a Chinese ferry, able to see with my own eyes sights which I had spent years dreaming about, trying to imagine. Now I could smell, feel and hear it all for myself. It was real.

Breakfast was watery rice porridge.

'This is pretty foul. I've got an idea. I've got some Coffeemate powder I purloined from a flight. Let's sprinkle it on. It might make it taste creamy and more bearable.'

'Hey, good for you, Louise. You'll make an intrepid traveller yet.'

The only Westerner we saw on that ferry was a Frenchman who spoke fluent Cantonese. After docking, he pointed out the way to the bus station.

The walk from the jetty revealed open-fronted shops and a market, where men dozed, stretched out on the top of the counters, amongst the produce. People sat on the pavement behind flat baskets, offering vegetables for sale. Girls in tight jeans carried pink umbrellas to protect themselves from the sun.

'You look shattered. I'll go on and get the tickets. Wait here with the bags, okay?'

Louise nodded and sank onto the dusty pavement.

'Yangshuo?' I repeated until someone pointed to one of the ticket desks.

I opened my purse like a trusting child opens its arms. The ticket clerk waved in the direction of a line of ancient wrecks in a dusty yard.

When I returned from the bus station, Louise was in tears. 'Within minutes of you leaving, I was surrounded by local people, who kept pointing and yelling in Mandarin,' she wailed.

'Well, what did you expect? They wouldn't be speaking English...'

'They were shouting at me, Rachael. One woman came up and pulled at my rings. I think she was trying to steal them.'

'No, I expect she was trying to advise you to take them off in case of thieves. I've told you about that before.'

'Well, it was all remarkably scary. I couldn't even move because of the bags.'

'Keep your chin up, Carruthers.'

We climbed aboard a ruined, rusty wreck, and found two forward-facing plastic seats with horsehair upholstery jutting up through the holes. Most of the others had been twisted on their axis through anything from forty-five to one hundred and thirty-five degrees, offering a variety of viewing angles.

'Yangshuo?' I asked. The driver waved us aboard. He turned to inspect our tickets. Cigarette fumes and stale alcohol assaulted our nostrils.

'I don't think this thing will even start, let alone transport us up into the mountains for a seven-hour journey. Just wait till the kids hear about our luxury coach journey in China,' I said.

As we waited, the bus filled up with locals, all smoking. The air was thick after ten minutes. When there was no clean air left to breathe, the driver ignited some machinery bearing no resemblance to an engine. The bus lurched forward then stopped. Five minutes later, we almost had whiplash injuries from jerking backwards and forwards as off we went, through the crowded streets and winding narrow alleys, stared at by curious eyes, onward, out of town into the hills, past pine trees, ferns, bamboo and clematis.

Rice terraces reminded me of the enclosures of medieval England, but shaped like ornamental ponds. Workers toiled in submerged fields, up to their waists in mud. The area was rich in vegetation and foliage, and very green. Farmers clad in coats and boots against the misty chill used ox-drawn ploughs, or hand ploughs without cattle.

We passed straw igloos on stilts. People got on and off the bus carrying small trees, or live chickens in bamboo leaf cages. Everybody shouted. The driver crunched the gears every time he changed them, and three times during the journey he did a U-turn, drove back for ten minutes, then without explanation turned round again to carry on along the bumpy road.

'My teeth are going to fall out; they're getting so loose from all this being thrown about! I'm glad I don't wear dentures. They'd end up out of the window!'

I loved Louise's sense of humour, and reminded myself to think of that next time she delayed our departure.

'Why do you think we've stopped?' she asked. 'What the hell was that?'

A loud boom rang out as workmen dynamited the road. We did another U-turn and drove across potholes, then turned off down a mud track. I was sure the bus would get stuck and we would have to get out and push. Every now and then, I enquired tentatively, 'Yangshuo?' which was greeted with a shake of the head and a "how can you be so pathetic?" look.

After six hours of banging and crashing, the bus screeched to a halt. A young man clambered aboard, covered in blood, shouting, and obviously in shock. He rode for ten minutes, explained his predicament to anyone interested, and got off abruptly at the next village. There was no sign of a medical establishment; only three huts and a garage. I wished I could understand what was going on.

High in the mountains on a winding road, we were enjoying a blast of fresh clean air through the ever open windows—no glass in any of them—when a tyre burst. There was a bang, and the bus veered across the road, slid out of control for a few seconds and came to a halt, kilometres from anywhere. Everyone got off and stood on spongy ground by the roadside, enjoying the fresh smell of soil and leaves in the drizzle.

For several minutes, the driver stood looking at the tyre, scratching his head in bewilderment. All of us passengers watched in silence as he crawled underneath and pulled out a rubber hose with which he inflated the tyre temporarily from an air supply under the bus. Louise clambered down a densely overgrown, slippery, steep, muddy slope to relieve herself. She picked her way down carefully but slipped, and within seconds was sliding down on her bottom, ending up inches away from a local woman squatting with diarrhoea. Shaken by this near miss, she pulled herself back up the slope using branches and hastily joined the other passengers for re-embarkation.

'I've just had a close encounter of the turd kind.' She was trembling.

The driver got back on board and drove very slowly down the mountain, the tyre gradually deflating until we could hear the screech of the metal rim on the road. After an hour, he pulled in to a repair station. We were ushered into an adjoining roadside café shack whilst the tyre was being fixed. Everything in the buffet smelled like cough syrup.

'What's this? I'm hungry.' I tasted a piece of what looked like sausage, then turned to look around for somewhere to sit.

'Oh, good Lord, look at this!' My jaw dropped when I took in the scene around us. As my mouth opened a half-chewed piece of the impostor sausage landed on my knees. 'Now I've seen everything.'

Seated on low stools in a dark corner of this roadside café, in this remote town, a group of locals sat entranced before a tiny black and white portable television, transfixed by the sight of Terence Stamp clad in a gaudy, gorgeous dress, miming to Abba's "Dancing Queen" as the film "Priscilla, Queen of the Desert" played out, subtitled in Cantonese.

***

Yangshuo

The journey, which should have taken seven hours, lasted twelve, and when we finally arrived at eleven at night, we both swayed for twenty minutes afterwards. But, joy of joys, the driver had dumped us in front of a modern hotel, with heating.

'Hey, Rachael, look at the notice on our wall. We've been warned.'

I walked over to read: "beware for smoking preventing conflagration".

'Nothing about this country will surprise me from now on, 'Louise said.

'We badly need this warm room after the cold draughts in the bus. Let's go and find a hot drink.'

We sat drinking chocolate with brandy in "M C Blues Café", where the owner, Jimmy, spoke English and served Western food. With relief, we ordered burger and chips.

'I'll never be snooty about Western food again.' I welcomed the familiarity with relief. If anyone had told me I would ever be glad to eat a beefburger, I would have laughed. Look at me now, relishing every bite. I wanted to immerse myself in Chinese culture. Forget it!'

By now, we both craved the company of other Europeans. We hadn't seen a Western face in days. There were lots of other travellers in the café, full of stories, advice and friendship, accompanied by the familiar music of Dire Straits, U2 and REM.

We went back next day for an enormous breakfast. Louise had enough to feed three people. As the mist lifted, I looked out of the window for the first time. The scenery was from the land of fantasy fiction. A giant troll might appear, or a prince seeking a lovely maiden to rescue, or a hero on his way to slay a dragon.

The village was surrounded by tall, odd-shaped peaks, covered with trees, reaching directly down to the roadside. Each hill was individual, rising out of the flat surrounding land like a huge molar. The tops were shrouded in mist, giving the whole scene an eerie, mystical appearance. I had seen paintings of this area of China, and always thought they were horribly exaggerated. Now I could see for myself that not only are they realistic, but they cannot ever do justice to the strange karst formations that spring up, in some places like a row of serrated teeth, in others, shaped like animals. I walked outside to look around while Louise was chomping on eggy toast.

'This feels like being in a painting, or in a magical land from a children's book,' Louise commented when she joined me.

'Apart from the weather, though, eh?'

It was pouring with rain. Mud splashed up our legs. The streets shone like mirrors, reflecting the peculiar shapes of the landscape. Everyone was plodding around in waterproofs and boots. Yet I couldn't help but be captivated.

'I hope to God we don't see many dead dogs. What was it they were called on Jimmy's menu?' asked Louise.

'Japanese baby, in the snakes and rats section. It's not okay to have dog on the menu in case tourists get offended, but Japanese babies? No problem!'

Turnips, squash, spring onions, tubers and greens were laid out for sale on the side of the road. There were a couple of canvas tents propped up against a concrete wall, with a "bike for rent" sign outside, but no sign of any bikes. Another Western-style café called "Planet Yangshuo" sported a bright yellow painted board displaying the menu, which included "Alcoholic—we got plenty" and "Jerry's Orgasmic Pancakes".

We separated after arranging to meet for a coffee in the crazy-sounding café. I wanted to look around and Louise wanted to find a cash machine.

'I've just been to the bank, Rachael, and I met a woman in there called Li. She acts as a guide, apparently, and lives from tips only. Good for her; quite enterprising. She's learned enough English to make her living and escape from work in the fields. Remarkable.'

Li was pretty, with a lively, intelligent face full of smiles. I liked her instantly. Of course, she was hoping for our custom, but she never made this obvious.

246

'I can take you up to Moon Hill tomorrow morning. You will see lovely views over Yangshuo and the countryside around.'

We had nothing else planned so agreed a time and a place, and went off in search of souvenirs. I wanted to get my sandals from Goa stitched, thinking it wouldn't cost much.

'How much? That's three times what they cost! Just keep them for yourself. I'm not paying that much. They're hardly worth anything.'

The street cobbler looked crestfallen.

'Tell you what, I'll give you half. Okay?'

He reluctantly accepted my offer.

By the time I went to collect them, I'd had a fit of guilt and paid his asking price. What had I been thinking of? They cost virtually nothing, so I was paying three times nothing. They were so thoroughly stitched, they'd hold together forever.

Our excursion began in a heavy downpour, via the thirteen-hundred-year-old Banyan tree at Chuanyan. We took motorbike taxis, with covered sidecar, to the base of the hill.

'Phew! I've just counted eight hundred steps!' Louise exhaled, wiping her wet hair out of her eyes. 'We're over half way up, though.'

By the time we reached the top we were drenched, but the view was spectacular, even through the mist and rain.

The other hills looked like an army of spectres which had been frozen en route. The fields below were sodden, shining brown mud in a mosaic of shapes. The river snaked its way through them, a few trees dotted here and there. Every metre of land was cultivated. After an hour's walk down, with willow and fern brushing against our faces, we tramped through the deep mud to Li's house, where she introduced her family.

Mum-in-law prepared duck, pork sausage, rice, vegetables and fresh green bamboo shoots on a tiny stove in a corner of the room.

'Take these, they are gifts for you.' Li handed us a soft brass bracelet each, engraved with the Cantonese for "good health and long life".

247

'They were made for my future grandchildren, but I had too many made. It is impossible to have so many grandchildren in China now. Our children will go to school until they are twenty, but the family has to pay. Most people borrow money from the government for this. This house is new. Our old family house finally fell down last year. We own the house, but we have to pay a fee to the government for it. It is not like a mortgage, as we have to pay it forever, but we have the security of being able to pass the house on to our family.'

After dinner, I went outside to the communal village toilet.

'We very proud of this. Not many villages have one.'

It was situated in a large concrete barn. There was an open trench, dug out of the soil, with a plank placed strategically over it for sitting, legs dangling into the pit below. The smell was overpowering. There was no running water.

'How does that all work?' I asked.

'We bury the faeces every now and then, and reposition the plank over a fresh area. Behind our house is a big cavern called Buddha Water Cave,' Li said. 'You want to see it?'

We were too wet, cold and tired to visit it, so plodded wearily back through the mud, the path lined with earth walls which were collapsing in the downpour. We had to walk along the top, as the mud on the path was deeper than our boots. The bus ride back into Yangshuo took only fifteen minutes.

'How about collapsing into our favourite café for a huge piece of chocolate cake and a glass of brandy?' Louise sometimes had some great ideas.

'Sounds like a good plan. And, while we're in thinking mode, why don't we move into the youth hostel opposite the bus station? I reckon there'll be more atmosphere there than in the hotel.'

'Your room is upstairs, the last on the right.' The hostel proprietor raised his eyes for a second from the room chart on his counter. In the front doorway, a skinny dog sniffed at a rubbish pile.

'Hmm, it's going to be very noisy in here. We'll hear all the din from people outside,' I complained to Louise.

'Well, the only noise I can hear is our washing!' Our wet, rain-soaked clothes were dripping from the makeshift washing line Louise had strung along a wall. The drops hammered onto the floor.

We wandered along the street to "our" café. Breakfast was not included in the hostel room price.

'Ow! My knees are aching from the climb yesterday. How about you, Louise?'

'Not too bad, remarkably.' She paused. 'You know, Rachael, there are loads of other people here. I bumped into a group of Australians, some English and even some Americans. There are so many people travelling around the world you can hardly believe it. Have you ordered breakfast? I must just nip to the loo. Order for me if you don't mind. Anything recognizable!'

She emerged after a minute. 'Rachael, you have to go into that loo! It's hilarious!'

On the toilet wall was a carefully hand-painted sign stating "no poo" alongside a sketch of a turd with a big red cross through it.

***

It was still raining next morning.

'Okay, boat day, come rain or come shine.' Louise said, looking up to the grey sky.

We had planned a boat trip down the River Li, hoping to hire cycles to get back from the nearest village, Xingping. We stepped onto a flat barge, painted red and yellow. The river was quite wide in places, but we could see both shores, lined with bamboo groves. The landscape was even weirder upstream. Some of the mountains had distinctive shapes, like Dragon Head Hill, Camel Hill or Carp Hill. Most of them looked like camels' humps reflected in the river.

'Unreal,' was all I could say.

We watched as a cormorant fisherman attached one of his bird's feet with string to his long, narrow bamboo boat. He put a ring around its neck to prevent it from swallowing the fish. The bird ducked its head into the river and pulled out a fish which the man threw into a storage basket. After a few minutes, he gave the bird its share of the catch, temporarily loosening the string.

'Wow, doesn't it look weird, seeing a cormorant bobbing up and down with a fish in its beak?' I looked at Louise, who was as enchanted as I was. 'At home, we're so used to seeing them flying free then diving from great heights into the sea. It's just so odd to see them attached to a river boat, working as a team with a man.'

Water buffalo wallowed in the shallows.

'I have definitely fallen in love with them! They have such beautiful faces, haven't they?'

Louise nodded.

We had passed a few other barges full of tourists, almost all Chinese, gazing transfixed at the strange formations along the route. Houseboats, complete with washing lines, lined the banks.

'Oh, Louise, I feel as if I'm in another world!'

'Yes, me too, and not for the first time on this trip.'

There was no jetty at Xingping so we had to hop ashore. We walked through the market, past a few empty stalls. A couple of people plodded through the rain in wellington boots, carrying umbrellas, but most of the streets were completely deserted, and many of the buildings had been boarded up. Villagers stared.

'I thought they were supposed to be used to foreign visitors here?' I wondered aloud.

Sacks of grain were piled against exterior walls, along with bicycles and piles of rubbish. Old-fashioned telegraph poles leaned drunkenly.

'Ooh look, Xingping's one and only telly aerial!' Louise pointed to a piece of metal hanging lopsidedly from the eave of a concrete dwelling.

'You hungry? Let's eat. There's a café. At least, I think it is.'

Inside, white walls and a Western fridge looked completely out of place. We pointed to a bowl of chicken and rice on one of the other tables. This was greeted with a frown and a glare of disapproval by both diner and café owner alike.

'Dunno what's wrong with them,' Louise said. 'We're only indicating what we want to eat. Not exactly a crime.'

'Maybe we've just committed some terrible cultural gaffe.'

'Oh well, better that than starve.'

We ate quickly, slightly unnerved by the hostile glares of our fellow diners, and left hurriedly.

'Shall we give up on the bikes idea, Rachael? Look, there's a bus station.' The rain was still teeming.

The road was long and straight. We sat on hard wooden seats, far too small for two European-sized bottoms, amongst crowds of locals going about their business. The women smiled; the men looked serious. We drove through green bamboo groves, passed through villages of straw huts raised on stilts, as children ran and played in the fields amongst workers bent low.

'Aren't we lucky to be here, getting a glimpse of what life must be like for billions of people?'

'Sara and Conrad and co wouldn't appreciate it though. I wonder how they're getting on,' I replied.

We're a bit like birds of passage, I thought. *Driven by optimism and curiosity, moved on by some kind of energy force from one destination to the next, stopping briefly in each new country. I am done for: I will never be able to give this life up.*

***

To: Wendy McKintock
From: Rachael Green
Subject: Giant sheep
Sometime in May—I think!!
Hi
I'm in a village called Yangshuo, in China, after the weirdest boat trip ever. This place is quite famous among backpackers

251

apparently. Don't ask me how I came to hear of it. Seeing as how you teach art and architecture, I had to tell you about it. The mountains here are really strange. You know those weird Chinese paintings of tall, thin hills that I always thought were just rubbish? Well, the hills here are really like that! Those paintings depict real places! We saw men using birds to catch fish: that's why there's so many in the paintings. And the houses are three-sided, with the front open to the street, so we can see right in, like in Vietnam. They're built between brick pillars, their roofs made of wood or corrugated iron. When there is an upstairs, it's marked by a heavily carved wooden balcony three quarters of the way up the height of the building, flush to the outer walls. You probably know the correct architectural term. From the front, the houses look like rows of letter Hs. They could have been homes or stables—probably both. The brick is exposed through peeling whitewash. They all look dilapidated. I suppose it's made worse by the endless rain turning them a depressing grey. The pavements, where they exist, are wide, cracked flagstones. Over one of the balconies, I can see long strands of rice noodles, looking like rope, I guess hanging out to dry. It looks as if a sheep has come along and left half its wool on the poles, though I've never seen a two-metre tall sheep, so I guess that theory is shot to hell! Anyway, gotta go. The connection will probably time out in a minute. Next stop Oz.

See you,
R, x

***

Ping An

'It says here, "The drive from Yangshuo to Ping An takes under four hours in good weather and traffic conditions, and the driver of the Golden Lion bus might play cassettes of traditional folk songs to help pass the time. The route takes you via the regional capital, Guilin, past subtropical trees such as chestnut, kumquat,

252

peach and orange, and you will pass some of the twenty thousand breathtaking limestone peaks in the area. The name Guilin means forest, and the yellow and white flowers of the cassia trees adorn its main boulevards." We could stop there on the way. We could do it, you know, if nothing goes wrong. The rice terraces near there are really famous. Well worth seeing.'

Louise eyed me sceptically while adjusting her headscarf.

We were heading by bus for the world-famous Dragon's Backbone Rice Terraces - Longji in Mandarin Chinese - just north of Guilin, for a whistle-stop visit before heading back to Hong Kong.

We decided to break the journey with a quick stopover at Guilin hospital to see the Department of Traditional Chinese Medicine, where you can pick up haemorrhoid killer pills, skin itch killer capsules or some sinew-bone regulation liquid. Never know when you might need them.

'Hey, Louise, I might get young smarty-pants Michael a tub of pills to invigorate yang and improve his sexual performance, or better still, some constipation tablets. I'm surprised they sell those. That's not usually the problem in China!'

We visited the electro qigong room, where one hardy visitor insisted on trying the shock treatment, having assured us that he really was suffering from "unhappiness"—the prerequisite for undergoing the therapy. He stood against a wall of peeling white paint while the doctor held onto two bare wires. A second doctor switched on the power and, after a few seconds, the "live" doctor grabbed the tourist's hands. We could almost feel the charge as the patient jolted for a second or two, after which he assured us that he felt much better and thanked the doctor profusely. I wondered if the British National Health Service might send an observer to learn this stunning technique.

We had paid a guide to accompany us. He suggested a visit to Guilin's tiger and bear park. After strolling past huge compounds where hundreds of tigers loped in a bored fashion, he called me to him. 'You come now. Time for show.'

Something alerted me. 'What show?'

'Oh, very good show. You will like. Come follow.' He grinned excitedly. He ushered us towards a stadium where an excited crowd was shoving its way along the rows to get ringside seats.

'What is the show exactly?' I enquired again, but before he could reply, I heard a low mooing from the other side of the stadium and immediately yelled, 'Come on, Louise, we need to leave. Right now!'

Startled at my unusually dictatorial manner, she shot to her feet instantly. As we hurriedly left the stadium, I glanced over my shoulder to see a cow being winched into the arena. We heard its shrieks and the charging roars of the tigers as we hurried out through the gates. Feeding time at the zoo will never appeal to me again.

The hapless guide was quite bewildered. 'This very special show in China. Many come. Very good, tigers tearing cow. Very funny, ha, ha.'

I began to shiver. Whether from the shock or the cold, I couldn't tell. 'Can you tell us how to get to Ping An, please?'

'Ah, yes. Bus. Over there, look!'

'Is that bus going to Ping An?' I turned to Louise. 'A bit too much of a coincidence, I reckon.'

'No, no. Bus go Sanjiang. Very good hotel there. You stay. You go next day Ping An. Small bus at hotel.'

'Will you please wait with us till the bus comes and tell the driver to drop us at San...what did you call it?'

'Jiang. Mean river. Okay, okay. I tell.' I forgave him his tiger show gaffe.

Sanjiang was drab. Lorries trundled slowly past us, belching smoke. The "very good" hotel had an impressive frontage and foyer, but inside—surprise, surprise—nothing worked. No water, no heating. Thin, faded cotton sheets barely covered the stained mattresses, and the chairs were too rickety to sit on.

'There's a restaurant downstairs. Let's take our chances.'

But the restaurant was closed. We asked at reception where we could find food. A thin, tight-lipped girl handed me a menu card in Chinese characters.

'Could we please have chicken and rice with green vegetables?'

'Wait. Give money. Come soon.'

'Aha, I think she's ordering food from somewhere else. How funny, getting a Chinese takeaway in China!' I laughed.

The chicken was less than lukewarm by the time it arrived, clearly from a restaurant some distance away. That night, I slept fitfully, cold and still hungry.

Next morning we made our way to a pretty fountain in a park opposite the hotel, where we had been told the Ping An bus would stop. A minibus pulled up.

'Do you think this is a private bus? There aren't any other passengers. How much do you think it will cost?'

'I don't know, Louise. We're just going to have to bite the bullet and hope for the best. We've come too far to turn back now. And we've been lucky so far.'

We never found out what the fare was: we gestured payment but the driver merely shrugged, yanked the handbrake and cranked the gearstick up and forwards.

Rocks and small boulders were strewn across the road, evidence of recent landslides, and I began to feel anxious. As we trundled along among azalea bushes, we glimpsed Yao minority women in colourful red and black embroidered costumes, their long hair piled on their heads.

The engine made a grunting sound, and the bus lurched to a stop.

'Oh no, not another breakdown.' Louise looked apprehensive.

'Stay in the bus, in case it's robbers.'

The driver turned to point at us then at the road in front. A pile of rocks blocked our way. He handed us a shovel each and we began to dig. After half an hour, the rocks had gone but, by now, it was teeming with rain. We boarded again. The bus wheels span in the mud.

'I know! I know what to do!' Louise hopped down onto the road and crossed over to a small bush.

'Help me break a couple of branches off, Rachael! We need to give the wheels something to grip.'

The driver looked on, leaning against his bus, smoking.

'He's not even going to help, is he?' I tried to look as outraged as possible without making him angry. He finished his cigarette and slowly climbed into his cab, where he leaned forward, crossed his arms on top of the steering wheel, and rested his head on his hands. 'I don't believe this! He's going to have a sleep now!'

We laid the branches right in front of the wheels and, sure enough, it worked. The bus lurched forward and, for a minute, I thought he was going to drive away without us, but he slowed to a halt and we jumped aboard.

We drove for another few minutes and pulled into a large car park.

'He let us do all that work and he could have walked along here in twenty minutes and fetched help. What a bastard.'

'Careful, Rachael, watch out, there's a young girl behind you.' Louise turned to the girl. 'Oh, your hair is lovely! Um, sorry. Do you speak English?'

She giggled in response.

'Your hair. Very long. Very beautiful.'

'They never cut it, apart from when it reaches the floor, when the cut section is woven into the new growth.' An older woman, whom I took to be a tourist guide—everybody here seemed to double as a tourist guide—approached.

'Sounds a bit like our hair extensions,' I said.

'Only women with children are allowed to take their hair down to show visitors,' the woman explained.

'That part doesn't sound a bit like our hair extensions.'

'How come you speak such good English? Your accent is perfect.'

'Thank you. I went to university in Guilin. Here in China, everyone must learn English if they want to get a good job. But for many it is very difficult. I have been lucky to get a guide job working here. We are beginning to get more foreign visitors, but it's mostly Chinese who come here. The terraces are very famous.'

We arrived at the foot of a gentle slope, where our guide friend left us. It was a ten-minute walk up the hill to the five-hundred-year-old village, or you could ride in a sedan chair to the top for a few yuan per person. Ping An is the closest village to the terraces. The name is supposed to mean peace, but the villagers pushed, shoved, shouted and screamed in order to get our business.

Some offered to carry our bags in a bamboo basket and, despite the later total chaos at the top to decide who carried whose bag in which basket, we were glad to take advantage of the service: the steps were steep. I climbed into the sedan, feeling guilty. If I felt bad then I felt a lot worse on the way up as my sedan bearers struggled under my weight.

Louise, being smaller and lighter, reached the top first, and smiled at me indulgently. 'Think of it like this. You're giving them money they couldn't have got otherwise.'

We ate a lunch of dark brown and green fern. We were told it was good for curing cancer. Afterwards, we hired a local guide for two days and walked further up the hill to "Number One Viewing Spot", where we looked down onto the spectacular rice terraces which apparently date from the Ming dynasty over seven hundred years ago.

We followed a path along one of the terraces, passing shrines where ribbons and gifts remained from a festival the year before. Depending on the season, the local terrace guide told us, the surfaces vary from reflective mirrors when raining, frozen white ribbons when iced over, bright green when sprouting young crops, to swaying streams of grass when the rice is fully grown. There are hundreds of them, rising eight hundred metres, a major construction feat, even nowadays.

From Ping An, we made our way back downhill to a bus and travelled along a road which had more potholes than surface to the Wind and Rain Bridge, an exotic structure built entirely from wood. Seventy-eight metres long, it was built without nails, and covered to protect users, hence its name. Five pagoda-shaped towers rose from the wooden floor, where hawkers squatted beside their wares in the hope of catching the eye of the few tourists.

I stopped at a wooden stall to examine a jar of dark liquid, thinking it might be honey. With amazing speed, my purse was open, money taken out, and the jar shoved into my hand. An old woman nodded at me, grinning in encouragement as she mimed opening the jar. After a couple of easy turns of the lid, I saw what it contained: pickled, cockroach-like insects. There were dozens of similar jars on sale; clearly a local speciality. To my horror, I realized that I was expected to taste, right there and then.

After Laos, I didn't dare risk an international incident, so I gamely stuck my thumb and forefinger in and pulled one out. I closed my eyes and opened my mouth, briefly recalling what I used to say to the kids when they were little: 'Open your mouth and close your eyes, and you shall have a nice surprise.'

Should I swallow whole, or crunch? I decided to crunch, in case I choked. The liquid was sweet; the corpse tasted of dust mingled with what I thought could be formaldehyde. When I could avoid swallowing no longer, I gulped it down, to rapturous applause and pats on the back. I had clearly undergone some kind of rite of passage.

'The Dong People Autonomous Region has its own language and traditions,' continued the guide. 'South-east China is populated by nearly three million of them. Many of the women still wear traditional black dresses trimmed with blue, pink and purple.'

We stumbled into one of their stockade villages where a small show was in progress. A selection of local dances and music was on offer and, at the end, we were invited to join in. A band struck up a winsome-sounding tune on a variety of panpipes and percussion as two rows of dancers stood in line, facing each other and bent low, holding two long poles each. They clapped these together in time to the music, and the dance involved stepping over each pole in time to avoid having your legs caught between them.

'Go on, have a go, Rache.'

It was harder than it looked. 'I'm going to have bruised ankles, for sure.'

On our return journey to Guilin, we passed several ancient waterwheels, still functioning to irrigate the land. Fishermen lined the shore, and giggling schoolchildren ran out from their classrooms to wave at us briefly before running back inside. At Guilin Airport, we paid our "airport construction fee" and boarded our flight, during which we were served with a packet marked "delicious food".

'What is in the packet, please?' I asked.

'It delicious,' the stewardess replied with a patient look.

'Yes, but what is it exactly?'

'It delicious.' She smiled again sweetly.

I never did find out, but the biscuity-looking snack tasted nothing like the promise of its name. It should have been called "tasteless food" instead.

As we rose into the air en route to Guangzhou, I looked down at the fields and houses of rural China and felt as if I had just returned from travelling a hundred years back in time.

***

Dear Sophie,

Well, darling, I've just phoned you. Really excited about seeing you! Glad you remembered to check your passport. Louise and I took our lives in our hands and flew here to Hong Kong on China Airlines. They apparently have the world's worst safety record. In the flight magazine, the president was proudly announcing a whole eighteen months of accident-free air travel!!

We simply couldn't face another long-distance rattling bus. We landed, grateful to be alive, after flying from Guilin via Guangzhou. We had arranged for the others to leave a message at the Qantas desk in Kai Tak Airport, so once we knew where they were, we taxied here and have now all met up again. We're staying in a bit of a dump, but it's clean and about the only budget place in H-K. The rooms are tiny. You can't stand; you have to crawl off your bed to the doorway, as the floor space is taken up with your pack—and Louise and I left our big packs at the left luggage place in the airport! We spent the day eating McDonald's (the others have been living on McDonald's for the last week as it is so cheap and right opposite the hotel), looking around the shops (I am trying to get a laptop), and watching a programme called "Hercules" on the telly. In the evening, we went for a beer in an English-style pub. A real taste of Hong Kong!! Louise carried her bag of dirty clothes with her, hoping to find a laundry, so we have nicknamed her the "bag lady". I probably shouldn't tell you this but there is a shop here called "Wan Long Phuc"!!! Don't you dare tell your dad. By the way, the Chinese don't spit as much as the Indians. Thought you'd like to know! I can barely contain my excitement that, in just over a week's time, I will finally see you walk through the arrivals hall at Sydney Airport. I am longing for that moment.

Your Mama

xxxxxxxxxxxxxxxxxxxx

***

Hong Kong
'Phew! It's eighty-nine degrees according to that sign.' Louise wiped her brow.

Michael stood watching the swirling crowds who busied themselves in and out of Hong Kong's Kai Tak Airport. 'Journey okay?'

'Coming in to land was amazing. I could see into people's windows. I could almost see what Mrs Wong was cooking in her wok!'

'Thanks for meeting us, Michael. How's it been for you all?' Louise asked.

'Okay, okay. Not bad, not bad.' How enlightening. 'The others are waiting in town. No point paying more taxi fares than we needed,' he went on.

'Taxi! Chungking Mansions, please.' Despite his sullen response, or perhaps because of it, I felt relieved

Hey, I've done a good job, I thought. *They survived on their own for a week in a foreign environment. I can let them go, leave them, and they'll cope. Perhaps I'm not such a bad mother, after all.*

What about Sophie, though? How will she cope with that massive long flight, all alone? God, I hope it doesn't traumatize her forever. She might end up hating flying. Someone might be horrible to her; frighten her. Oh God, what if the plane crashes? What if...

'Here we are!' Sara, Conrad and Gecko were smiling, waving in welcome.

'Well done, you guys! Where are we staying?'

'Some dump of a place with minute rooms, but it's cheap and close to all the shops. Called Something or Other Mansions,' Conrad answered.

'Yes, Michael's told me the name already, but where is it exactly'?

They all pointed at the building in front of us.

'Oh, I see. Yes, it is a bit shabby. Oh well, it's only for one more night then we're off to a proper home. How bad can it be inside? Hmm, don't answer that. You didn't contact Lyn at all?'

'No, Ma. We didn't need to. We had fun sorting things out for ourselves. Michael's been brilliant, too. He found us the rooms.'

Sai Kung in the New Territories was where we were to stay for a few days with my friend who had moved here ten years before.

Lyn's house was ultra-modern, minimalist, shining with glass and steel, pastel colours offsetting quality ornaments collected from her worldwide travels. A framed photograph of Ayers Rock at dawn dominated the main wall; a stone statue of one of the kings of Kampuchea embellished the marble-topped mantelpiece; and views over the bay beyond Sai Kung port and surrounding hills gleamed through the wide picture windows. In the far distance, tiny islands rose from the flat, azure sea.

We took tea in the jasmine-scented garden, a full English tea with scones, jam and cream, served by Lucy, Lyn's Filipino maid, who lived in the cupboard under the stairs. Sara was shocked by this at first until Lucy explained that her "room" was twice as big as the corner she had occupied back home, and that she was able to support a family of six on half the wages she was earning as Lyn's maid.

After tea, Lucy led us to a swimming pool, shared with other residents, to watch Lyn's children play in the water whilst she worked at her computer. By nine o'clock, eyelids heavy, we were all ready for sleep.

'Wakey, wakey, I'm going to take you to see Stanley Market,' Lyn called next morning. 'You may as well see as much as possible while you're here.'

Sara groaned as Michael sat down at the breakfast table eagerly, helping himself to cereal and toast.

'Wow, first proper food for months.'

Conrad and Gecko did not emerge, but the promise of an English breakfast stirred the rest of us. Louise, Sara and I were sharing an enormous attic studio. Lyn's accommodation did not run to three spare doubles, so we had split into the two sexes: the boys in a small triple, and the girls in the studio, each on our own futon between the architect's drawing board and the astronomical telescope.

'Listen, honey,' I told Lyn. 'I'm not keen on visiting the market. Remember how I hate shopping?'

'Okay, I get it. You can have a drink instead at a place I know. I'll come back and pick you all up there after a couple of hours.'

I sat in a café while Sara and Louise whiled away a happy hour or so buying up T-shirts, silk shorts and hair decorations for next to nothing. Michael had decided to stay at Lyn's and enjoy the luxury of home comforts.

In a few days, I'd be reunited with Sophie. The guilt and the loss that had accompanied me for the last three months still weighed me down. But not as painfully as before. Somehow, there'd been a shift. I still ached for her, missed the sound of her voice, and her shy smile. But I would see her again soon, and would continue to see her for the rest of my life. I recalled the Indian family who'd had to sell their daughter because they couldn't afford to feed her. What did life look like to them? My guilt was crass and self-indulgent in comparison to what they were forced to do to survive. I had time to think, to ponder and wonder and question, while others—the majority—could not afford the luxury of a respite from the daily fight for existence. Whatever emotional damage I'd done to Sophie was surely reparable if I just held on to love, not trying to make amends.

***

Although Lyn had lived in Hong Kong for ten years, she had no sense of direction, and we drove round the Happy Valley Racecourse three times before finding the correct route home.

'I'm better in the southern hemisphere. I never get lost in New Zealand.'

'Yeah, yeah. We've all heard that one before...'

'Tomorrow we're going on the famous Star Ferry. We'll go across to Lantau.'

'We?' I queried. 'Are you coming with us? That's great. Thanks, Lyn. I know you're busy working. I really appreciate you giving up time to look after us.'

The Star Ferry manoeuvred awkwardly yet confidently into its berth. I closed my eyes and listened to the shouts, the reversing engines, the rush of the sea beneath the propellers. Tens, or possibly hundreds of thousands had crossed to Central on this transport.

'Back to civilization, eh? How does it feel, Conrad?'

'It doesn't matter where you are. It's what's in your head that counts.'

I was impressed by my son's wisdom. I had spent hours analysing the difference between living in the East and West, and he had already worked out what really mattered.

'God knows what's going on in my poor demented brain,' I shook my head in response.

'Best not to go into that.' He smiled affectionately.

'You're right, though. Citizens of Planet Earth, that's what we are.'

'Yeah, okay, don't get carried away.'

On Lantau Island, the Buddha at Po Lin monastery beamed down from his thirty-five metres. From a distance, he looked like a giant chess piece. His hands were in the "protection" position, one raised, one on his lap. On his right palm was the Buddhist wheel, and his chest bore the swastika, symbol of peace.

'Come on, Sara, love. We haven't got all day! What are you looking at, anyway?'

Sara was immobile, transfixed, staring down at a snake swallowing a frog which twitched every two or three seconds as it made its way slowly down the reptile's body.

Inside the monastery, giant bronze urns held incense; its pungent aroma prickled our nostrils. Saffron-cloaked monks hurried silently across the courtyard, averting their eyes. Some smiled coyly but shook their heads if a camera was lifted. Huge iron gongs stood in the shade of palm trees. Inside the main hall, tasselled lanterns illuminated rows of golden Buddha figures, bowls of fruit, lamps, candles and other offerings lined up in front of walls inlaid with jewels and silver.

Nearly a year ago, I'd made my resolution to make this journey happen. Now, I made another: to really listen to my children in future, to stop interpreting and anticipating and figuring out my strategy for response. I wasn't the only one who'd felt isolated. I'd been self-obsessed, thinking I couldn't cope with the grief of losing David. It was like a form of insanity. I had made decisions "while the balance of my mind was disturbed". Truth was, I'd always been like that—headstrong, determined, relentless. It was all about survival. I was as scared of life as everyone else. When people asked me last year what I was running from, I took offence and struggled to answer. Maybe I was running from me, just as David had. I must have been like that snake, consuming everyone in my path as I kept myself alive.

During the long, hot, tortuous bus ride back down to the small harbour, we passed groups of locals playing cards, chattering noisily. Once on board the ferry home, we scoffed bowls of noodles with chopsticks, and watched coastal fishing villages glide past. Old ladies with agile thumbs were playing with electronic hand-held games, whilst smartly dressed businessmen shouted into their mobile phones.

'Bussi jam, mgoy.' Louise had been dying to try out the only phrase she knew: 'Next stop, please.'

'Gwaipo,' someone muttered with a grin. Later, Lyn told her this meant "female white devil".

'That's the last time I practise my Cantonese, then.'

'No wonder they stare, there's so many of you! From behind, you could be mistaken for a Japanese family—if you weren't so big, or so badly dressed!' Lyn laughed.

With only two more days left in Sai Kung, Louise and I felt the need to explore locally. A shark warning was in force, but we were determined to take a boat ride. Birds were chirping, cicadas were trilling. A cow strolled past on its lonely way uphill. A toothless old lady agreed to row us around for an hour in her sampan. It was misty, hot and very humid.

We stepped from boat to boat, through oily water littered with floating plastic bottles, paper bags, discarded food cartons and rusty tins. The sampan was half-covered by an arched awning supported by bamboo slats, various items of laundry hanging from the highest part of the dome. A linoleum-covered bench seat offered space for two Chinese-sized passengers. We had to sit side on, facing outwards, away from one another, which made conversation a bit difficult above the noise of the woman's endless shouting. She seemed to be in dispute with every other boat owner in the harbour.

***

'It's our last full day. Please can we go back into town?' Sara wheedled. 'There's nothing for us to do round here.'

The Chinese Emporium at Tsim Sha Tsui was a shopper's wonderland. Sara stuffed her bag with wall fans, joss sticks, napkins, place mats, an inlaid tray, and chopsticks with stands.

'Where the hell are you planning to put all that, sis? You've got no flat now, remember?' Both she and Conrad had given up the leases on their accommodation at home.

'I'm going to post it all back to Grandpa and ask him to store it for me.'

Sara had it all worked out. When it came to spending my money, there were no obstacles she couldn't overcome. This time, however, there was another motive.

'Mum, there's something I need to tell you.'

'Oh no, how much have you spent?'

'No, nothing like that. You know me and Michael...'

'Michael and I, dear,' I began. Oops, so much for my resolution to listen.

'Oh, for God's sake...Michael and I...have decided to live together when we get home.'

'Oh, that's good, darling...'

266

'No, wait. We want to go back after Australia. He can't take more time off before he starts a proper job. And I can't stay away if he's there. I really love him, Mum. We really love each other.'

'Well, I reckon you've both seen each other at your worst, under all sorts of trying circumstances: sitting by roadsides, vomiting, runny tums, stressed out... If you've survived that, you should be okay, I think! Good luck. And, hey, less money coming out of my pocket, too!'

I still had my doubts, but my new "I don't know it all" policy required me to keep shtum.

'Well, me dears, I need something to eat. Let's go and try some dim sum. You can only get it in the morning, apparently. There's a restaurant right here.'

'What the fuck is that?!' Conrad laughed as he sat down at the table, aghast at the colourless dumplings on his plate. 'I'm going over the road to the McDonald's. Back in a tick.'

'Really, Rachael, you can't expect them to appreciate the subtleties of oriental cuisine. You know what they say about horses and water,' Louise said.

Conrad rejoined us with a polystyrene box full of burger and chips. We struggled to hold dumplings between chopsticks while he used his fingers, grease running down the side of his palm. An image of Sophie eating her favourite takeaway Japanese food took shape in my brain.

'What's on your mind, Ma?'

'She'll be leaving your dad's now. She's already on her way to us.'

My two kids stopped and smiled. We exited the restaurant, stood still on the wide, crowded pavement, and grinned at each other. People jostled and shoved but we ignored them, just for a few seconds, all sharing the same anticipation.

'You wan' copy watch?' A man approached, shifty-looking eyes darting from side to side.

'I've heard you can get fake Rolexes for next to nothing here. It's completely illegal. Let's go and have a look. I might get one for Dad,' Sara said with a conspiratorial smile.

The man led us between the shops, to a back alley, where people were lying beside rubbish bins, their opium-glazed eyes following us with accustomed suspicion. We climbed a rickety staircase, crept silently along narrow corridors, heads bent low in the confined space, to a small, dark room where the dealer banged twice gently on the door before easing it open.

Open briefcases crammed full of expensive-looking watches, some diamond-studded, were laid out on a trestle table. They weren't real, but passed for genuine. Just the sort of thing David would like, I thought bitterly, then felt instantly ashamed. Sara picked a fake gold watch and strap, and nervously asked how much. She was answered in English by a fat, bug-eyed, ugly man with podgy fingers, whose multi-layered belly flapped over the top of his pants as he rocked back and forth on the legs of his chair. His shirt was spattered with food stains. He held a bowl of food under his chins, his face enveloping the food which he sucked in through thick, flabby lips.

'Michael, it's only fourteen pounds sterling. Can you lend me it in yuan till we get to Australia? My dad would love it.'

Michael gently lowered his hand into his pocket. I knew what he was thinking: if they were real crooks they would be sure to steal the rest of his cash. Even when we left the building, he was looking tentatively over his shoulder.

'Oh look, darling, the time's wrong. Can you set it for me?' Sara looked at him sweetly.

'Sure.'

What confidence.

He pulled the winder out from its hole, and began to turn. Once he'd adjusted the time, he was about to hand the watch back when he noticed the winder had fallen out. By sheer luck, he caught sight of it lying in the dusty alley. Days later, crushed with humiliation, he was still trying to repair the now completely useless watch.

On the way home, we stopped at a brightly-coloured fairground where a stage was the focal point of an open-air auditorium.

'Let's stay for a while. We're not in a hurry,' I suggested.

Half an hour later, we reeled from the high-pitched squealing sounds emanating from the mouths of magnificently costumed, puppet-like mannequins moving stiffly around the stage to the accompaniment of clashing cymbals. We departed rapidly.

'That was just like the puppets in Vietnam, remember?' I said. Silence was the response.

'Stay there, Mother! Has anyone got a camera handy?'

I stood still and smiled, flattered by my son's interest.

It was weeks before I saw the developed photo—of me grinning under the sign "Wan King Path".

***

To: Wendy McKintock
From: Rachael Green
Subject: G'day mate
03 June

Hi

Well, here we are, about to leave Asia for Australia.

You asked about Sophie. The last few weeks have been...I guess you'd say, enlightening. God forbid, but I think I've learned something. Which is—ta dah!—that I'll never know if I've done the right thing, leaving her behind. It wasn't my choice, but I didn't put up much of a fight. She was always worried about her dad being lonely, so I guess on that level it was the right thing.

David's such a technophobe that he doesn't even have a computer, but I've managed to keep in touch using fax shops and the odd email via his colleagues who are much more computer-savvy than him! Mostly, though, I've been writing to her, so I am personally acquainted with a dozen post offices between London and Hong Kong.

I've spoken to her on the phone a couple of times, but the connections were bad and we could hardly hear each other. It cracked me up the first time when she said 'I miss you, Mum.' It felt like someone had stabbed me.

I wallowed in self-pity for a couple of days then got bored with myself. I figured it was up to me how I dealt with it. I could either spend the following months feeling bad, which wouldn't put right what had actually happened—I had gone off on a three–four month trip and left her with her dad—or I could put my guilt to one side and get the most out of every minute of the trip. I could always come back to the guilt later! *Oh hi, guilt. Here I am, back again to give you an airing. How's it going?* So, yes, I guess I've finally forgiven myself.

I've emailed Tess and Dan in Hounslow and asked them to meet her from the Guernsey flight and take her to Heathrow the next morning. Knowing Tess, she'll get her an upgrade to first class—she can be very persuasive!

I'm sorry to hear your time with your Texan is nearly up. No more 'yee haw!'s coming from your bedroom, then. Enjoy your last few rides, kid.

This will be it from me till the Land of Down Under, when I'll email again, in about a month. Oh wow, just realized Sophie will have been and gone by then! Wonder how I'll deal with that?

R

x

***

The aircraft hauled itself up into the sky. The main onboard meal was "Fillet of cod Szechuan style, with turmeric rice and stir-fried green beans"—a last taste of the Orient.

The next three months were going to be a challenge for us all. I planned to rent an apartment in Cairns for me, Conrad and Gecko. After travelling with Sophie alone for some quality mother–daughter bonding, I would return there to live. Louise was going off on an Oz bus tour by herself, and Sara and Michael would find a place of their own, in Sydney. Those who could would get themselves jobs to re-inflate my dwindling funds. There would be Western-style houses, garages, transport, shops and restaurants. We would be returning to the once-familiar world of a work routine, buying and cooking food, and other domestic chores.

'I wonder how we'll all handle this after so many weeks of freedom. And then there'll be the feeling of having to stay put in one place, after so much movement. I suspect it's going to be hard, and will change us all again.'

'You certainly won't be the people you were when you set off,' Louise replied.

'You look deep in thought, Mum. What are you and Aunt Louise talking about?'

Sara and I used to talk at length until Michael had joined us, and I was longing to share my latest ideas with my daughter.

'Come over and sit next to me, darling, please, just for a while. Louise, do you mind swapping? I haven't had a talk with Sara for ages.'

'No worries. I'm going for a walk around anyway.'

'How do you feel about re-entering the so-called civilized world, darling?'

'Relieved, of course! Don't get me wrong, it's been fascinating, but I'm looking forward to telly and steak and stuff like that. Aren't you? Did Aunt Louise really say "no worries"?' I ignored her sarcastic question.

'To be honest,' I said, 'part of me is afraid to leave the spiritual peace of the East. Although there is so much hardship, the serenity of the people and the landscape is what I'll remember most.'

'Oh God, here she goes again. Wind her up and off she drones. Hold on, sis, I'll rescue you in a minute.' Conrad grinned down at us as he passed along the aisle. Cheeky sod.

'I've been thinking a lot about what reality is. Before we came on this trip, I thought I knew what the world was about, in a way. I wasn't interested in religion, or in anything that couldn't be proved. But now, we've seen so much that it's as if everything I thought I knew has been turned upside down in my head. Even what happened with your dad. I was so sure he was having some kind of crisis and should have sorted it out. I didn't see how lonely he must have been, once he realized he didn't love me anymore. Nothing's black or white, right or wrong, but everything is "both...and". I see that now.'

Sara nodded, trying to look interested, but I could see she wanted to get back to snuggling against Michael's chest.

'Do you remember that boyfriend I had after your dad left who talked to trees? He said they were wise.'

'Yeah, the boring one with halitosis, who was a macro-vegan or something and only ate lentils.'

'Yes, him. He believed that everything on earth was part of the same whole universal being. Well, I reckon that if our thoughts are chemically or electrically induced in our brains, or however they are, then they must also form part of the universe. There are so many other things in our world we can't see, like sound waves for example, so why couldn't each one of the countless billions of human thoughts be like a group of particles, that can move across space–time as waves, then change back into particles when someone becomes consciously aware of them?'

'Hang on a minute. I haven't a clue what you're talking about. Is this that quantum stuff you've been reading about?'

'Only my understanding of it, which is probably off the wall.'

'You can say that again!'

'Okay, Conrad, enough.'

'*Ladies and gentlemen, we are expecting some turbulence as we are having to fly through a storm. Please return to your seats and make sure your seat belts are securely fastened. We are unable to continue our drinks service during this time, and the toilets are now out of use.*'

I put my head back and shut my eyes. If Sophie has to fly through this storm too, I thought, she'll be scared. After putting her through months of missing us, she'll be alone and frightened on the other side of the world, and I can't hold her hand.

The plane lurched, creaked, then plummeted so fast that the overhead lockers flew open. Coats and bags fell out onto shocked passengers' heads. Before the screaming got out of control, a uniformed figure made for the PA system mic.

'It's alright,' said the stewardess. 'Please stay calm. It's nothing to worry about.'

Sure enough, the plane levelled out and began to rise. The cabin crew began to restow the fallen property.

'Ladies and gentlemen, this is your captain speaking. As you know, we have just passed through an air pocket. Unfortunately, this has caused a slight problem. The power transfer unit has malfunctioned, which means we've had to shut down one of our starboard engines to avoid the risk of a small fire breaking out. This is nothing to worry about. We can fly the plane on the remaining engines, and it is something we practise in the simulator regularly. Shutting down the engine is a precautionary safety measure. We will be landing in Sydney on time. Thank you for your attention. I'll make a further announcement on our approach to Sydney.'

I pressed the call button. Within seconds the stewardess was at my side. 'How can I help you, madam?'

'Is this storm getting worse?'

'I'm afraid I don't know, but we are ahead of it and we shouldn't experience any more turbulence. We expect to be landing on time.'

'Yes, but my daughter is also flying into Sydney in a couple of hours. Can you find out what the weather forecast is like for the next few hours?'

'I'll do my best.'

The cabin was buzzing with conversation about the storm damage. No one had had time to think; it had all happened so quickly. But the relaxed atmosphere in the cabin was gone. There was now tension; anxious faces looking around at each other. People's backs stiffened; voices sounded strident, edgy.

Louise leaned over my shoulder. 'Rachael, have you seen my sponge bag?'

'Just borrow mine,' I sighed.

'I can't, I need to wash my important little places.'

'What?'

'You know, my private parts.'

'Oh, right, okay. Sorry, haven't a clue. And I'm a bit distracted right now, Louise. I'm worried sick about Sophie's flight coming in to land in this storm.'

'Now where could I have put it? Remarkable!' She hadn't even heard me. How could she be so insensitive?

'Hmm, yes, it is, quite.'

Sara raised her hands up and out then pulled a face whilst performing an elaborate mime which clearly conveyed: 'She wants to have a strip wash in an aircraft toilet? She's really lost it.'

As Louise headed for the aft toilet, a narrow, deeply wrinkled face turned to me from over the back of the seat in front. 'Do you mind if I take part in your conversation? I couldn't help but hear what you were saying. I'm very interested in your ideas. I'm a philosopher, you see.'

'Er, um...' What conversation did he mean? Surely not Louise's "little places"?

'Let me introduce myself. How very rude of me. My name is Christopher Fitzpatrick. I'm going to Sydney to give a lecture. I do hope you don't mind my interrupting. May I sit alongside you? There is an empty seat.'

He looked odd: his lazy left eye turned up and outwards, so I couldn't decide if he was looking at me or the bulkhead. But what harm could he do in a packed aircraft cabin? And it would at least take my mind off panicking about Sophie's flight.

'I suppose that's fine, please join us.'

Gecko was unaware of the proceedings, nodding to his Walkman, his mouth drawn down at an appreciative angle. Conrad flicked through the in-flight magazine.

'Um, well, what I was going to say was that, well, it's difficult to explain, but suppose our psyche comprised not only the actual thoughts and feelings created in our brains, but also our as yet unformed thoughts and feelings, plus the previous thoughts and feelings of the whole of humanity, waiting to be recreated in a slightly different form, with different bias or emphasis, depending on our state of mind? Does that make sense?'

'Yes, yes, do go on.'

'So what we see depends completely on us. Our state of mind can affect what we think we see. And the way we observe anything will also have an impact on the result.'

Gecko rose from his seat and winked at me as he passed by.

I gave the stranger a brief rundown of what we were doing, and how I'd been trying to make sense of the world since my expectations for my family's future had disappeared. 'I thought we'd grow old together. I thought we'd be bouncing grandchildren on our knees. My husband leaving was the most painful thing ever to happen to me, and that includes giving birth!'

'I've just given birth—to an enormous turd in the rear loo.' Gecko returned to his seat. 'I wouldn't go in there if I were you.'

'No idea of appropriate behaviour, that young man. Sorry. He's not my son.'

'Don't worry about it. You were saying?'

'I felt as if I was stepping through a veil when I made my decision to take this journey. Our dreams, past-life recollections, even insanity, clairvoyance, déjà vu, fortune telling, extra-terrestrial life—blah-blah-blah, all that stuff—they could all be real events existing in different layers of reality. These layers could be vertical, horizontal, three-dimensional or circular, it doesn't matter. What do you think? I don't know anything about physics, but I've done a lot of reading in the last three months. Now I wish I'd done science at school. I was always good at languages, you see, and couldn't do maths to save my life, so I dropped science as soon as I could. I'm sorry if I sound like an ignoramus.'

'Don't apologize, my dear. Most of us experience movement through what you call "layers" at some time in our lives, don't you agree? The possibility is sheer magic, the wholeness, the completeness of it, of these infinite instants all happening at once is sublimely comforting; perfectly secure. And quite beautiful. Dare I say divine?' He beamed with enthusiasm.

Sara rose. 'Look, Mum, I'm sorry, but I'm really knackered. I love hearing your ideas but my brain hurts at the moment. I can't think when I'm tired.'

'You been listening to Mum's drivel?'

'I heard that, Conrad!' I glowered at him over the back of my seat.

'Sounds like she's met someone as barmy as her,' Sara whispered as she settled down next to Michael.

***

Louise tucked her hair neatly into her headscarf, adjusted her large gypsy hoop earrings, and made her way back towards her seat.

'You'd better sit next to us, Aunt Louise. Mum's pulled.'

Louise wore her scarves like a turban, an art which I had never mastered. She was wearing a long, padded embroidered jacket over linen trousers. Underneath, her tunic top was belted at the waist, emphasizing her curves. I glanced down at my flowing wrap-around skirt and felt ashamed of my frumpiness. Just about everything I owned was baggy and unflattering, and for the first time, I cared.

'Excuse me, sir. We are landing soon. Will you all be sitting where you are now for landing?'

The philosopher returned to his own seat. As he rose, he said, 'Perhaps we can have a drink together. I'm staying here for the next week. Do call me once you're settled.' He handed me a card.

'He's quite dashing. Shame I won't have time for him. But I really should make more of an effort. You never know, I might meet someone in Australia. I'm going to buy some new clothes in Sydney.'

'Good plan, Mum!'

How it was that both Sara and Sophie had inherited their aunt's fashion sense, I didn't know, but I was relieved that they had developed their own styles and not mine.

When he worked in a bank, Conrad had felt uncomfortable in suits. They never seemed to fit his gangly frame, and he was far happier in shorts. Would they ever settle back into normal jobs, I wondered. Had I actually done them a great disservice, bringing them with me? Was it really because I wanted them to see the world, or because I was afraid of doing it alone?

I closed my eyes again but was too wired to sleep. Only two or three more hours to go till I would see her. What if her plane crashed? How would I ever go on living? Or what if ours did, and Sophie was robbed of her brother and sister as well as her mother?

There's nothing for it but to make it work out, I thought. I must act like a proper mother, stop trying to be their friend, stop this eternal trying to please, and face up to my responsibilities. I have to grow up, quick. I can't undo the past, but I can do my utmost to change the way I am for the future. If I beat myself about the head, I won't be any use to them. If I carry on ignoring things I don't want to deal with—like smoking dope—I won't be doing them any favours.

'*Ladies and gentlemen, we are now making our final approach into Sydney Kingsford Smith Airport. Please return to your seats and fasten your seat belts. The local time is oh-seven-fifteen and the outside temperature is twenty-five degrees.*'

The stewardess returned. 'You'll be pleased to hear the weather is improving at Sydney. Don't worry about your daughter's flight. The storm will have passed by the time they land.'

'You're not too bad when it comes to mothers, you know, Ma. None of my mates' mothers would have the guts to do this.' Once again Conrad leaned over me from the aisle, on his way back to his seat.

'Oh, thank you! I'd just been wondering if it's all been worthwhile, and then you say that and I feel so happy!'

'Of course it's been worthwhile, you daft bat. It's been brilliant! Best thing to have happened, ever! Sara and I have had a ball.'

'And Gecko, do you think?'

'Don't worry about him. He's weird. Bit of a selfish git. But it's been okay having him around, really. And Michael's not bad either.'

'And you haven't minded having Aunt Louise along with us?'

'To be honest, I'd rather it had been just us, like at the beginning. But once Michael and Gecko came on the scene, she's been good company for you, so that's okay. Right, I'm off back to my seat now.'

'*For your safety, please make sure that your seat belt is fastened, your seat back is in the upright position, and your table is stowed in the seat in front.*'

We were pushed back into our seats as brakes screamed and tyres squealed.

'*Ladies and gentlemen, please remain seated until the aircraft has come to a complete halt and the captain has switched off the seat belt sign. Please make sure that you take all your hand luggage with you, and be careful when opening the overhead lockers as some items may have shifted position during the flight.*'

'Remarkable, how I'm here, on the other side of the world, and just a few months ago I was on the verge of suicide. Leaving Andrew was the best thing I've ever done. I still feel guilty about it, but he'll be alright after a while. Anyway, just want to say thanks for letting me come along with you.'

'It's been great having you with us, Louise, really great. You are such good fun.' I didn't mention my lack of choice.

'We must keep in touch! And maybe I'll see you back in Guernsey. Who knows?'

She leaned forward to kiss my cheek.

'Of course we'll see each other again. Anyway we haven't even disembarked yet—let's not get too emotional!' I grinned.

278

'Thank you for choosing to fly with Qantas. We wish you a safe onward journey.'

The engine noise died away.

By now, I was shaking with emotion. I turned to face Sara and Conrad. Tears flowed into the corners of my mouth as I smiled. 'We'll be seeing her little face in less than two hours!'

'Cabin crew, doors to manual and cross check. Ladies and gentlemen, welcome to Australia.'

***

Epilogue

Sydney Airport

The doors slid open. A group of dishevelled passengers appeared and their eager faces searched the arrivals hall, seeking friends, relatives, lovers, business partners. We stood in silence, hardly daring to breathe. Well, apart from Gecko, who was busy chatting up the girl next to him.

The doors slid shut. I realized my hands were shaking. Sara had tears in her eyes. Conrad was pale. It had been over an hour since the flight landed, and surely most of the passengers had emerged by now.

I trembled violently. Bile rose in my gullet. My stomach churned. Conrad came and stood close beside me, supporting me, his arms around me. Sara buried her face into Michael's shoulder.

'There's something wrong. I know there is. This just doesn't feel right.' My voice cracked as I spoke.

'Mum, we should go and ask someone. There's probably a simple explanation. She could be...'

'Don't. Please.'

My ears rang. Voices sounded distant. I couldn't make out what they were saying. Where was I? What were Sara and Conrad doing here? Why had someone changed the world?

'I can't...'

Then a scream. I gasped. I shut my eyes. Again, a full throated, piercing screech.

'There she is! There she is! Look!'

'Oh wow! You're actually here!'

She was running towards me, beaming. Her brother and sister scooped her up in turn before letting her wriggle free to come to me. I squeezed her till I feared she might pass out.

'G'day, madam. One daughter, safely delivered into your hands. Will you sign here, please? Oh, and we can take this off now, you'll be pleased to hear, young lady.'

She lifted the UM sign and slipped it over Sophie's head.

'And you'll be needing your bag, I think. I'll just hand it over to Mum.'

'S'okay, I'll take it.' Michael stepped over.

'Wow! You're really here! Wow, wow, wow, wow, wow! It's so fabulous to see you! What was the flight like? Was it bumpy? Were you scared? Did they look after you? I asked Tess and Dan to make sure you got special attention.'

'Give her a chance to answer, Ma.'

'Did you get all my letters?'

'How the hell is she supposed to know that?'

'Oh, I suppose that was a bit of a dumb question. But I counted. I wrote you twelve letters in all. And Sara's written five. Don't suppose you know how many you received, do you?'

Sophie bit her lower lip and frowned.

'Oh, well. Never mind. And did you remember to bring your diary? I want to know everything about what you've been doing...aah, I can see you didn't. Don't worry, darling, it doesn't matter. It doesn't matter a bit. I'm just thrilled to see you.'

'Enough of the Spanish Inquisition, eh?'

Then the floor beneath us shook.

'God, did you hear that bang? What the hell was that?' The muscles on Conrad's face tightened.

'Sounds like that thunderstorm's back with a vengeance! Remarkable!'

Suddenly all hell broke loose. Sirens wailed, people ran in all directions, shouting, screaming.

'Oh, thank God you landed before…'

'That wasn't a thunderclap,' Michael stated, his voice betraying a nervousness I'd not observed in him before.

'Well, what else could it have been?' Instinctively, I pulled Sophie to my side.

'Ssh! Listen! Listen to that! Ssh, Mum, they're making an announcement. Quiet!'

'What?'

'May I have your attention please. This is an announcement for customers awaiting the arrival of Air China flight CA64 from Singapore Changi. We regret to announce that, due to an unexpected incident, this flight has had to make an emergency landing. At present, we have no other information. Please await a further announcement.'

'Come here, all of you, please.' In the pandemonium, it came out almost as a whisper but, without hesitation, they gathered around me. Even Gecko responded instantly.

'Group hug, no arguments. Thank God we're all safe. Thank God.'

As the ground shuddered, so did I. We may have "suffered" a lot of inconvenience, disappointment, and discomfort, but we were together, safe, and alive. It struck me at that moment how fragile life is, how quickly and suddenly it can end. As I stood trembling with a mixture of fear and relief, I made another momentous decision: from now on, I wouldn't be seeking more from my life, I would be relishing every moment of it.

Also available from Acclaimed Books Limited

The Tour Guide Life by Maureen Moss

Rachel's Shoe by Peter Lihou

The Causeway by Peter Lihou

Book by Peter Lihou

Golden Promise by Heather Whipp

Druid's Bane by Phillip Henderson

Maig's Hand by Phillip Henderson

The Arkaelyon Trilogy by Phillip Henderson

Coming soon...

The Legend of Oofty Goofty by Russell Estlack

Seven Cities of Gold by Russell Estlack

All for One Guinea by Peter Rogers

Larnius' Revenge by Phillip Henderson

500 Years An Island Family by Peter Lihou

Available in paperback and Kindle formats from Amazon worldwide.

See the entire catalogue, reviews and author interviews at www.acclaimedbooks.com

Printed in Great Britain
by Amazon